Barbary Baseball

BARBARY BASEBALL

The Pacific Coast League of the 1920s

by R. SCOTT MACKEY

McFARLAND & COMPANY, INC., PUBLISHERS
JEFFERSON, NORTH CAROLINA, AND LONDON

Cover photo: *Ike Boone (Tony Pirak)*

British Library Cataloguing-in-Publication data are available

Library of Congress Cataloguing-in-Publication Data

Mackey, R. Scott, 1955–
    Barbary baseball — the Pacific Coast League of the 1920s / by
R. Scott Mackey.
        p.   cm.
    Includes bibliographical references (p.   ) and index.
    ISBN 0-7864-0055-2 (sewn softcover : 50 # alk. paper) ∞
    1. Pacific Coast League — History.   2. Minor league baseball —
West (U.S.) — History.   3. Baseball players — United States — Registers.
I. Title.
    GV875.P33M33   1995
    796.357′64′0979 — dc20   94-44985
                                                                          CIP

Manufactured in the United States of America

McFarland & Company, Inc., Publishers
    Box 611, Jefferson, North Carolina 28640

To my wife Barbara,
my daughter Lauren,
and my son Rod

Table of Contents

Acknowledgments   ix

Introduction   1

1 Rocked by Scandal   5

2 1920 — The PCL's First Dynasty   15

3 1921 — The (Un) Lucky Beavers   29

4 1922 — The PCL as a Third Major League   43

5 1923 — Civil War   57

6 1924 — The Great Six-Day Bicycle Race   73

7 1925 — Team of the Decade   90

8 1926 — One for the Angels   108

9 1927 — A Buzz in Oakland   123

10 1928 — No Tears Due or Justified   141

11 1929 — The "Other Team" Shares the Glory   159

12 In Their Own Words   178

13 The All-1920s Team   193

Appendix: The Players   197

Bibliography   213

Index   217

Acknowledgments

This project would never have happened without the help of several people.

First, let me thank the former players—Lou Almada, Dolph Camilli, Carl Dittmar, Tony Freitas, Dallas Locker and Gus Suhr—who graciously agreed to be interviewed. An assist goes to Don Runcie, who recorded two interviews with his uncle, Vernon first baseman Dallas Locker.

A special thanks goes to John Spalding, author of *Always on Sunday: The California Baseball League, 1886–1915*. John painstakingly reviewed the manuscript, correcting factual errors, recalculating batting averages, and offering stylistic and organizational suggestions that significantly helped the book. His work in verifying and correcting names in the appendix was particularly appreciated.

Similarly, Dick Beverage reviewed a late draft of this work, offering valuable advice. As president of the Pacific Coast League Historical Society, Dick helped me contact the families of former players and others with photos, memorabilia or anecdotes about the 1920s.

Vincent Stanich, a baseball fan who saw firsthand many of the players discussed in this book, provided anecdotes, access to his record books and other information, and offered the initial encouragement for undertaking this book.

Dan West performed the yeoman's share of the early research, studying yards of microfilm to find the nuggets of information. In like manner, June Owens of Shields Library at the University of California, Davis, added hours and hours of critical help.

Bill Conlin, legendary sportswriter for the *Sacramento Bee*, picked up more than one lunch tab and spent considerable time helping me flesh out information, particularly in Chapter 10.

Dick Beverage, Bill Weiss and Dick Dobbins participated in the selection of the "All-Decade Team," and their experience and knowledge of the subject helped immensely.

Tony Pirak, Doug McWilliams, Vic Pallos, John Spalding, Don Hazel-

ix

wood, Kay Roper and Bob Brady provided many of the photos contained in the book. A special thanks goes to John Outland, whose father, George E. Outland, photographed approximately 200 PCL players during the 1920s. Many of these rare photos appear in this work thanks to John.

Robert Hoie, of the Society for American Baseball Research (SABR) critiqued a research paper I wrote on the Seals and helped provide additional information about the draft. Bill Deane, Senior Research Associate, National Baseball Hall of Fame, and Steve Gietschier of the Sporting News Archives provided research materials and information. Peter C. Bjarkman, "Doctor Baseball," offered much encouragement and advice.

Dan Lovitt shared a draft of his article-in-progress, "Seattle wins the pennant! Seattle wins the pennant!", which helped me write Chapter 6.

Robert Bluthardt, chairman of the SABR Ballparks Committee, furnished information on PCL ballparks and sources for further information.

Dozens of others offered help along the way. To all of you, thanks. One person who did so without realizing it: Hank Greenwald, radio announcer for the San Francisco Giants, whose insights and anecdotes not only brought the magic of baseball into my home, but also inspired me to tell this story.

Thanks also to my parents, Dave and Betty Mackey, who nurtured my love for the game.

And finally, this book would not have been possible without the love of my family. To Barbara, I thank you for supporting—and for putting up with me—during the course of researching and writing this book.

Introduction

Why write a book about the 1920s Pacific Coast League?

Because it is hard to imagine another time or place in minor league history filled with as many great stars, teams or characters as the PCL of the 1920s. This was the West Coast's major league. And while it may have resided a notch below the National and American Leagues in the official hierarchy of organized baseball, it was not for lack of quality or color.

More than 90 all-time great minor leaguers as recognized by the Society for American Baseball Research, hundreds of major leaguers, and nine future Hall of Famers—Earl Averill, Harry Hooper, Sam Crawford, Lefty Gomez, Ernie Lombardi, Mickey Cochrane, Tony Lazzeri, and Paul and Lloyd Waner—starred in the PCL during the decade. Rosters were filled with major league names, either those on the way up, those on the way down, or those who simply preferred the PCL and its long seasons, decent pay and exciting style of play.

In an era when the minors were more than a prelude to the majors, the eight Pacific Coast League teams gave the baseball-mad West Coast more than its money's worth.

Sandwiched between the end of World War I and the Great Depression, the 1920s were a rollicking age of unprecedented wealth, good cheer and decadence. It was a self-indulgent decade of speakeasies, gangsters, "wild" music, sexual freedom, and conspicuous consumption. Known as the Roaring 20s, The Jazz Age, The Lawless Decade, The New Freedom and the New Era, 1920s America abounded with bullish enthusiasm, and journalists and historians have characterized it as the Golden Age of Sports. Not even the Black Sox scandal could dampen popular enthusiasm for a generation of larger-than-life stars like Babe Ruth, Red Grange, Jack Dempsey, Gene Tunney, Walter Hagen, The Four Horsemen, Big Bill Tilden, Bobby Jones and others who would emerge and endure beyond the decade.

The Pacific Coast League betting scandal, uncovered just slightly before the 1919 Black Sox scandal came to light, presented a grave threat to the game both on the coast and nationally. Baseball was on the ropes. Only a style of play that could match the big and bawdy times could hope to survive.

Nationally, Babe Ruth stepped in to save the game, becoming a figure of legendary proportions, and one the nation could embrace. Out on the coast, there emerged a league of sluggers likely never to be seen again. A juiced-up ball first appeared in 1920, ostensibly because of a better grade of yarn, and then an even livelier ball came onto the scene in mid-decade, a cork center the source of its new vigor. The limited ban on spitballers and "freak deliveries" gave hitters a better chance still. Suddenly the emphasis on station-to-station baseball and "doing the little things" to win games went out the window. Raw power was in vogue. And fans flocked to the ballpark.

The ballparks themselves were cozy bandboxes that made for slugfests the likes of which have never been equalled over such a sustained period. It was mainly men, dressed in suits and hats, who filled the grandstands. Some came to root, others to gamble, still others to drink. In spite of the Volstead Act, drinking went largely unchecked at most Coast League parks. Not even prohibition could squelch the alliance of booze and baseball. The most notorious paradise for drinkers was called, appropriately, the Booze Cage at San Francisco's Recreation Park. Prior to prohibition 75 cents bought a shot of whiskey and the best seat in the house; after prohibition, a Booze Cage ticket delivered the same seat and the right to tip an illicit flask without reper-cussion.

On the field the consumption was more conspicuous: teams played a 200-game schedule, packing a seven-game series against a single opponent into every week from the first of April till mid–October; hitters collected 300 hits a season, sluggers belted out 40, 50, even 60 homers; and players and um-pires exchanged fists as often as insults. It was big, bawdy baseball—the kind of play that fit perfectly on what was still being called the Barbary Coast.

In the boardrooms of team owners and league officials, emotions ran just as high. The 1920s saw continuous battles between warring league factions. They fought over minor business issues, and over policy matters like the draft and league independence that had profound long-term ramifications. Their egos large and their mouths unchecked, the eight owners produced fireworks virtually every time they entered the same room. Sometimes this meant marathon shouting matches; other times it meant violence.

Controversy swirled about the Pacific Coast League from its origins. When the league began in 1903 it was an "outlaw league" unrecognized by organized baseball, which viewed any organization outside its purview as a pariah. It competed with the Pacific National League, a recognized class C league, for West Coast preeminence. The Coast League won the battle, driv-ing the PNL into extinction. The ruling body of the minor leagues, the Na-tional Association of Professional Baseball Leagues, soon recognized the strength of the PCL and accepted the league into the family of organized baseball in 1904 as a class A circuit. At the time class A was the highest rating a minor league could receive, demonstrating the respect the PCL had earned after just one year. Six teams comprised the league in that inaugural season: Los Angeles, San Francisco, Sacramento, Oakland, Seattle and Portland. Except for 1907 and 1908, when only four teams competed, the PCL maintained a six-team organization, with some minor shifts in member cities. A war-shortened 1918 season threatened the league as it did minor leagues across the country, but the PCL rebounded the following year by fielding eight teams, the size it would remain until 1962.

Most of the talent in the league came from the West, a preponderance from the baseball-rich San Francisco Bay area. Players were white, quite often the sons of Italian and Irish immigrants. Occasionally a player came off college campuses like Stanford University, the University of California, or the University of Southern California, but for the most part kids came from the sandlots, went to the low minors and then worked their way up to the Coast League.

Though there were a few Native Americans and an occasional Latin, the color line was strong in the 1920s. Except for preseason exhibition games against touring Negro league teams, black players never blessed PCL ballparks during the decade.

After the 1920s the minors began to lose much of their independence as the pernicious major league farm systems devoured minor league after minor league, leaving in their wake only memories of a time when a city's team was its own—not that of a major league owner several thousand miles away.

In the 1920s, West Coast fans paid more attention to the Coast League than they did the National and American. More than 7,800 games would be played by a thousand players during the decade. Some of the ballplayers were great, some mediocre, but all of them are worth remembering. It would be impossible to write about more than a fraction of these players or the games they played. This book does not attempt the impossible. It does try to do something simple: to keep the place and time known as the Pacific Coast League of the 1920s alive so that all of us who came later can enjoy it.

Chapter 1

Rocked by Scandal

The slight morning chill had already disappeared as bright blue skies shone over the City of Angels—fitting weather for the final day of the successful 1919 Pacific Coast League season. By the ninth inning the baseball looked the color of saliva, tobacco juice and infield dirt, its pristine whiteness having vanished long before. Vernon pitcher Wieser Dell gripped the ball in his fingers, took his stretch and looked over at first base, where Los Angeles Angel Rube Ellis took his lead. There were two outs in the ninth, the tying run on first and the league championship on the line.

More than 22,000 had packed Los Angeles's Washington Park for the Sunday morning game that would decide the PCL pennant. After 8⅔ innings, they had gotten their money's worth.

At the plate, Bert Niehoff represented the Angels' last chance for the game and the pennant. Dell delivered his pitch. Niehoff chopped it wide of the mound, Dell fielded it cleanly, but his hurried throw to first sailed wide. Ellis, however, trying to take an extra base on the play, sped for third. The throw from first came on a line across the diamond to nip Ellis at the bag. The season was over. After seven months and 181 games Vernon had won the 1919 Pacific Coast League pennant.

By almost any measure 1919 had been an unqualified success. Crowds neared capacity in all eight Pacific Coast League cities during one of the most hotly contested pennant races in league history. Even Seattle, fielding its first PCL team in 13 years, and Salt Lake City, the most remote of Coast League cities, drew exceptionally well. Every team turned a profit, the level of play was outstanding, and fan support was growing. The league looked solid, the outlook bright. It would come as something of a shock, then, when less than a year later the league was shaken to its knees, its future gravely threatened.

The first rumblings of trouble came in November 1919, when the Pacific Coast League directors—the eight team owners—went on record as opposing gambling, suggesting a problem in their ballparks. This order of business came minutes after the hiring of a new league president, William H. McCarthy, to whom the owners gave the directive to stop the gambling.

Gambling at baseball games was nothing new in the Pacific Coast League, or the major leagues for that matter. Wagering on ballgames had been around as long as the game itself. Both the National and American Leagues had experienced betting scandals, though the granddaddy of all scandals, the Black Sox scandal wherein the Chicago White Sox deliberately lost the 1919 World Series, would not come to light until later in 1920. Between the 1919 and 1920 seasons the issue of gambling at major league parks drew headlines. Gambling was on the rise and organized baseball and gamblers were fighting a battle over the reputation of the game. By the end of 1919, gambling's pervasiveness and the absence of laws with any teeth would have encouraged any betting man to lay money on the gamblers' winning this battle.

Scandal had not afflicted the PCL, and McCarthy shared the directors' desire that it never would. As long as gamblers operated openly at ballparks, questions remained about the legitimacy of the game being played on the field. And to baseball fans, crooked ballgames were anathema.

One did not have to be a detective to witness betting at ballparks in the Pacific Coast League. The gamblers hardly cowered from view; the loud men in fancy fedoras openly clutched fistfuls of money, which often changed hands on the outcome of an at-bat or even a pitch. The more serious money was bet on the outcomes of games or on a series of games. This business, too, was usually conducted in public view, usually in a favored section of the ball-park, such as the upper unreserved grandstand above first base at San Francisco's Recreation Park and the right-field grandstands at Seattle, for example. One day during 1919, the activity grew so heavy in Seattle that authorities could no longer look the other way, and 20 gamblers were hauled away to jail.

When league officials met in San Francisco the second week of January 1920 they spent a full day talking only of gambling. They drafted an extensive declaration of principles, and for the first time the league president was given the authority to ban known gamblers from ballparks; previously, only an individual club had authority under league bylaws to do so at its ballpark. To prevent gamblers from following clubs from ballpark to ballpark, photographs would be circulated among clubs so that banned gamblers could be identified.

The anti-gambling plan amounted to the toughest in organized baseball, demonstrating the owners' and league officials' resolve against gambling. For several of the owners, their staunch anti-gambling stance turned out to be more bluster than substance. When it came time to choose between self-interest and morality, more than one club owner came up lacking. This hypocrisy would soon create a schism that divided the league for four years.

The PCL's tough stance did curb gambling during the 1920 season, but it did not end it. Gamblers simply became more careful and less open in their activities. Some men were banned from ballparks, but by and large the more serious of the lot either found a way into the ballpark, or did their betting outside.

The increased scrutiny also confirmed McCarthy's worst fears when it exposed rottenness at the edges of the game. The first news of corruption in the ranks of Pacific Coast League players came barely a month into the season, when Charlie Graham, manager and part owner of the San Francisco Seals, announced the release of pitchers Tom Seaton and Casey Smith. A tight-lipped Graham would not reveal precisely what the two players had done, but he alluded to their gambling on games and consorting with gamblers. Left unsaid was whether the players had actually conspired to lose ballgames.

For Seaton, this was getting to be a habit. A few years earlier he had been tossed off a semipro team in Oxnard, California, for throwing games for money. He had supposedly mended his ways, pitching six years in the major leagues without incident. Now almost 33 years old, he was one of the best pitchers in the league, winning 25 games for the Seals in 1919. Smith, too, was counted on heavily by Graham and the Seals. The ex-infielder-turned-pitcher was seen as a potential Coast League star with a chance at the majors.

Graham's decision to cut the two players drew praise from owners and newspapermen around the league. *Sporting News* columnists hailed his unselfishness in putting the game above his own ballclub, for Graham's action almost certainly would cost his team the pennant. A San Francisco writer, whose pen name was Seal Rock, wrote of Graham's action: "Folks out this way are wondering why some of the big league clubs do not take the bull by the horns and fire some of the players that are suspected. It was that courage [by Graham] that appeals to the fair-minded fans who want clean baseball, and his action did more to clarify the situation than reams of talk and blustering."

Any sting Graham might have felt over losing two of his best players was eased by the adulation he received from virtually every corner. On the field, however, the Seals dropped quickly from their first place position and by summer fell into the second division; the loss of two accomplished pitchers, and the accompanying effects on morale, hurt the Seals badly.

Seaton and Smith vehemently denied the charges and threatened to sue the Seals and the league. The threat to litigate against the league meant that the players believed Graham had not acted alone in releasing the players, but had consulted with fellow San Franciscan McCarthy. Indeed, McCarthy appeared to be acting in concert with Graham; on the heels of the manager's actions he banned three of San Francisco's better known gamblers from ballparks throughout the league. He then warned Seaton and Smith that they were not welcome anywhere in the PCL.

McCarthy's angry assault on gambling came on the afternoon of Monday, May 10. That night he and a lady friend strolled casually down a San Francisco street not far from Recreation Park, home of the Seals. As the couple neared a restaurant, they were startled by Roy Hurlburt, who asked if he could speak privately to McCarthy. Hurlburt was one of the three gamblers McCarthy had banned only hours before. Warily, the league president acceded to the man's request, preparing for the heartfelt denial of the wrongly accused. Instead, as he neared the curb, McCarthy took a sucker punch in the jaw, which knocked him to the ground, where he barely avoided a kick to the head. Seconds later, back on his feet, McCarthy squared off with Hurlburt, landing at least one blow. Standing more than six feet tall, McCarthy had been described in several quarters as a physically imposing figure. Before the fight proceeded much further, however, a San Francisco policeman stepped in to end the confrontation.

An outraged San Francisco police chief promised to step up the campaign against the gamblers by sending plainclothes detectives to the ballparks. McCarthy vowed to become even more zealous in banning gamblers, even though he admitted that California had no laws to support his unilateral action. As far as he was concerned, the gamblers could take him to court.

Neither Tom Seaton nor Casey Smith filed suit, and they did not play again in the PCL. Later in 1920, the two ballplayers surfaced for a time with Little Rock of the Southern League. Aware of their alleged activities on the West Coast, the Southern League president would not allow the players into the league. After a court action and a league vote, the players remained outlawed from the Southern League.

A month after the run-in with Hurlburt, McCarthy visited Washington Park in Los Angeles, home field for the Los Angeles Angels and the Vernon Tigers. Shortly after his visit, police officers raided the right-field bleachers, the popular spot for gamblers, netting 11 suspects. Only hours later, the gamblers paid their $10 bail and were back on the streets. Some of the suspects later received a small fine, while the charges against others were dropped.

The run-in with Hurlburt and the lack of statutory support notwithstanding, McCarthy's campaign began to gain momentum. Not only did he have obvious violators arrested and expelled, he also instigated undercover investigations. Word on the street was that several gamblers were cooperating with investigators. Some gamblers became more cautious, others continued their activities unabated.

McCarthy continued to apply the pressure, and as he proceeded he soon discovered a cancer in the ranks of the league. In August, Vernon first baseman Babe Borton admitted to bribing Salt Lake players to throw ball games during the week of September 22, 1919. Worse still, Borton claimed that the entire Vernon team had pooled their money to create a slush fund of more than $2,000, with which it bribed members of other ballclubs. Suddenly, the glory days of Vernon's 1919 pennant looked less than grand. Not only was the Vernon flag tainted, but the rest of the league was sullied as well.

Portland writer Roscoe Fawcett wrote that the 1919 pennant should be torn off Vernon's flagpole, adding, "There is no more room for tarnished pennants than there is for tarnished ballplayers."

Among the names implicated in the scandal were Salt Lake's best players and PCL marquee names: 1919 batting champion Bill Rumler, PCL veteran Harl Maggert and pitchers Ralph Stroud and Charley "Spider" Baum. Another name that surfaced in the allegations was Hal Chase, the ex–major leaguer who had been accused of throwing games as far back as 1910 and who had been suspended in 1919 by the New York Giants for the same reason. Chase helped orchestrate the fix of the 1919 World Series and also bribed Chicago Cub Lee Magee to throw games in 1918. Even in the wake of the Seaton and Smith case, several PCL players continued to socialize openly with Chase, who was unwanted as a player, but who had become a fixture in PCL ballparks.

Borton, allegedly in cahoots with Chase, was caught paying Maggert an unspecified sum of money. The two players claimed the money was for the settlement of a craps game bet. Soon enough Borton revealed the truth. He had bribed Maggert to do less than his best in the September series between Salt Lake and Vernon. Maggert admitted accepting the bribe. Salt Lake dismissed Maggert outright. Ignoring pleas from Maggert's tearful wife, McCarthy followed up Salt Lake's action by suspending the player from the league.

Vernon suspended Borton "pending investigation." This apparent equivocation in the face of a baldfaced bribe angered many in baseball, who felt Borton should be summarily banned.

McCarthy's investigators swooped in, targeting the Salt Lake and Vernon ballclubs. In addition to applying pressure to players, McCarthy, a former grand jury foreman, put up a $5,000 reward for anyone supplying evidence to support Borton's claim that the entire Vernon club had created a bribery fund.

Soon, fearing that their names might come out in the investigations, several players came forward with details about bribe attempts. One of the first to do so was Ralph Stroud, the Salt Lake pitcher who won 14 games and lost 11 in 1919. One of his losses came during the stretch drive, Stroud claimed, when Borton offered him $300 to lose intentionally. Stroud says he declined the money and had legitimately lost the game. After the game Borton sought out Stroud and offered him the money. Stroud refused it. A few days later Stroud walked off the Salt Lake team, supposedly over a contract dispute. Borton claimed Stroud left because he had bribed the pitcher not to pitch another game against Vernon. The Stroud-Borton exchange had become common knowledge among players around the league.

The Los Angeles Angels, who lost the 1919 pennant by an eyelash on the last day of the season, felt that Borton's bribing of players had cost them the title and the $10,000 prize that went with it. Stroud bore the brunt of the

Angels' wrath as he was taunted mercilessly during a Los Angeles–Salt Lake series in the summer of 1920. Angel Manager Red Killefer led the verbal assault. A distraught Stroud turned to his own manager, Ernie Johnson, and explained how Borton had approached him the year before. Not much later he signed an affidavit saying that he had been offered—and had refused—a bribe from Borton. Baum filed a similar affidavit, saying that Borton and Chase had approached him to throw ball games during the 1919 pennant race.

As fan outrage grew, McCarthy vowed to launch a full-scale investigation. Stroud and Baum were allowed to continue playing, but McCarthy insisted on suspending Rumler because he admitted accepting money. Rumler's suspension would start one of the most bitter feuds in PCL history. That it could do so can only be attributed to the self-interest of Salt Lake owners Bill Lane and Jack Cook.

Rumler admitted accepting money from Borton. It would have been difficult for Rumler to deny it because payment was made with a bank draft signed by Borton and endorsed by Rumler. Also, investigators uncovered a letter from Rumler to Borton that, circumstantially, was incriminating.

Instead of a bribe, Rumler claimed he and Borton had simply bet on the outcome of the pennant race, with each man betting against his own team. According to Rumler, Borton approached him in July 1919 with the following proposition: "It begins to look as if either one of us might cop this year's pennant and the $10,000 which the boosters have hung up. Let's arrange a trade whereby both of us can get a little cut in on the melon; if Vernon wins I'll owe you $250 and if Salt Lake wins you pay me $250."

Rumler accepted the "trade," justifying it thusly: "Dozens of such trades are made each year in the major leagues and I'll wager there are many of them pending on the two big league championships right now. I'll dare anyone to produce any evidence that I ever laid down on any club I have ever drawn money from, or that I ever wagered a cent against my club. I did merely what hundreds of other honorable ball players have done and, what is more, I made no secret about it."

Incredibly, Rumler claimed his bet was merely a hedge against losing the pennant, which even if true was no less despicable than accepting bribes for losing ballgames. Borton scoffed at Rumler's claim, stating that the $200 was to encourage the player to fake an injury during the stretch drive so that he would miss a week-long series against Los Angeles. The Salt Lake owners supported Rumler, apparently believing his story that he had not accepted a bribe and understanding his justification that it was common practice to bet against your own team. The fact that Rumler was one of Salt Lake's most popular players and that he was worth a lot of money to a major league team may have contributed to the two owners' gullibility. Prior to the allegations against him, Rumler had been coveted by several major league teams, most notably the Boston Braves, which projected him as a starting outfielder.

Amid the maelstrom of suits and countersuits that came about during the scandal, Lane threatened to sue McCarthy, who suspended Rumler indefinitely. Noting that the bylaws forbade the president from suspending players for longer than 10 days without authorization from the league, Lane planned to schedule a league meeting to overrule McCarthy. About the same time Rumler announced his $50,000 lawsuit against McCarthy.

McCarthy knew that Rumler had been encouraged by the Salt Lake owners and that he was in for an epic battle on which the future of the Coast League might depend. "If Rumler can collect $50,000 from the Coast League, then we had just as well shut up shop, for Borton and Maggert and Seaton and Smith can all come in and ask for damages," he said. "I think if a suit is brought it will be with the idea of frightening the directors into reinstating Rumler next year."

A special league meeting was held in San Francisco during the last week of September 1920 to determine Rumler's future. Lobbying on one side were Bill Lane and Jack Cook, on the other McCarthy. While on the surface it would seem that McCarthy would easily win this battle, the president knew better. After all, it had taken 15 ballots the previous December to elect him. The most vocal opponents had been Oakland owner Cal Ewing, Seattle's William Klepper and Portland's William McCredie. McCarthy eventually defeated incumbent Allan Baum, 5–3, despite Ewing's best efforts. Los Angeles owner Johnny Powers at first supported his nominee, sportswriter Harry A. Williams, but eventually he joined the McCarthy faction.

McCarthy vowed that if the owners overruled him he would resign. Even without McCarthy's vow, the vote was more than a vote on Rumler; it was a vote on McCarthy and his authority as league president. Just before the meeting was to begin, McCarthy received a stroke of luck. News of the fixing of the 1919 World Series — the Black Sox scandal — came to light. The nation was outraged. An anti-gambling fever spread across the country, fueled by angry editorials in newspapers from San Francisco to Boston. Even Rumler admitted that nothing could have hurt him worse. "That Chicago scandal makes it all the tougher for me," he said.

Undaunted, Lane argued his case, agreeing that Rumler used "poor judgment" in consorting with a player like Borton, but that he was innocent of wrongdoing. Without accusing Rumler of bribery, McCarthy simply pointed to the player's affidavit, in which he admitted to betting with Borton on the outcome of the season. In the president's view, that was enough to warrant a five-year suspension from the league. Dr. Charles Strub, majority owner of the Seals, angrily defended McCarthy and further asserted that Rumler had accepted a bribe. In addition to the $200, Strub claimed, Rumler also received Borton's assurance that the Vernon team would do what it could to let Rumler hit safely.

At the conclusion of the meeting, the owners sided with McCarthy, 7–1.

A three-person committee of McCarthy, Graham and Ewing was then formed to investigate the charges that the entire Vernon team had conspired to bribe its way to the 1919 pennant. Forming the committee was a concession on McCarthy's part; the move reduced his unilateral power to conduct his own investigation and act on the findings. This was important to Ewing and McCredie, who resented the muscle-flexing McCarthy had already displayed during his brief tenure, disregarding the power the senior owners had earned in the league.

At a time when unity was critical, politics was taking precedence over a desire for the common good. This became evident to most of the writers covering the PCL scandal. The *Los Angeles Times*, unimpressed with the PCL committee plan, published an editorial beseeching the Los Angeles Grand Jury to launch an investigation into the case. Wisely (at least as far as the future of the Pacific Coast League was concerned), the Los Angeles District Attorney's office agreed to a grand jury inquiry.

The season ended on October 17. Less than two weeks later several members of the ballclub, as well as players from around the league, appeared in Los Angeles before the grand jury. Portland sent a contingent of Manager Walter H. McCredie and players Art Koehler, Del Baker, Frank Farmer (a player on the 1919 team), and Red Oldham. More than 25 players, writers, owners and managers were on the original list of witnesses.

Leading off the witness parade was Babe Borton, who spent two hours excoriating his ex-teammates and repeating claims that they conspired to fix the 1919 season. Maggert followed, saying that Borton and Vernon infielder Bobby Fisher approached him, Eddie Mulligan, Jean Dale and Rumler to fix games. A bank draft for $500 from Borton to Dale convinced the grand jury that Dale had accepted a bribe. Dale, who pitched in the Texas League in 1920, refused to leave his home in St. Louis to participate in the proceedings.

McCarthy presented an affidavit from Salt Lake catcher Edward Spencer stating that he, too, had been offered a bribe from Borton. In one of the few humorous moments of the investigation, Borton responded to Spencer's claim that he was offered $1,760: "I may have offered [Spencer] a bribe, but not for that much."

Portland second baseman Paddy Siglin's affidavit stated that Borton offered him $100 to stay out of the lineup for a week. Seattle first baseman Rod Murphy claimed that gambler Nate Raymond offered him $3,000 to throw ballgames in August 1920. Further, Murphy asserted, Raymond boasted about having earned $50,000 from gambling on PCL games in 1919.

Other players testifying included Vernon's Hugh High, Tommy Long, Willie Mitchell and Bill Essick. Ralph Stroud also appeared and affirmed his earlier affidavit, while Portland players Dick Cox and John Glazier both presented affidavits damning Borton. After a week of testimony Chief Deputy District Attorney William Doran said that at least five of the eight teams in

1919 were crooked and that the 1919 pennant race "was a game of bunking the public."

The picture of the scandal that was emerging had Borton in the center, offering bribes to players on the Salt Lake, Seattle and Portland teams. To complete the picture, two questions remained to be answered: Who had accepted bribes and who had bankrolled the operation?

To the first question, only three players were caught with money received from Borton: Maggert, Rumler and Dale. If the other players had accepted money, it was likely in cash and thus untraceable. Commenting on players' denials of having accepted bribes, one juror remarked that many of the players appeared to be lying.

To the latter question, there were two claims. Borton stuck by his original assertion that the Vernon players had bankrolled the bribery pool and, further, that his former best friend and roommate, Bill Essick, ran the show under his authority as manager. The other camp held to the view that Borton was lying out of fear of reprisal from the gamblers, and that he was acting as go-between for serious gambling interests that included Nate Raymond.

The grand jury investigation proceeded in fits and stops as jurors juggled a heavy schedule of investigations, including a couple of celebrated murders. On December 11, six weeks after the inquiry had begun, the grand jury announced its findings: the Vernon players were absolved of conspiring to bribe opposing players. The jury found that Borton had worked in concert with Raymond, and perhaps other gamblers, to try to fix games. In addition, it found sufficient evidence to charge Rumler and Maggert. Dale was not charged. The charge was criminal conspiracy in colluding to throw ballgames in the Vernon–Salt Lake series in Los Angeles in October 1919. None of the four men were present when the indictments were handed down. Judge Frank Willis then issued a warrant for their arrest and set bail at $1,000.

The investigations had netted little more than was already clear. Rumler remained the only player charged who denied his guilt. The grand jury's work did exonerate Vernon and restore some credibility to both the 1919 and 1920 pennant races; however, the breadth and depth to which gambling had infiltrated the Coast League game was more troubling than the vindication of a single team. It seemed likely that other players had accepted bribes, considering the frequency with which Borton offered bribes and the universal nonchalance with which most players regarded such offers. Very few players questioned showed outrage or anger—except over being singled out in the scandal. Until McCarthy started digging up facts, players did not come forward voluntarily with their reports of bribes or bets offered to them or their teammates.

There was no question that gambling had seeped deeply into the Coast League. The grand jury had revealed that; the next move was up to the league.

The Pacific Coast League owners, President McCarthy and other league officials gathered in Sacramento a few days before Christmas for what would prove to be one of the league's stormiest sessions. The order of business was to establish tougher regulations against gambling, but the two-day meeting quickly deteriorated.

McCarthy blasted those club owners who put their own interests before the league's or the good of the game. "This league needs a housecleaning among club owners as well as players," he shouted angrily, adding, "Jack Cook is at the bottom of most of the trouble." He then insinuated that Portland, Seattle and Oakland had also not done a good job of policing gambling in their ballparks.

Lane would not let the Rumler issue drop, arguing that McCarthy could not suspend the player—essentially finding him guilty as charged—until the player had his day in court. McCarthy held fast.

Lane and Cook rallied support from McCredie, Ewing and Klepper, forming a four-team bloc calling for the president's ouster. The Seals' Strub, along with Johnny Powers from Los Angeles, Lewis Moreing of Sacramento and Ed Maier of Vernon not only supported McCarthy, but offered to double his salary to $10,000 annually. Soon the shouting escalated and then erupted into violence when Cook punched John Powers. Powers retaliated, knocking Cook out.

Tired of the bickering, McCarthy resigned and walked out of the meeting. After McCarthy left, things calmed a bit and the owners voted to offer him a raise to $10,000. The vote was reported in the papers as being unanimous, though this was likely for public relations reasons. After all, how could the league let go the man responsible for starting its cleanup? Even those owners opposed to McCarthy must have recognized this.

Yet when 1920 came to a close, the Pacific Coast League had no president, low public confidence, and the team owners were hopelessly divided. Lane expressed the dismay that many of the eight owners must have felt: "What has got into the boys [owners]? It seems to be getting worse and I am mighty tired of it. I hope to sell out my interest in the Salt Lake club and step out. Life is too short to be doing what we are doing at these meetings."

Lane received more bad news when it was announced the last week of December that charges were dropped against Rumler, Borton, Maggert and Raymond. Judge Willis explained that nothing under California law prohibited throwing baseball games, and, therefore, the players could not be charged with criminal conspiracy. The judge then admonished the four men for their actions, adding that he wished they could be prosecuted.

A trial was Lane's last chance for vindicating Rumler. Now there was no hope to reinstate the player, or to sell him to another ballclub. For Lane, his fellow owners, and for William McCarthy, the year that had begun with optimism and promise ended with rancor and despair.

Chapter 2

1920 – The PCL's First Dynasty

As the bribery scandal raged off the field during 1920, on the field a baseball season continued to be played. In the thick of the race were five of the Pacific Coast League's eight teams, including the Vernon Tigers, pennant winners in 1918 and 1919. On paper the Tigers were the team to beat in 1920. But constant assaults against the team's character dogged them all year, jeopardizing their run for a third consecutive pennant.

In addition to hearing fans, opposing players and the press excoriate them with charges that their 1919 pennant had been "bought" with bribes, Vernon players had to defend their 1918 flag as well. That year a "work or fight" rule, issued by the federal government in response to World War I, shortened the Coast League season to slightly more than one hundred games. Vernon beat runner-up Los Angeles by a game in the win column and, therefore, claimed the title. Following the regular season, a nine-game series was played. To Vernon fans, the series was little more than an exhibition; to Angel fans, it was a playoff series to determine the true Coast League champion. When the Angels won five of seven games, they claimed the crown. Vernon pointed to their own superior regular season record to stake their claim. Though the Reach guides for several years show Los Angeles as the 1918 champion, today's official PCL records credit Vernon with that honor.

Since joining the league in 1909, when the PCL grew from four teams to six, Vernon had to fight to gain even footing with their big-city neighbor to the south. Vernon's owner, Ed Maier, tired of his squabbles with Los Angeles owner John Powers over rights to Washington Park, decided to sell the club prior to the 1919 season.

Maier, a successful brewer, found a willing buyer in Roscoe "Fatty" Arbuckle. By 1919 Arbuckle was one of the nation's biggest celebrities, with his comedic talent and fan appeal compared to Charlie Chaplin's. Two years earlier he had set Hollywood on its ear when he signed a three-year, $3 million deal with Paramount. Arbuckle would fall in a national homicide scandal in

1921, but in 1919 he was awash in both fame and money. Arbuckle, however, hesitated at buying the club outright, instead insisting on an option to buy the club for Maier's asking price of $65,000. Maier agreed, and Arbuckle and his associate, Lou Anger, ran the ballclub for the 1919 season.

When the season ended, Arbuckle's team had won the pennant and turned a $30,000 profit. Now all Arbuckle had to do was exercise his option and pay up. But Arbuckle balked, dismayed over his inability to secure a 10-year agreement with Powers to use Washington Park. He also did not want to pay Maier the $65,000 in full. "Cash was demanded," he said, adding that "cash dealers of that size are not a habit in baseball. So I guess I am through with baseball."

Maier held similar bad feelings. In recounting his woes, Maier referred to "Fatty Carbunkle" and his fake money. "Next time I sell out there had better be some real money on the line," he said.

So the 1920 Tigers faced the season with two questionable titles under their belt and a reluctant owner controlling their fate. Not only did he appear reluctant to be associated with the Tigers, Maier sounded downright truculent toward his ballplayers.

"I do not want mechanical players," Maier declared prior to the start of the 1920 season. "I do not want those who play for the 'first and fifteenth.' I will not tolerate umpire baiting and I will not stand for a listless club, regardless of the fact that it may be a winner."

Maier's comments came in response to allegations that his team played dirty, charges that stemmed from the 1919 Junior World Series with St. Paul of the American Association. In that series between Double A champions, not only did Vernon players taunt and bait umpires and opponents, but they started several fistfights as well. At the close of the series, a riot erupted and an American Association umpire was beaten by Vernon fans. Eastern writers labelled the Tigers and their fans "thugs" and "hoodlums" who damaged the good name of baseball.

Maier may not have been pleased, but he did not clean house, realizing that he owned the most talented club on the West Coast. He gave manager Bill Essick a raise and a three-year contract, rewarding him for piloting the team to its two previous titles and absolving the skipper of blame in the Louisville debacle. Essick was also named general manager and he went to work shoring up the lineup. In 1920 he had more latitude than in the past as the roster size was increased from 16 to 18 players for the period between May 1 and September 15. Before and after these dates, clubs could carry as many players as they needed. Since the season was expanded to 28 weeks in 1920, Essick and the league's other managers needed an ample supply of players for the grueling 200-game season.

Vernon's first priority was to find a third baseman to replace Bob Meusel, who had been sold to the New York Yankees. Just prior to the start of the

Carlisle Smith (Don Hazelwood)

season, the Tigers signed J. Carlisle "Red" Smith, who came from the New York Yankees as part of the deal that sent Meusel east. Smith, a 30-year-old veteran with nine years of major league experience, was coming off a 1919 season in which he hit .245 for the Boston Braves.

Other question marks in the lineup included a pitching corps that had lost starters Joseph Finneran, Rex Dawson and Byron Houck, as well as thin catching ranks that dropped off dramatically after starter Al DeVormer. Pitching and catching depth were critical in any league; they were especially so in the long Pacific Coast League seasons.

On the positive side, Essick returned three players who had been tabbed

Hugh High (George E. Outland)

as PCL all-stars in an informal poll of fans conducted by a Los Angeles sports-writer. Shortstop Johnny Mitchell and outfielders Chester Chadbourne and Hugh High led a lineup that was solid from top to bottom.

Essick was not lulled into a sense of false security, and at the beginning of the season he predicted the PCL race would be tight. "I fail to see any soft spot anywhere," he said. "The field will be so strong that it is unlikely that any club will show an average of .600 at the finish. The club that wins the 1920 race will not finish above .575 or .580." San Francisco and Los Angeles looked the toughest, according to Essick, who also gave Seattle a chance, even though the Indians were only in their second season and had finished an abysmal 62-108 in 1919.

Veteran PCL observer Abe Kemp, quoted in the *Sporting News*, con-curred with Essick, and even called Seattle "the team to beat" for the PCL

Chester (Chet) Chadbourne (George E. Outland)

crown. The Indians did not live up to their advanced billing in the early season, getting off to a 9-21 start. They occupied the cellar, with a record well below .500, through the middle of July.

Vernon's season begins

Vernon opened their season in April with a 7-4 win over the San Francisco Seals. Their opening day lineup held solid for most of the year (1920 season statistics in parentheses): Johnny Mitchell, ss (.270, 1 HR); Chester Chadbourne, cf (.286, 3 HR); Hugh High, lf (.288, 4 HR); Frank Edington, rf (.272, 3 HR); Robert Fisher, 2b (.310, 2 HR); Babe Borton, 1b (suspended in bribery conspiracy, statistics stricken from books. Replaced in lineup by Edington, Hamilton Hyatt and Arthur Mueller during last weeks of season); Red Smith, 3b (.292, 1 HR); and Albert DeVormer, c (.242, 3 HR).

Wieser Dell (George E. Outland)

Not everything clicked for Vernon at the season's outset. Pitching appeared especially shaky. On April 17, Los Angeles pounded Vernon pitching for 19 hits in a 21–9 win. Pitcher Walter Smallwood struggled in the early going, while Art Fromme missed all of April with whooping cough.

On May 2, Vernon sat in third place with 14 wins and 13 losses. Pitching was not the only culprit in the lackluster start. The team still needed another catcher, and the hitters were not hitting. Particularly weak against left-handers, the team's lack of punch left them at the bottom of the league in batting average.

Vernon's fortunes improved slightly in early May when Houck agreed to terms and reported to work. This bit of good news was soon offset by the departure of Wieser (pronounced "Wheezer" and spelled this way in many accounts) Dell, who joined an industrial league in Richmond, Utah. An electrical company agreed to pay the pitcher $550 a month to pitch and work yearround. Dell's leaving was a ploy to extract more money from Maier, and the pitcher gave the owner something to think about when he threw a two-hit shutout against Oakland in his farewell game on May 9.

A month later Dell returned, reportedly frightened by the National Commission's threat to ban for five years those players in organized baseball who violated their contracts. The commission's action came at a time when players in the majors and high minors were jumping their teams (or threatening to) to play in industrial or outlaw leagues, where high profile players could draw large salaries, at least for the short term. These players were coddled by their adoptive teams, as evidenced by Salt Lake's Nick Cullop, who left his club to join an outlaw Idaho league. Salt Lake manager Ernie Johnson went to Idaho to convince Cullop to return, only to be escorted out of town by the marshall and a hundred baseball fans threatening to lynch the interloper. Before he departed, Johnson did locate Cullop at the local hotel, where the locals were "bowing the knee and uncovering every time he [Cullop] yawned." In spite of the star treatment, Cullop returned to Salt Lake shortly after the commission announced its intended ban.

Dell's return in June sparked a resurgence of the Vernon team. The team played .600 ball for the month, led by Dell's five wins. For the year, the 33-year-old right-hander went 27-15 and compiled a 2.99 ERA. Offensively and in the field the Tigers received clutch help from an old veteran: 34-year-old Scotty Alcock. Save for a cup of coffee in the major leagues in 1914, Alcock was a career minor leaguer who was both versatile and reliable. During the season he played every position, including spot relief pitching. Alcock went quietly about his job and was a fan favorite. The only mark against him came on June 17 when he made his first error in nearly two years.

The last week of June, the struggling San Francisco Seals came to Washington Park for a seven-game series—the standard work week for PCL teams in the 1920s. Weakened by the release of pitchers Tom Seaton and Casey Smith, the Seals limped into town having lost consecutive series to Los Angeles, Salt Lake and Sacramento. Their luck would not change. During the first four games of the series, San Francisco managed just one win. Then on Saturday, June 26, Dell blanked the Seals, 1–0 in 10 innings, outdueling Johnny Couch.

The following day, Vernon swept a doubleheader, winning 1–0, and 4–3 on Mitchell's three-hitter. In both games Vernon scored the winning run during their last at-bat. The series dropped the Seals from third to fourth place. As July began Vernon trailed first-place Salt Lake by one-half game.

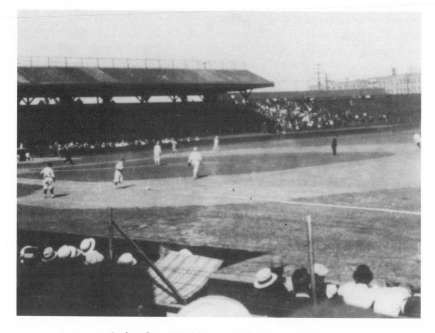

Action from Washington Park (Ray Medeiros)

Pitching, a concern at the season's outset, was now coming through. Middle infielders Johnny Mitchell and Robert Fisher continued to play well. Mitchell's play drew the attention of Yankee scouts and by mid-July the big league club asked Maier to name his price for the shortstop. At season's end he went to the Yankees for an unspecified sum. As a team the Vernon hitters struggled. Most disappointing were the outfielders. Of the quartet of High, Chadbourne, Edington and Tommy Long, only High hit above .280 (.288), and as a group they produced just nine home runs. In an attempt to add more offense to the lineup, Essick moved Smith from third to right field and brought Hap Morse off the bench to play third. The experiment failed; for the year Morse managed only a .230 average and no home runs.

First-place Salt Lake, meanwhile, thrived on the strength of their hitting. Earl Sheely, Bill Rumler, Ernie Johnson and Harl Maggert led the Bees' attack. With the exception of Ralph Stroud, however, their pitching was weak. Their one-dimensional aspect rendered the Bees vulnerable. "Salt Lake is out in front now," wrote the *Sporting News*. "But should something happen to Sheely, Rumler, Johnson or Maggert, the club would limp along."

The assessment proved prophetic. A few days later Salt Lake lost both Rumler and Maggert to the betting scandal. The team clung to first place in late August, but the loss of the two leading hitters eventually caused the Bees to tumble, ending up a disappointing fifth at the season's close.

Vernon assumed first place on August 27 while they sat idle, watching the rain fall in Seattle; down in Los Angeles, Salt Lake lost the first of five straight to the Angels.

Seattle rebounds

While Vernon, Salt Lake, Los Angeles and San Francisco battled for the top spot, Seattle slowly began to fulfill its preseason promise. The Indians caught fire during the summer, winning eight straight series to rise from the cellar and surpass the .500 mark. By the first week in September the team had reached third place. Much of the credit had to go to club president William Klepper, who never stopped dealing for a combination of players who could bring credible baseball to the PCL's northernmost city. The resurgent ballclub became the toast of Seattle, drawing crowds of 10,000 to 12,000 for weekend games and 3,000 to 5,000 during the week to dilapidated Rainier Park.

Vernon did not receive the same fan support. Allegations that the entire club had conspired to bribe its way to the 1919 pennant inspired jeers for the local ballclub. Rather than succumb to the adversity, the Vernon players thrived on it, banding together to hold onto first place as the season entered its final 60 games.

The Seattle Indians arrived in town the first week in September. As the two teams approached the doubleheader finale on Sunday, the Tigers held a four games to three edge in the series. The morning game would feature the pitching and defensive battle of the year.

The durable Wieser Dell squared off against Seattle's Harry Seibold. Neither pitcher seemed overpowering, Dell yielding a run in the third, Seibold one in the fourth. Dell in particular was having a terrible time finding the plate. When he did, Seattle hit him sharply; nevertheless, he blanked the Indians from the fourth inning through the ninth inning. Seibold settled down after his rocky third inning and though he was not fooling the Vernon batters, they managed only to hit ground ball after ground ball to the waiting Seattle infielders. The game turned into a test of wills between the two pitchers as they labored through 16 innings. By the top of the seventeenth, Dell had given up 14 hits and walked eight. He had not, however, given up a run for 13 innings. His luck ran out when Sammy Bohne hit his second double of the game to drive in the go-ahead run. Seibold shut down Vernon in the home half of the seventeenth to win 2–1. His was a masterful six-hitter, which seemed even more incredible given that he struck out only one batter on the day.

The afternoon game had to be called because of the length of the morning marathon. Thus the series ended at four games apiece. Seattle's streak of winning series had ended, though hardly conclusively. Not only had Seattle won the tension-filled Sunday game, but they had frustrated the Tigers on Saturday as well, when the home team had the tying run on base in the bottom of the ninth but could not push it across. Taking the loss in the Saturday

Frank Shellenback (George E. Outland)

game was Frank Shellenback, who came within 24 hours of what could have
been a memorable major league career.

Shellenback and the spitter

Shellenback had pitched for the Chicago White Sox in 1918 and 1919,
winning 10 and losing 15. The six-foot-two right-hander showed major league
promise, with a cumulative 3.06 earned run average. He held out for more
money for the 1920 season, whereupon Chicago owner Charles Comiskey sold
him to Vernon—just 24 hours before the start of the 1920 season. Still only
21 years old, Shellenback's future appeared bright until the major leagues
banned the spitball and other "freak" deliveries such as the shine ball (where
a pitcher applied paraffin wax to the ball) and the emery ball (a ball scuffed
with an emery board) in December 1920. Only those pitchers on active rosters
in the majors during 1920 were exempted from the clause.

In 1920, Shellenback threw a good fastball, which he complemented with a spitter. Arm trouble in 1921 took much of the heat off his fastball, forcing him to rely on the spitball. Though still young, he could not master another legal pitch and never made it back to the big leagues. Though the PCL toyed seriously with the idea of banning freak deliveries, it opted instead to grandfather in players who had used the pitches prior to the major league ban.

For Shellenback the story was not all bad. The 1920 season launched one of the truly great minor league careers, in which he pitched for 18 years in the PCL for Vernon, Sacramento, Hollywood and San Diego. He won 295 games in the circuit, with 361 complete games and 4,185 innings worked. All are PCL records that still stand.

Ironically, Shellenback attributed his longevity (he pitched up to age 40) to the spitter. "It was an easy pitch to throw," he said. "There was very little strain on the arm."

He also staunchly defended the pitch against those who outlawed it. "The reason agitation against the spitball began was because of the cheating that accompanied it. Pitchers used to camouflage in every way. They'd use the mudder, the emery and the shine ball and in every violation the spitter was always blamed," he said.

After his playing days, "Shelly," as he was affectionately known, went on to an exemplary career as a coach and scout. He worked as a pitching coach for the Boston Red Sox, Detroit Tigers, and New York Giants. Giants manager Leo Durocher called Shellenback "one of the greatest assets the Giants had. There was not anything about pitching that he did not know. I took Shelly's word on anything about pitching."

The ex-pitcher also did some managing and there, too, he excelled. At San Diego he managed Ted Williams, convincing the youngster to give up a career as a pitcher in favor of playing every day in the outfield.

Shellenback's best year as a pitcher came in 1932 with Hollywood, when he went 26-10 with a 3.12 earned run average. In 1920, his 18-12 record and 2.71 earned run average were a big part of the Vernon success.

Vernon withstood the continual pressure of Seattle, Salt Lake, San Francisco and Los Angeles to hold onto first place through September. The Angels, on the strength of a 23-7 run from the last week of August through the last week in September, vaulted into second place with a record of 94-83, six wins behind Vernon's 100-79. Seattle remained in third place at 93-82, an eyelash ahead of San Francisco.

As the teams prepared for the final month of the season, the Chicago Black Sox scandal broke, stoking the anti-gambling sentiments that had simmered all summer long on the West Coast. Fan sentiment against crooked ballplayers, along with the pressures of a pennant race, produced some ugly moments.

During a Vernon–Los Angeles series in the third week of September, the

Angels assaulted the Tigers with jabs about their "buying" the 1919 pennant. Robert Fisher took umbrage at Red Killefer's barbs and the two tangled, starting a bench-clearing brawl. Later, Killefer and Frank Edington exchanged blows. In the stands, the teams' two owners, John Powers and Ed Maier, continued their feud, engaging in a heated argument in full view of fans.

The two teams did manage to play some baseball, with the Angels taking five of the seven games. By October 2, the Angels had clawed their way to second place, just two games behind Vernon. San Francisco and Seattle were also playing well, and all three teams occupied second at one point during the week.

With two weeks remaining in the season, the Tigers travelled to Salt Lake, where they won four out of five games (the Sunday doubleheader was cancelled because of rain). San Francisco could not keep pace at Sacramento, losing five of seven games. Los Angeles lost its momentum, winning only two of its seven games against Seattle.

With a week to play, Vernon's chances were enviable, though the Angels, Seals and Indians all had mathematical chances to unseat the defending champions. Los Angeles, at four games back, had the best shot, especially since their concluding seven-game series was against last-place Sacramento. Any Angel hopes for victory were dashed on Thursday, October 14, when they lost their second game in three days. Sacramento went on to take five of seven in the series, playing the spoiler for the second consecutive week. In so doing they climbed past Portland into seventh place. The Seattle Indians benefited the most by Sacramento's inspired play, completing a magnificent turnaround to finish second.

Vernon officially clinched the pennant on October 14, with a 5–3 victory over Portland. The Tigers chased Herman Pillette in the second inning when they scored all five of their runs. As he seemed to be all year, 33-year-old Wieser Dell was on the mound for the crucial game. Dell went the distance, closing out a remarkable year in which he pitched 370 innings.

Turbulent off the field, and hard fought on it, the 1920 season established Vernon as the team to beat in the 1920s. The ballclub overcame accusations and diversions that might have derailed lesser teams, demonstrating that it had character to go along with talent. As hitters the Tigers came back from a slow start to finish third in the league, with a team batting average of .273. That mark would prove to be the lowest average for a pennant winner during the entire 1920s; in fact, only five ballclubs would hit under .273 during the decade. The ballclub also lacked power. Hugh High, their leading home run hitter, hit only four four-baggers. In Vernon's defense, only six players in 1920 reached double figures for home runs. Both home runs and batting averages rose dramatically during the decade, thanks to an increasingly juiced-up ball.

But above all, the Vernon team won on defense and pitching. Defensively, they led the league with a team fielding percentage of .972 — a mark only four teams would equal or exceed in the decade. The pitching staff was unquestionably the team's strength. In addition to Dell and Shellenback, Willie Mitchell (25-13, 2.38 ERA) and Bill Piercy (13-10, 2.44 ERA) had outstanding seasons.

Vernon rose not only to the top of the pack in 1920, but they also removed the tarnish from their disputed pennants in 1918 and 1919. As the first ballclub to win three straight pennants, the Vernon Tigers of 1918 through 1920 laid claim to the Pacific Coast League's first dynasty.

1920 Final Standings

	W	L	Pct.
Vernon	110	88	.556
Seattle	102	91	.528
Los Angeles	102	95	.517
Salt Lake	95	92	.508
Oakland	95	103	.480
Sacramento	89	109	.449
Portland	81	103	.440

Team batting leaders

Average:	Salt Lake — .295
Runs:	Salt Lake — 983
HRs:	Salt Lake — 91

Individual batting leaders

At-bats:	Morrie Schick, San Francisco — 810
Average:	Earl Sheely, Salt Lake — .371
Runs:	Dennis E. Wilie, Oakland — 135
Hits:	Hack Miller, Oakland — 280
2B:	Brick Eldred, Seattle — 59
3B:	Sam Crawford, Los Angeles — 21
HR:	Earl Sheely, Salt Lake — 33
RBI:	not available
Total bases:	Earl Sheely, Salt Lake — 420
Stolen bases:	Rod Murphy, Seattle — 63

Individual pitching leaders

Winning percentage:	Ralph Stroud, Salt Lake—.667 (26-13)
Games won:	Buzz Arlett, Oakland—29
Games lost:	Ken Penner, Sacramento—23
Most games:	Samuel Lewis, San Francisco—63
Most shutouts:	Wieser Dell, Vernon—7
Most complete games:	not available
Most innings:	Buzz Arlett, Oakland—427⅓
ERA:	James Scott, San Francisco—2.291

Chapter 3

1921 – The (Un) Lucky Beavers

Vernon's three straight pennants were a first in the PCL, yet at least one other franchise could stake claim to being the league's first dynasty. Between 1903 and 1920, no franchise won more Coast League championships than the Portland Beavers. The team took five titles, including the 1906 championship and consecutive flags in 1910 and 1911, and 1913 and 1914. Only the Los Angeles Angels could match this record over the league's first 17 years. Indeed, Portland was a proud franchise, supported by fans and viewed by media and baseball men as one of the class outfits of the PCL.

The beaver had long been Oregon's mascot, adorning the Oregon territorial seal. When it achieved statehood, Oregon dubbed itself the Beaver State. So in 1906, when the *Portland Telegram* ran a contest to name the local PCL franchise, the editors chose Beavers over such other unofficial monikers as Browns, Giants and Ducks. Soon the team's winning ways prompted many to refer to them as the "Lucky Beavers."

After 1914 the team was not so lucky. The ballclub's fortunes plummeted, with ineptitude on and off the field. The decline culminated in the 1921 season when the franchise hit rock bottom.

Just as the good times in Portland could be credited to Judge William W. McCredie and his nephew Walter McCredie, so could the bad times be blamed on the two men. They operated the ballclub for 16 years, the judge serving as majority owner and president and Walter managing the ballclub on the field.

The McCredies acquired the team in 1904 for $9,000 from a group of owners that included Max Fleischner and Frank Spencer. The team they inherited had finished comfortably in the league's cellar. Relying on the judge's business acumen and community connections and Walter's baseball experience (he was an ex-player who won the California League batting championship with Oakland in 1902 and played a year with the Brooklyn Superbas of the National League in 1903), the McCredies hoped to rebuild the woeful franchise.

Results came quickly. In 1905 the team went 94-110, a marked improvement over the 79-136 finish of the year before. More importantly, the Beavers fought their way to fifth place in the six-team circuit, a game ahead of cellar-dwelling Seattle. The following year may have been Portland's best ever. Again, they beat out Seattle—this time by 19½ games. Instead of fighting for the cellar, however, the two former doormats vied for first place, which Portland won with an astounding record of 115-60. Their .657 winning percentage remained a PCL record until 1934. The turnaround was complete. Success followed success for the next eight seasons, but after the 1914 season the McCredies lost their magic touch.

Portland was perhaps the hardest hit of all PCL franchises during the war years. With travel costs and restrictions a concern, the Coast League teams decided against traveling to Portland during the season, and they voted to shift the franchise to Sacramento. Pacific Coast League President Allan T. Baum wired Judge McCredie and reluctantly informed him of the move: "It is with regret that I have to record the leaving, although perhaps only temporary, of one of the Pacific Coast League's staunchest and best friends."

His PCL franchise may have moved to California, but the judge stayed active in the game by entering a new ballclub in the Northwestern League. Walter became the manager of the Salt Lake City Bees; the job offer demonstrated the respect he had earned from the league's other owners. As it was, the 1918 season was an abridged affair in which McCredie guided Salt Lake to a fifth-place—48-49—season. The Sacramento franchise, outfitted with several ex–Beavers, finished a half-game ahead of the Bees. A year later Walter and the judge were back in charge of the Portland Beavers. Their enthusiasm for the game, however, seemed to have waned.

The Sacramento franchise remained and Seattle rejoined the circuit, thereby expanding the league to eight teams for the first time. Portland, faced with building a new team essentially from scratch, now competed with seven other ballclubs for players. The team they put together in 1919 beat out only newcomer Seattle, finishing with a 78-96 record. In 1920 the team fell to 81-103 and last place. Fans found this finish appalling, especially since Seattle, in only its second season, finished in second place and played perhaps the most exciting baseball in the league.

Fans who had cheered the return of their beloved Beavers in 1918 began to question the organization's commitment, and calls commenced for new ownership. Memories of the glory years had faded; all that remained was the litany of failure brought by the McCredie family.

As early as August 1920, the judge vowed to build a team in 1921 that would challenge for the pennant. He denied rumors that the ballclub was for sale, though fans could see improvements at the Vaughn Street Park go wanting while the McCredies unloaded players for cash.

Vaughn Street Park, located at 24th and N.W. Vaughn Street, had seen wonderful days. During the 1910s, the ballpark hosted standing-room-only crowds for the season's opening ballgame, and Portland claimed the unofficial record for opening-day attendance at 16,000. Sometimes referred to as Recreation Park or Lucky Beaver Park, the ballpark was built in 1901 for the Portland franchise in the Northwest League. The ballpark was owned by Portland's street railway company until Tom Turner, who came to own the Beavers, also bought the park in 1927. The original structure consisted of a small, wooden grandstand behind home plate. These stands were razed and larger ones constructed for the National Track and Field Games held as part of the Lewis and Clark Exposition of 1905.

Seven years later, the park was rebuilt and seating capacity expanded to 12,000. The rebuilt stadium featured outfield bleachers and covered grandstands that rimmed the playing area from first base to home and all the way down the left-field line. It was constructed of wood and stood virtually unchanged until 1955, when it was torn down. Groundskeeper Rocky Benuvento tended the ballpark from 1927 until its demise, and was credited with saving it more than once from errant cigarettes that threatened to set the wooden stadium ablaze.

Rebuilding the Beavers

The new year had barely begun when Walter McCredie shortened his off-season vacation, leaving his ranch behind and committing himself to making his Beavers winners again. The 1920 season had been humiliating and talk once again commenced among PCL directors about tossing the franchise out of the league. The talk, as usual, proved idle, but McCredie knew that if the ballclub was to compete in 1921, virtually the entire 1920 team would have to be replaced.

Tex Wisterzil was sold to Seattle, Biff Schaller to Beaumont. Paddy Siglin was traded to Salt Lake for Marty Krug, and John Glazier was sold outright to Omaha. Lu Blue had been sold late in 1920 to Detroit and outfielder George Maisel went to the Chicago Cubs. The deals left open three infield and two outfield jobs. About the only roster spots that were secure were catcher Del Baker, outfielder Dick Cox, infielder Marty Krug, and pitchers Sam Ross, Syl Johnson, Harry Polson and Herman Pillette.

An angry Judge McCredie expected players from the Blue deal with Detroit and the Maisel deal with Chicago, charging that the two major league clubs had reneged on their agreements. Detroit's Frank Navin claimed that Portland was offered several legitimate players and that McCredie refused them. McCredie's charges irritated Chicago president Bill Veeck, who said the Cubs bought Maisel for $37,500 and agreed to pay an additional $5,000 or turn over two players. Several players were offered, according to Veeck, but all were rejected, including outfielder Don Brown, an ex–major leaguer who would hit .309 and wallop 15 home runs for Salt Lake in 1921. Therefore, the $5,000 was paid to complete the deal.

The dispute revealed a problem the McCredies — and other PCL owners —
had in dealing with major league clubs. Even before 1918, when the PCL refused to have its players drafted, many PCL teams had a "working relationship" with a major league franchise. Working relationships are not to be
confused with farm clubs, which flourished in the 1930s and forever changed
the minor league game. Working relationships were less formal and usually
lasted as long as the Coast League team owner and the major league club's
president enjoyed cordial relations with one another.

Typically, a working relationship was established when a major league
team wanted a particular player on a PCL ballclub. An agreement was struck
and the PCL team usually received players and cash in return for the coveted
player. If the PCL club had other potential major leaguers, the two ballclubs
might talk about doing business again. Sometimes a major leaguer was sent
to a PCL club for a year of seasoning and was returned to the majors the following year. When he did return, the minor league club often was compensated.
From one transaction, a steady exchange of players could result for two or three
seasons, thereby establishing a working relationship.

The Seals enjoyed a working relationship with Detroit in the early 1920s,
and increasingly with Pittsburgh as the decade wore on. Vernon and the New
York Yankees had a strong working relationship, while Los Angeles worked
with both Detroit and St. Louis. Los Angeles developed something more than
a working relationship with the Chicago Cubs in late 1921, when Cubs owner
William Wrigley bought the Angels. As evidenced by Detroit's involvement
with several clubs, these relationships were not exclusive; a major league team
could deal with other PCL clubs, and PCL clubs could deal with other major
league clubs.

The McCredies did not play the "working relationship game" well in the
1920s. After years of enjoying successful relations with Cleveland, built largely
on the friendship between Judge McCredie and Cleveland's Charley Sommers,
the team entered several deals with major league clubs and always seemed to
come out on the short end. The Detroit and Chicago deals were good examples.

Since help from the majors appeared remote, the McCredies turned to
the open market of minor leaguers. The judge told reporters: "I am willing
to pay $2,500 apiece for three more players, if we can secure them, or we
would go higher than that for one I have been after." Hardly extravagant, the
$2,500 was a reasonable amount for a low-end-to-average Coast League
player.

When the season began on April 5, the Portland lineup featured few stars
(1921 season statistics in parentheses): Art Bourg, rf (.216, 0 HR, played in
only 16 games); Ike Wolfer, lf (.274, 2 HR); Marty Krug, 2b (.274, 7 HR);
Dick Cox, cf (.301, 5 HR); Jim Poole, 1b (.330, 20 HR); Willis Butler, 3b
(.241, 0 HR); Del Baker, c (.276, 0 HR); and Wes Kingdon, ss (played in fewer
than 10 games — no stats available).

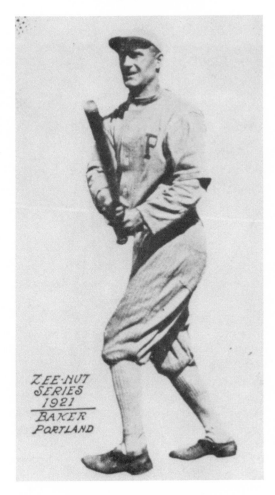

Del Baker (Don Hazelwood)

Only Cox, Baker, Pillette, Bourg and Kingdon had been on the roster the year before, and the latter two did not last long in 1921. Wolfer and Cox held down the outfield, though Bourg gave way to Walter Genin (.259, 3 HR); Poole and Krug anchored the right side of the infield all year. Poole turned out to be one of the league's best first basemen and one of Portland's few bright spots. Gus Fisher (.288, 4 HR) shared catching duties with Baker. To replace Wes Kingdon, Portland used a shortstop-by-committee approach, with George Grantham (.305, 1 HR), Clyde Young (.169, 0 HR), Tommy Mee (.211, 0 HR), and Hazen Paten (.211, 0 HR) all logging innings at the critical position. At third base, Baker played in only 44 games, giving way to hard-hitting Sam Hale (.342, 9 HR) for most of the season.

Dick Cox (George E. Outland)

Walter McCredie juggled his lineup and his roster constantly during the year. Knowing he lacked high caliber players, McCredie petitioned the league to expand rosters from 18 to 22, hoping that quantity might somehow overcome the team's lack of quality. Mercifully, the league's owners agreed to let every team carry up to 20 players during the heart of the season.

Portland's fringe players were little more than semipros fresh out of high school or college. At one point in the summer, the ballclub had four pitchers on the roster without previous professional experience. Their lack of experience produced moments of humor such as an episode reported in the June 30, 1921, issue of the *Sporting News*:

> Portland started Ralph Coleman, a young college pitcher, in a recent game against Los Angeles, and he was doing nicely until Rollie Zeider pulled

a trick on him. With two men on bases Zeider was coaching third. He suddenly called: "Throw me that ball." The young pitcher did as ordered, Zeider stepped aside, the ball rolled away and the runners scampered home. Coleman lost the game 4–3.

On the other end of the spectrum, Walter McCredie attempted to resurrect the career of Harvey "Specs" Harkness, the 33-year-old ex–Cleveland Indian, who had last pitched in the majors in 1911. Harkness pitched batting practice as a first step toward returning to action. It became clear that Specs could not recapture his old form, and he was let go just a few weeks after his comeback had begun.

If Portland fans found any of this amusing they did not show it. The ballclub was too pitiful to be funny. After the first seven-game series against the Seals in San Francisco, it became apparent just how bad the ballclub was—they lost seven straight. From day one they occupied the cellar. Before the season was two weeks old writers labeled the franchise a "weak sister," and "not of PCL caliber." By the start of the third week, fans were loudly calling for Walter McCredie's ouster.

Every deal the club made was ripped by fans. First they criticized the ballclub for not taking Morris Rath from Seattle in the deal for Tex Wisterzil. Then they said the club missed an opportunity to acquire Vernon's Tommy Long, who was traded out of the league to Shreveport. When the McCredies traded the popular Wes Kingdon for Ike Wolfer, the fans really began to wail, ignoring the fact that Wolfer had outperformed Kingdon.

When Portland sold two of its best pitchers—Harry Polson and Rudy Kallio—to Salt Lake in the middle of June, the fans and media accused the McCredies of making a quick buck before unloading the franchise. Judge McCredie countered that he had unloaded the veterans to give more youngsters a chance. He also intimated that he would like to sell Cox, Wolfer and Poole, possibly to major league ballclubs.

The rumors flourished. First, a group of Portland businessmen was to buy the ballclub; then, Bill Rourke of Omaha, Nebraska, supposedly offered $79,000 for the franchise. Two weeks later, Rourke's reported offer had grown to $130,000.

On the field the Beavers played consistently bad baseball. Just past the season's halfway point, they were 12½ games back—of seventh place. Their 22-74 record buried them deep in the cellar, 42 wins behind league-leading San Francisco.

As the season continued, the situation only grew worse. A month later they were 52 wins behind San Francisco. The *Sporting News* was outraged and one of the PCL beat reporters wrote: "That town [Portland] has been pretty well shot by losing teams and a change in ownership and management would be a good thing for Portland and the league."

Jim Poole (George E. Outland)

Portland's fans agreed and refused to support the team. In the final homestand, when the Beavers had the chance to spoil the pennant hopes of Los Angeles, 36 fans poured through the Vaughn Street turnstiles for the Saturday game. Earlier, Seattle proposed moving their series from Portland to Seattle, where gate receipts would be larger. Portland agreed, but San Francisco's Charlie Graham blocked the move, arguing an unfair home-field advantage for the pennant-contending Indians.

Portland's miserable season ended on October 2. Their 51-134 (a .276 winning percentage) finish stands as the worst in the first 41 years of the Pacific Coast League. The team's record for the year shows that they could not beat anyone; they failed to play .500 ball against any of their seven opponents. The

Ike Wolfer (Don Hazelwood)

club did manage to win 14 of 29 from Salt Lake, which had also been labeled a sub–PCL quality team by several *Sporting News* beat writers. San Francisco and Sacramento pretty much had their way with Portland, going 25-3 and 23-4, respectively, against them. The club hit .272—dead last; they fielded .957—next to last; and, only one pitcher had an earned run average under 4.00–Syl Johnson, whose 3.82 ERA was good enough to earn a 12-26 record. Only one other pitcher in the league lost more ballgames—teammate Herman Pillette.

Herman Pillette
The next to last day of the season, Saturday, October 1, Portland's Herman

Pillette lost his thirtieth game of the season. Even on a bad team, 30 losses is an ignominious achievement. Herman Polycarp (Old Folks) Pillette, however, was not a bad pitcher.

Born the day after Christmas in 1895, the 25-year-old Pillette had knocked around the minors since 1917, finally landing at Portland in 1920 in time to lose three late season games. In 1921 he became the staff workhorse, appearing in 55 games and throwing 326 innings, a career high. Judging by the numbers, Pillette would not appear to have been effective, allowing 378 hits, 152 earned runs and a 4.20 earned run average. He set his career high in walks (104), but with the number of innings he pitched, that statistic was misleading, especially since he logged 141 strikeouts. The Detroit Tigers saw promise in Pillette, making yet another deal with McCredie, who found the $40,000 and seven players the Tigers offered for Pillette and Syl Johnson enough to overcome his indignance over the Lu Blue deal.

Pillette went on to have an outstanding season with the Tigers in 1922, earning a 19-12 record and 2.85 earned run average, the second lowest mark in the league. The following year, he slipped to 14-19, 3.85 ERA, and then pitched only a part of the year for the major league ballclub in 1924.

At 29 and out of the major leagues, Pillette's career was far from over. The six-foot-two right-hander returned to the Coast League in 1925, again landing on a last-place ballcluba—the Vernon Tigers—for whom Pillette lost 26 games and won just 11. Following the 1925 season, however, there was no looking back for Pillette, who pitched a record 23 years in one minor league. In addition to Portland and Vernon, he pitched for the San Francisco Missions, Seattle Indians, Hollywood Stars, San Diego Padres and Sacramento Solons.

His career ended in 1945, just weeks short of his fiftieth birthday. In all he won 264 minor league games and lost 264 (3.62 ERA), an admirable record considering some of the ballclubs he pitched for. Pillette's major league record of 34-32 (3.45 ERA) was respectable, and gave his son Duane something to shoot for in his eight-year major league career (1949–1956). Alas, while Duane won four more games than his dad, he lost a total of 66.

The McCredie era ends

Portland fans wishing for the McCredies to sell out had their wishes granted in late October when a group headed by William Klepper bought the Beavers for $150,000. Klepper and partners James Brewster and brother Walter Klepper planned to make the franchise a community effort by selling ownership shares in the club to local businessmen.

"Portland is a good baseball town," Klepper declared. "The town is more than pleased to see the change and we are going to put Portland back on the baseball map."

Klepper's purchase caught most observers by surprise. A week before,

Walter McCredie told reporters that a deal to sell the club was nowhere in sight and that "I'm going to tackle it [managing] for the 19th season in a row." McCredie's math (it would have been his eighteenth season for the Beavers) and foresight were wrong.

Two weeks before McCredie's pronouncement, William Klepper had been part-owner and president of the Seattle Indians and Brewster had been secretary-treasurer; they did not seem candidates for buying a rival PCL franchise. But the two men were ousted by Seattle's majority owner, James Boldt, who was displeased about the ballclub's off-field dealings. Most of all, Boldt was miffed at late season deals sending pitcher Bob Geary to Cincinnati and outfielder Bill Cunningham to the New York Giants. The loss of the two players all but ended Seattle's 1921 pennant hopes.

Even the other owners viewed the sale of the two star players with concern. San Francisco's Doc Strub promised to pass a league rule prohibiting owners from selling players to teams out of the league until the season ended. Klepper protested. "It's my money and I'm going to protect it." After heated debate at the winter meetings, the other PCL owners sided with Klepper.

The paunchy and garrulous Klepper was persuasive in most matters and viewed as an astute dealmaker who had quickly turned the Seattle franchise into a contender after its 1919 re-entry into the league. Sometimes, however, he played a little fast and loose. He promised a new stadium, or at least the addition of double-decked stands, and other improvements at Vaughn Street, but they never happened. He then virtually assured fans of a first-division finish in 1922, only to have the team finish seventh. But what really landed Klepper in hot water was the hiring of Seattle player-manager Bill Kenworthy.

Not long after Klepper left Seattle, he lured Kenworthy away from Seattle and signed him to a Portland contract. This outraged Boldt, who claimed that Kenworthy had violated his contract with Seattle and that Klepper had tampered in the matter. Kenworthy argued that his contract had a clause making him a free agent if he was not satisfied with the terms of his 1922 contract.

Soon Major League Baseball Commissioner Kenesaw Mountain Landis became involved, asking to see the telegrams sent between Klepper and Kenworthy following the 1921 campaign. The commissioner found enough evidence in the telegrams to suspend Klepper until January 1, 1925, and fellow owner James Brewster until January 1, 1924.

Klepper turned to his fellow league owners for support, declaring that Landis had overreacted in the matter and that, furthermore, he did not have direct jurisdiction over the affairs of minor league owners. The league directors met in August 1921 and agreed to protest Landis's decision. The vote to do so was close, the argument heated. At one point, Klepper and Doc Strub nearly came to blows. McCarthy called for tossing Klepper from the league,

but backed down when opposed by Oakland, Salt Lake, Portland and Los
Angeles.

Landis responded with an apparent equivocation on his decision regarding
Klepper: "My decision dealt with baseball matters and distinguished from
purely internal corporate administrative affairs. The PCL is not required to
cease relations with Portland if Klepper's activities are limited to purely internal, corporate administrative affairs." As one writer put it, "The Portland
President can count the gate receipts and can sign a player's pay check, but
he can't make a player tip his hat to him and say 'Howdy, Boss.'" Landis had
saved face and avoided a federal court case.

Klepper went back to running the team, virtually ignoring Landis's ruling, though he did speak through the Beavers' secretary at Pacific Coast
League meetings. Kenworthy remained ineligible to play or manage for Portland until 1924. Klepper's second choice as manager for the 1922 season — Al
Demaree — was also nixed by Landis for playing in an outlaw league. Tom
Turner managed the ballclub for awhile, though pitcher James Middleton
skippered the club for most of the second half of the 1922 season and into
1923.

Three years after buying the ballclub, Klepper tired of the hassles with
his fellow owners. He unloaded the ballclub for $250,000 to Turner, who had
strong ties with the Philadelphia Athletics, particularly with John Shibe, the
Athletics' vice president. The purchase marked the beginning of a long association between the Portland Beavers and the Philadelphia Athletics.

The pennant race of '21

Despite Portland's travails and a dismal performance by a Salt Lake club
that somehow managed to hit .303 and still lose 110 games, the Pacific Coast
League enjoyed one of its most competitive seasons ever in 1921. Five teams
won more than 100 games and six teams finished above .500. It proved to be
a hitter's year, signalling the start of rising batting averages and power statistics for the decade. Overall, the league batting average was .288, up 19 points
from 1920. Home run production jumped by 73 percent, with 598 roundtrippers hit during the season.

From the outset San Francisco looked like a team of destiny. Their seven-
game sweep of Portland to start the year shot them into first place, a position
they would hold 22 of the season's 26 weeks. Early on Sacramento wrested the
lead from the Seals, while Los Angeles nabbed the top spot at the end of the
season.

Jimmy O'Connell, a 20-year-old first baseman, led Seals hitters with a
.337 average and 17 home runs, numbers that would land him on the New
York Giants in two years. Other Seals on their way to the majors included
shortstop Ike Caveney (.325, 11 HR), who went to Cincinnati in 1922, and
third baseman Willie Kamm (.288, 13 HR), whom the Chicago White Sox

purchased for $100,000 after the 1922 season. Lefty O'Doul led San Francisco's pitchers (25-9, 2.39 ERA) and managed to hit .338 in 136 at-bats. O'Doul could not carry the ballclub by himself, though. Lack of pitching depth proved San Francisco's undoing and led to their ultimate third-place finish.

Dogging the Seals all year were the Sacramento Senators, the "little guys" from the league's smallest city and the second weakest hitters (next to Portland). This was a team built on defense and speed; their 247 stolen bases far and away led the rest of the league. Paul Fittery and Bill Prough had big years on the mound, while third baseman Charlie Pick (.328, 13 HR) and outfielder Buddy Ryan (.320, 9 HR) led the offense. In addition to Marty McGaffigan's 55 thefts, three other Senators stole 40 bases or more: first baseman Fritz Mollwitz (47), outfielder Merlin Kopp (45) and Pick (43).

The speedy ballclub could not catch the eventual pennant winner, the Los Angeles Angels. Not considered a threat at the season's outset, the Angels played up to these modest expectations, lumbering along in the middle of the pack through most of the summer.

On August 15, Vernon's Frank Shellenback shut out the Angels and the ballclub fell 12½ back of the Seals with little more than a month and a half to go. From this point on the Angels caught fire and the Seals faltered. A week later, the Angels had made up five games on the leaders. Though probably coincidental, the Angels' charge came about the time the ballclub was sold by Johnny Powers to William Wrigley, Jr., who agreed to buy the franchise on August 29 for $150,000.

The Angels gained their momentum largely at the expense of the Portland Beavers. Just as the Seals feasted on the Beavers in the first half of the season, so did the Angels in the second half. Twenty-one of their final 51 games came against Portland, including a Coast League record 13-game series at Washington Park. In all, the Angels won 16 of the 21 games against the Beavers, enough to beat Sacramento by 1½ games and San Francisco by 2.

More than anything, pitching won the 1921 pennant, especially that of Victor Aldridge (20-10, 2.16 ERA) and Otis "Doc" Crandall (24-13, 3.13 ERA). Managed by Red Killefer, the Angels finished sixth in club batting and last in home runs, but their 186 stolen bases and league-leading 91 triples point out that they, too, were a team that relied heavily on speed to win games. The team's leading hitters included outfielders Sam Crawford (.318, 9 HR) and Jigger Statz (.310, 2 HR) and shortstop Jim McAuley (.299, 0 HR).

Two fast, light-hitting teams had beaten all others in 1921. As the decade progressed, however, the game's emphasis would change. Power, not speed, would win ballgames and attract fans, reflecting the general tenor of a society that increasingly admired action and bravado. The era of home runs and big innings was dawning on the West Coast.

1921 Final Standings

	W	L	Pct.
Los Angeles	108	80	.574
Sacramento	105	80	.568
San Francisco	106	82	.564
Seattle	103	82	.557
Oakland	101	85	.543
Vernon	96	90	.516
Salt Lake	73	110	.399
Portland	51	134	.276

Team batting leaders

Average:	Oakland — .305
Runs:	Salt Lake — 1,044
HRs:	Salt Lake — 122

Individual batting leaders

At-bats:	Paddy Siglin, Salt Lake — 784
Average:	Hack Miller, Oakland — .347
Runs:	Paddy Siglin, Salt Lake — 156
Hits:	Paddy Siglin, Salt Lake — 270
2B:	Paddy Siglin, Salt Lake — 67
3B:	Dixie Carroll, Los Angeles — 22
HR:	Paddy Siglin, Salt Lake — 22
RBI:	not available
Total bases:	Paddy Siglin, Salt Lake — 409
Stolen bases:	Marty A. McGaffigan, Sacramento — 55

Individual pitching leaders

Winning percentage:	Arthur Reinhart, Los Angeles (15-5) — .750
Games won:	Wieser Dell, Vernon — 28
Games lost:	Herman Pillette, Portland — 30
Most games:	Sam Lewis, San Francisco — 56
Most shutouts:	Lefty O'Doul — 7
Most complete games:	not available
Most innings:	Paul Fittery, Sacramento — 361
ERA:	Vic Aldridge, Los Angeles — 2.16

Chapter 4

1922 — The PCL as a Third Major League

When the San Francisco Seals sold Jimmy O'Connell to the New York Giants in 1921 for $75,000, the baseball world was shocked. Never before had a minor league player brought such a sum. After all, Babe Ruth was sold along with two other minor leaguers for a mere $25,000 in 1914.

Just when baseball men had stopped reeling from the O'Connell deal, Seals President Dr. Charles Strub announced in June 1922 the sale of third baseman Willie Kamm to the White Sox for $100,000 and three players. The San Francisco Seals made headlines on sports pages across the country. Although well known in organized baseball, the Seals — under owners Alfie Putnam, Doc Strub and Charlie Graham — were now gaining national attention for their ability to develop ballplayers and make deals.

As early as December 1921, emboldened by the sale of O'Connell, Strub pronounced that the Pacific Coast League was entertaining thoughts about becoming a third major league. At the National Association of Baseball Leagues meetings in Buffalo he riled East Coast writers by saying that he would possibly introduce a resolution at the next Pacific Coast League directors meeting to declare the PCL a major league.

"We consider that the Pacific Coast League is or soon will be a major league," Strub said to a gathering of sportswriters. "Our average players now are the equal of those who are warming the benches of the so-called big leagues. We estimate that approximately 60 percent of the regular material now playing in the East was originated on the Pacific Slope. If we are to be a developing ground for the major leagues it is obvious that we can never hope to achieve major league proportions. Our patrons, who are in cities ranging from 300,000 to 700,000 population, have learned to expect major league baseball from our league, and we intend to give it to them. We feel that if we are to be successful in doing this, we must consider ourselves on a par with the Eastern majors."

Though his remarks were mainly volleys designed to end talk about reinstating the drafting of PCL players, Strub incited a great deal of debate. Francis Richter, publisher of *Sporting Life* and editor of the *Reach Guide*, echoed the mainstream major league view when he wrote:

> This [Strub's pronouncement] was to be expected of this erratic and comparatively isolated league, which has become so swollen with pride over several successful years and recent sales of stars at enormous sums, that it takes its "near-major" pretensions seriously, and imagines that it can succeed in the event of rejection by Organized Baseball, as a real major league.

But a *Sporting News* editorial in December 1921, though primarily referring to the interest generated in the California Winter League, affirmed that West Coast baseball had its proponents in the East as well:

> You can't get away from the Pacific Slope when it comes to affairs baseball. They develop the players, make the deals, play the game—yes, even start the scandals. It will be well for our self-centered baseball people east of the Rockies to keep the thing in mind. There is something besides climate that makes the game so popular on the Slope.

The Coast League had been exempt from the draft since 1919, when it joined four other minor leagues—the International League, American Association, Western League and Indiana-Illinois-Iowa League—in refusing to be subjected to the draft. McCarthy and the other owners, even if they did not believe the PCL would immediately become a major league, remained vehemently opposed to re-entering the draft. The lone draft proponent was Oakland Oaks owner J. Cal Ewing, known in PCL circles as the "Father of Baseball." Ewing favored the drafting of PCL players by the majors because it cleared the way for PCL ballclubs to draft players in the lower minors. To Ewing this meant he could acquire young players for the draft price of $2,500 instead of the open-market price that was often double that.

Ewing had been one of the PCL's founders and had served as league president from 1907 through 1909. Widely respected, he still served as the PCL's primary representative at meetings of the National Association, the minor league governing body. In fairness to its proponents, the draft system in effect in 1922 would not have ravaged minor league teams. No more than one player could be taken from any single minor league ballclub. Conducted around World Series time, 21 minor leaguers were tabbed by major league teams in the 1922 draft. The 1923 draft saw only 16 players selected, as many major league teams sought to make their own deals with minor league clubs prior to the draft. By subjecting itself to the draft, the Coast League would have allowed major league teams to take its best players for $5,000. Even an advisory committee of major league owners agreed that the $5,000 price was unfair, and they proposed boosting the sum to $7,500, at least on a yearlong trial basis.

Jimmy O'Connell (Don Hazelwood)

Ignoring Ewing's pleas, the Coast League directors rejected the offer in January. Within weeks the two other Double-A leagues—the American Association and International League—followed suit.

A showdown between major league interests and the three top minors appeared imminent. Judge Landis was an advocate of the draft, claiming that it provided players with the chance to move up the ranks and into the major leagues.

"A situation where one group of ball players can be boxed into a minor league, and can advance higher only at the whim of their employer, is intolerable and un–American," Landis declared. "So long as I am in this job, I will fight for the full restoration of the draft."

An open market system would also have given players a chance to advance, but Landis felt that a drafting system and its limit on the price paid for a player helped keep the costs down, benefitting both the major and minor leagues. A draft also kept a minor league with major league aspirations—such as the PCL—at a lower status than the majors.

Strub's associate, Charlie Graham, argued against the claim that the PCL was hindering player advancement, stating that major league owners were simply greedy. "They assume that there are only two leagues of any consequence and all the other leagues exist merely to be used for the purpose of the major leagues," Graham said. "They fail to realize, for example, that to the people of San Francisco the most important thing in baseball is the San Francisco team. To our people, the American or National League race is a secondary consideration."

Interviews today with a handful of fans from the era confirm Graham's contention—to West Coast baseball fans the National and American were "the eastern leagues." Eighty-one-year-old native San Franciscan Bob Schroth summarized the view of many fans: "For my friends, family and myself, we paid very little attention to anything but the Seals and the Oaks. As far as we were concerned the Pacific Coast League was it."

Even for the players, the PCL was not necessarily an inferior alternative to the majors. The PCL's monthly salaries were not bad, and the longer PCL season helped boost a player's income to a level that sometimes exceeded major league pay. Tony Freitas, who played for the Sacramento Solons in three decades—1920s, 1930s and 1940s—declined to play for the St. Louis Cardinals, preferring the PCL. "As far as I was concerned the Pacific Coast League was where I wanted to play and where I belonged," he said.

For a player like Freitas, the draft would have been forced servitude. Of course, the majority of players wanted to get to the majors, and the draft was their best ticket for getting there. For those unfortunate players who had major league talent but whose minor league owner demanded too much in payment, draft exemption often meant extra years playing in the minors rather than in the National or American Leagues. The draft, on the other hand, pulled qualified players up the ladder, whether the minor league owner wanted it or not. To a player with major league aspirations, the draft was not such a bad thing.

Whether Strub's threats to form a third major league had worked, or the major league owners were in no mood to fight, the draft issue died prior to the start of the 1922 season. The Pacific Coast League had scored a significant victory over the majors and retained its independent status—a status it would need if it ever hoped to become an equal to the National and American Leagues.

The PCL as a major league
Could the Pacific Coast League have succeeded as a major league? To do

so it would have had to pay players the same salaries as the two existing majors. That meant it had to draw enough fans to generate revenues to support such salaries. *Los Angeles Times* writer Matt Gallagher believed such talk was premature, noting that only San Francisco and Los Angeles were of sufficient size to support major league quality baseball.

By 1920, Pacific Coast League cities had the following populations according to U.S. Census figures: Los Angeles, 577,000; San Francisco, 506,000; Seattle, 315,000; Portland, 258,000; Oakland, 216,000; Salt Lake, 118,000; and Sacramento, 66,000.

Gallagher said the region needed about five more years of growth before it could sustain major league baseball. *Oakland Tribune* writer Eddie Murphy, a disciple of Ewing's, pooh-poohed such talk: "No doubt every baseball club owner in the Pacific Coast League and every fan supporting the league would like to see such a rating given to the organization, but a chance of that happening inside of 50 years is about as good as Babe Ruth coming to the Oaks next season."

San Francisco and Los Angeles each supported two teams, drawing well over a million fans a year to the two areas. These were major league cities in everything but name. Los Angeles, in particular, was in the midst of an explosive growth that was shaping the city's future for the rest of the century. Between 1920 and 1930 the city more than doubled in size, and by the 1930 census over 1.2 million people lived there.

At the other end of the spectrum, Sacramento and Salt Lake remained too small to draw fans in major league quantities. Sacramento played its Sunday morning game in Stockton to expand its fan base, while Salt Lake did something similar in 1921, playing at least one home game a week in nearby Ogden. Not that the West Coast was not wild about its baseball; Coast League fans may have been the most rabid baseball fans in the country. The league had twice the ratio of seating capacity to population as the two major leagues.

Population versus seating capacity, top five baseball leagues, 1920*

League	Population of cities in league	Stadium seating capacity	Seats/pop.
National	12,655,308	199,000	0.016
American	13,594,014	215,000	0.016
International	2,879,000	70,400	0.024
Amer. Assoc.	2,423,000	94,500	0.039
PCL	2,100,000	92,400	0.044

*Source: *Sporting News*, February 16, 1922

More importantly, the Coast League filled these seats. The eight PCL ballclubs drew about two million fans each year during the 1920s—about equal to its population base. That was less than half the annual average for the National and American Leagues, each of which averaged about 4.5 million fans a season during the decade. However, this 4.5 million represented only a third of the population base for National and American League cities.

Since PCL ticket prices were comparable to those in the major leagues, the league's revenues were about half those of the American and National Leagues. The average salary in the majors was about $7,000 by the end of the decade, not quite double the salary a Coast League player could expect. Some PCL stars did earn major league salaries; Jimmy O'Connell reportedly earned $10,000 for his lame-duck 1922 season with the Seals.

O'Connell was an exception, however. If it wanted to attract the players for a third major league, the Coast League needed to pay higher salaries across the board. For that it needed to generate more revenue. Expanding its ballparks was a possibility, but without star players to draw fans, it was likely larger parks would simply mean more empty seats. The league needed the players first if it was to draw fans. Such an investment in players could have stretched budgets on several ballclubs to the breaking point.

Even if the PCL owners had the financial wherewithal to load their teams with top major league talent, the rest of organized baseball would not have stood idly by. Since most players were under reserve, they would have had to jump their teams to play on the West Coast. Signing such players would have earned the PCL banishment from organized baseball and relegated it to outlaw status. The Pacific Coast League could probably have made a go of it as an outlaw. San Francisco, Los Angeles and Oakland regularly outdrew teams like the Boston Braves, who attracted only 2.5 million fans through the decade. To many players, the PCL was preferable to languishing on a perennial second-division club like Boston.

Essentially, during its draft-exempt days, the PCL operated as a third major league—albeit a lesser one—but the league never went so far as to give itself the upgraded label. The outlaw Federal League had collapsed earlier, and the Coast League directors had to consider whether such a fate could befall them if they became an outlaw league.

The gamble hardly seemed worth it; the league enjoyed much success the way things were and major league status looked like it might evolve naturally. For the time being at least, the real battle for the owners was to maintain the league's draft exempt status. That gave teams control over their star players and the right to make large sums of money by selling them on the open market.

One other entry into major league baseball was possible—the expansion of the existing National and American Leagues to the West Coast, specifically San Francisco and Los Angeles. That eventually happened, of course, but the remoteness of the two cities did not make such a move feasible in the 1920s given the cost of lengthy train rides to and from the West Coast.

The Seals

Maybe they were not a major league ballclub, but the 1922 Seals were exceptional. The 1921 ballclub had not been bad either, until thin pitching finally caused their downfall in the last month of the season. Since taking over the ballclub in 1918, the Seals' owners had never won a pennant and the 1921 defeat had been the most frustrating of all. They were eager to change their luck in 1922.

The "Vanderbilts of Valencia Street," as the team's owners were called, were an odd triumvirate. First there was G.A. "Alfie" Putnam, the consummate promoter and businessman with a knack for making a buck. Putnam was responsible for player acquisition and sales, as well as the bottom line. Like many baseball executives, he measured his success as much by debits and credits as wins and losses. In a letter to *Sacramento Union* columnist Vincent Stanich, Putnam pointed to his success in selling players and generating revenue, characterizing his reign with the Seals as "a baseball record that has never been equalled by any one owner or executive of any club in Minor League baseball."

Then there was Charlie Graham, the 44-year old former player and ex-*Sacramento Bee* reporter who managed the Seals from 1918 through 1921 before realizing his talents lay more in executive management. Graham had played in several leagues, mainly in the California minors, though he did log 31 games for Boston in the American League. In 1912 he bought the Sacramento franchise, then teamed up with Strub and Putnam to buy the Seals prior to the 1918 season. He was a capable manager, though some of his techniques were somewhat unorthodox. One of Graham's favorite spring training conditioning exercises consisted of taking players to the local golf course (usually near Boyes Hot Springs, north of San Francisco) and having each player hit a golf ball as far as he could. The player then sprinted to the ball and, without pause, hit it again. The hitting and running were repeated until the player was exhausted. Though no evidence indicates that the Seals were exceptionally conditioned, there is reference to their being the best golfing team in the PCL. After four years of managing the Seals, Graham admitted that he had become too close to the players to provide the discipline they needed, so he gave way to Jack "Dots" Miller and moved into upper management. He was regarded as the "baseball man" among the Seal executives.

Doc Strub was not a shy man. This was evident even before he bought into the Seals. Strub had already achieved celebrity in San Francisco for his billboards and advertisements around town promoting his dental practice. "The advertising dentist was how he was known," according to Stanich, who noted that one could not avoid Strub's ads around town even if he wanted to. The three men assembled championship ballclubs with their keen eyes for talent and their shrewd dealings. In addition to O'Connell and Kamm, the Seals made a bundle selling players. Some of their biggest deals included: Paul Waner and Hal Rhyne—$95,000 for both; Frank Crosetti—$55,000 + three players; Roy Johnson—$50,000; Gus Suhr—$42,500 + one player; Earl Averill—$35,000 + two players; and Smead Jolley—$25,000 + one player.

When they did not sell players, Putnam put on boxing matches at Recreation Park or baseball tours with players such as Babe Ruth or Ty Cobb to swell the club's coffers. The profits were invested in stars on the rise as well as major leaguers eager to pad their statistics in the Coast League's cozy ballparks with their 200-game seasons. The teams they built during the 1920s proved to be the class of the West Coast. Besides the New York Yankees, the San Francisco Seals were quite possibly the most successful professional sports franchise of the 1920s. The 1922 ballclub differed little from the 1921 team, except that they now had a new manager, Dots Miller, an ex–major leaguer with no managing experience. Miller soon became one of the most popular people in San Francisco. Easygoing and likeable, he devoted much of his free time to charities and local causes. Each weekend that the Seals were at home, Miller conducted a free baseball clinic for local sandlotters.

Graham refuted claims that he would call the shots behind the scenes, rendering Miller a figurehead manager. As the season progressed, it became clear that Miller had indeed been given control of the team on the field; it also became clear that this was a team that could win no matter who managed it. The 1922 Seals lined up like this: Gene Valla, lf (.333, 1 HR, 48 RBI); Joe Kelly, rf (.333, 5 HR, 68 RBI); Willie Kamm, 3b (.342, 20 HR, 124 RBI); Bert Ellison, 1b (.306, 16 HR, 141 RBI); Jimmy O'Connell, cf (.335, 13 HR, 92 RBI); Hal Rhyne, ss (.285, 0 HR, 93 RBI); Pete Kilduff, 2b (.287, 6 HR, 75 RBI); and Sam Agnew, c (.337, 11 HR, 61 RBI).

Most prominent among the reserves were outfielders Charlie See (.307, 1 HR, 40 RBI) and Sacramento castoff Pete Compton (.306, 8 HR, 43 RBI), and catcher Archie Yelle (.254, 0 HR, 24 RBI), who alternated with Agnew as the starter.

The Seals started the season with a decent but not spectacular pitching staff of Jim Scott, Oliver Mitchell, Bob Geary, Fred Coumbe, Daka Davis, Ernie Alten, Claude Gillenwater and Herb McQuaid. Scott (25-9, 2.22 ERA) and Mitchell (24-7, 2.90 ERA) pitched well all year long. Geary (20-9, 2.52 ERA) overcame some shaky games at Recreation Park to post outstanding numbers. Davis (1-6, 5.55 ERA), Gillenwater (1-2) and McQuaid (4-3, 3.78 ERA) were cut loose during the season, while Coumbe (10-7, 3.40 ERA), Alten (13-10, 3.55 ERA) and midseason acquisition Pat Shea (6-6, 2.51 ERA) pitched well in spots.

Oliver Mitchell (George E. Outland)

By the end of summer, however, it was apparent that the Seals could not count on a pennant with this staff. Midseason bolstering was needed if the team was to win the final pennant battle.

The 1922 pennant race

For the first time, the PCL directors established a $20,000 pool of money to be awarded to the top seven ballclubs. The first place team received $6,000 to be divided among its players, the second place ballclub got $4,000, third place $3,000, fourth place $2,500, fifth place $2,000, sixth place $1,500, and seventh place $1,000. This was an incentive for teams to battle all year long, even if they were out of the pennant race. More spirited baseball, it was hoped, would draw more fans during the waning months of the season, when attendance traditionally dropped off in towns with non-contending teams.

In the end, the bonus plan failed to generate a noticeable improvement in play or additional interest from fans. Only three teams voted to continue the bonuses — San Francisco, Vernon and Sacramento (which finished last and therefore was the only team not receiving bonus money).

The bonus plan did not work because the 1922 Coast League race very quickly settled into a three-team affair. At the top were the only teams to win pennants since 1914 — San Francisco, Vernon and Los Angeles. These three were the only ballclubs to finish above .500 in 1922. Vernon and Los Angeles were the only two ballclubs with returning managers, and this proved one of their major strengths.

Under the direction of manager Red Killefer — brother of Chicago Cubs manager Bill Killefer — the Angels played steady baseball, hovering near the .500 mark through mid-July. Just as in 1921, the 1922 Angels were a relatively weak-hitting ballclub that relied on speed and pitching. The team suffered a serious blow on June 22 when pitcher Elmer Ponder fell while attempting to catch a pop fly in practice, tearing his pitching shoulder and ending his season. Ponder, a preseason acquisition from the Cubs, was 10-2 at the time of his injury and was counted on as the ace of the staff.

The role of ace would eventually fall upon Nick Dumovich, probably the biggest surprise of 1922. The 20-year-old pitcher from Sacramento recorded a mediocre 8-7 record in 1921, so it seemed unlikely that he would go on to a 20-11 record with a 2.36 ERA in 1922. Lefty Thomas (18-11, 2.98 ERA), George Lyons (17-17, 2.70 ERA) and Tom Hughes (17-9, 3.08 ERA) also turned in decent seasons. Doc Crandall (17-19, 3.65 ERA), usually a mainstay, suffered a down year.

While Los Angeles pitchers had unspectacular won-loss records, they enjoyed excellent earned run averages. This reflected an offense that was only sixth in the PCL in batting average and scoring. With Jigger Statz's departure to the Cubs, the Angels lost a certain .300 hitter. When 42-year-old Sam Crawford left prior to the season in a dispute over playing time, the ballclub lost another proven hitter. Left to lead the attack were first baseman Art Griggs, who enjoyed a career year (.338, 20 HR, 129 RBI), outfielder Babe Twombly (.300, 2 HR, 79 RBI) and third baseman Charlie Deal (.331, 6 HR, 87 RBI). Though the team kept pace all year with the Seals and the Tigers, they could not rise above third place, finishing 16 games behind the pennant winners.

Bill Essick's Vernon Tigers averaged more than five runs a game — second best in the league and nearly a full run a game better than the Angels. His team also featured excellent pitching, with three 20-game winners: Jesse Doyle (20-15, 3.13 ERA), Wieser Dell (23-17, 3.17 ERA) and Bill James (21-12, 3.27 ERA). As good as they were, none of the three could match Frank S. "Jakey" May, the staff ace who went 35-9, posted a 1.84 ERA and struck out

238 batters—numbers that were good enough to win the PCL's pitching "Triple Crown" (wins, ERA, strikeouts). The left-hander could possibly have won 40 games had he not missed a month of the season due to injury. Known as "Joker Jake" by his teammates for his sense of humor, May played one more season for the Tigers before returning to the major leagues. He stayed in the majors until 1932, ending his career with 4 2/3 innings of work for the Chicago Cubs in the World Series.

Though they certainly had superior pitching, on paper the Tigers were no match for the Seals. Even *Los Angeles Times* writer Matt Gallagher admitted that the Seals had the most talent in the league, with no apparent weakness at any position. Bill Essick, now in his fifth season as manager, was the only reason the ballclub stayed on the heels of the Seals, according to Gallagher, who credited the skipper with deft use of his pitchers and for admirably juggling the day-to-day lineup.

On Sunday, September 24, Essick had jockeyed his ballclub dead even with the Seals after trailing all season long. With 22 games remaining, the teams had identical 114-63 records. Each club would play three more series. San Francisco travelled to play Sacramento and Los Angeles before concluding their season at home against Oakland. Vernon hosted Seattle, then travelled to Oakland, and returned to Los Angeles to play the Angels. The last week of September, Vernon won five of seven from Seattle while San Francisco was doing the same against Sacramento. With two weeks to go, the two teams remained tied.

On Tuesday, October 3, the Seals broke the deadlock. While the Tigers were rained out in Oakland, the Seals lost to the Angels in dramatic fashion. Harry Courtney yielded two runs in the bottom of the ninth, handing the Angels a 4–3 win over the Seals. Vernon led the league by a half game.

The next day both ballclubs lost, the Angels beating San Francisco, 6–2, while Oakland scored a ninth-inning run off Jakey May to beat Vernon, 2–1. To make up for the Tuesday rainout, Oakland and Vernon played a doubleheader on Thursday, October 5. In the first game, Buzz Arlett, in his last year as a fulltime pitcher, threw a three-hit gem to beat the Tigers, 1–0. Wieser Dell, who had thrown a no-hitter against the Oaks on September 21, was the hard-luck loser against Arlett. The hitters finally got untracked in the second game as Oakland pounded Vernon by a score of 11–8. Vernon had lost three straight.

In Los Angeles, San Francisco capitalized on Vernon's losing streak, recapturing first place on Thursday, October 5, with a much-needed shutout that ended their own two-game skid. The score was 3–0 and featured the pitching of Doug McWeeny, one of the three pitchers acquired in the Willie Kamm deal with the Chicago White Sox. Shovel Hodge (2-2) and Harry Courtney (5-2, 1.89 ERA) also came in the deal, adding depth to the Seals staff.

McWeeny proved the difference between the ballclub's near-miss 1921 season and its 1922 success. Though he started the year with the White Sox, he still managed to work 175 innings for the Seals, winning 15 and losing seven, with a 2.78 ERA. The six-foot-two, 190-pound right-hander threw a lightning fastball with outstanding control. Whereas the 1921 pitchers tired and floundered during the season's last two months, in 1922 the relatively fresh arms of McWeeny, Hodge and Courtney boosted the staff.

The Seals picked up only two more wins against the Angels and lost the series three games to four. Fortunately for the San Franciscans, Oakland drubbed Vernon five games to two, with Ray Kremer and Arlett splitting four of the wins.

Entering the final series, the Seals held a precarious two-game lead. The stage was set for the season's final showdowns: Vernon and Los Angeles, Oakland and San Francisco. The matchup of traditional rivals promised two spirited series. Vernon and Los Angeles held little love for one another; the Oaks and Seals had even less.

The roots of the discord between the ballclubs started at the top. Vernon's Ed Maier had fought for years, first with Angel owner Johnny Powers and later William Wrigley, over the Angels' territorial claims to the Los Angeles area. In the Bay Area, the owners of the two local ballclubs did not seem to see eye to eye on anything.

Cal Ewing had actually owned the Seals for a time and had been credited with saving the franchise during some tough times. One of the Coast League's founding fathers, Ewing opposed his cross-bay counterparts on some major issues of the previous couple of years: the draft, the Bill Klepper suspension, the handling of the 1919 betting scandal, and the bonus plan. In fact Ewing refused to contribute to the bonus fund so the Seals paid his share. The two teams also disagreed about the merits of the league's president, William McCarthy. Ewing believed he was little more than a servant of the Seals.

In 1922, for the first time, the Oaks played all their home games on the east side of the bay in Emeryville. Previously, the Oaks played only two games a week in the East Bay and the remainder of their home games at San Francisco's Recreation Park.

The move was a gamble for Ewing. He knew he could have counted on regular support from the voracious San Francisco baseball fans, but the price the Seals demanded to use Recreation Park was a point of contention. Across the bay, the population was half that of San Francisco's, and local fans had been sporadic in their support. Saddled with a sixth-place team, as they were in 1922, attendance was disappointing.

He felt that part of the reason the Oaks crowds were not larger could be blamed on Strub, Putnam and Graham. When the Seals were on the road, their owners booked semipro games at Recreation Park. Back in the 1920s, weekend semipro games drew a couple of thousand fans—fans that might have travelled across the bay to watch the Oaks. Ewing appealed to McCarthy, who rejected the appeal, and then to Commissioner Landis, who ruled that the semipro games were a violation of Oakland's territorial rights. The Seals stopped the ballgames, but to keep fans coming to the ballpark they leased a "play-by-play" electrical sign, which was erected near the entrance to the park and kept fans informed about how the Seals were doing on the road. Given the cool relationship between the two teams, Ewing could not have been happier if his was the team to spoil the Seals' pennant hopes.

Following a Tuesday rainout, the series began and it looked like the Oaks just might knock the Seals out of first place. Harry Krause completely shut down San Francisco for a 1–0 win. Any ideas the Oaks entertained about spoiling the Seals' hopes died when they lost the next four games, including the second game of the Saturday doubleheader, 4–1, that proved to be the pennant clincher.

Vernon could hardly blame their lost pennant hopes on the Oaks' collapse, because down in Washington Park Vernon's hitters suddenly stopped hitting and the team lost four of the first five games of their series with Los Angeles. Sunday they rebounded to beat the Angels 7–3 in the first game of the doubleheader, but by then it was too late.

The final game of the season for the Angels—the second game of the Sunday doubleheader—was called off because of darkness. The Tigers' season ended with a tied score. The Vernon Tigers had come so close, but in the end they came up 4 games short. At Recreation Park, the deadlocked second game of the doubleheader was also called, but for a different reason. The umpires ruled that it was impossible to continue the game with the thousands of happy fans rejoicing on the field, celebrating the Seals' first pennant in five years.

1922 Final Standings

	W	L	Pct.
San Francisco	127	72	.638
Vernon	123	76	.618
Los Angeles	111	88	.558
Salt Lake	95	106	.473
Seattle	90	107	.457
Oakland	88	112	.440
Portland	87	112	.437
Sacramento	76	124	.380

Team batting leaders

Average:	San Francisco — .298
Runs:	San Francisco — 1,085
HRs:	Salt Lake — 138

Individual batting leaders

At-bats:	Chet Chadbourne, Vernon — 830
Average:	Paul Strand, Salt Lake — .384
Runs:	William Lane, Seattle — 166
Hits:	Paul Strand, Salt Lake — 289
2B:	Paddy Siglin, Salt Lake — 60
3B:	Chicken Hawks, Vernon — 15
HR:	Paul Strand, Salt Lake — 28
RBI:	Bert Ellison, San Francisco — 141
Total bases:	Paul Strand, Salt Lake — 451
Stolen bases:	William Lane, Seattle — 60

Individual pitching leaders

Winning percentage:	Jakey May, Vernon — .795 (35-9)
Games won:	Jakey May, Vernon — 35
Games lost:	Paul Fittery, Sacramento — 26
Most games:	Jakey May, Vernon — 53
	Jess Doyle, Vernon — 53
Most shutouts:	Jakey May, Vernon — 7
Most complete games:	not available
Most innings:	Buzz Arlett, Oakland — 374
ERA:	Jakey May, Vernon — 1.84

Chapter 5

1923 — Civil War

On September 5, 1923, Seals skipper Jack Miller died; on that day the Seals were leading second-place Sacramento by six games. The likeable San Francisco skipper had been in and out of the hospital for weeks, suffering from an unspecified illness. He passed away in a sanitarium in Saranac Lake, New York, and was laid to rest in his hometown of Kearney, New Jersey, in a funeral ceremony attended by John McGraw, Miller Huggins and other baseball dignitaries. The passing of the 36-year-old San Francisco manager dampened what had already been a troubled season in the Pacific Coast League. Once again, off-field squabbles overshadowed the play on the field, so severely polarizing the league that outside intervention was needed to restore order.

It seemed fitting that when Miller's Seals and the surprising Sacramento Senators squared off the last week of September to play the season's most important series, somberness filled the ballpark. The American flag flew at half staff, and crowds at all Coast League ballparks stood for a moment of silence in memory of Jack Miller.

According to the *Sporting News*, interim manager Bert Ellison told the injured and depressed Seals as they prepared to take the field for the first game of the series: "We're badly crippled. The pennant is at stake and then some. Remember our late manager Jack Miller. Jack's biggest wish was to win another pennant. Every one of you fellows loved him. Now I'm going to ask you to give me everything this week, but do it for Jack Miller."

And the Seals did, winning six games and tying a seventh. Though they had lost Willie Kamm and Jimmy O'Connell to the majors, the 1923 Seals were another powerhouse. The emergence of a 20-year-old newcomer named Paul Waner (.369, 3 HR, 39 RBI) compensated for O'Connell's loss just as the arrival of major leaguer Eddie Mulligan did Kamm's. To the rest of the league, the Seals appeared to have an endless supply of talent. Bob Geary (21-11, 3.64 ERA) and Doug McWeeny (20-12, 3.91 ERA) led the team in wins. Despite reports of strife among the players, Ellison managed to hold the Seals together, earning a contract to manage the ballclub for two more years.

Action from a game at Recreation Park between Vernon and San Francisco. Speed Geary is pitching, Archie Yelle is catching and Oskie Slade is batting. (George E. Outland)

Sacramento went on to finish second with a 112-87 record, a major improvement over their last place finish the year before. Only San Francisco had a more balanced ballclub. The Senators could hit, posting a team batting average of .298 led by catcher Art Koehler (.356, 10 HR, 95 RBI). They could also field, leading the league with a .968 fielding percentage. And they could pitch, featuring a staff of Bill Prough (20-11, 3.60 ERA), Moses Yellowhorse (22-13, 3.68 ERA), Harry Thompson (18-12, 3.76 ERA), Paul Fittery (15-14, 3.84 ERA), and Bill Hughes (14-13, 3.91 ERA)—Sacramento's best set of arms in several years.

Salt Lake sluggers

Bright as the Sacramento story was, perhaps the biggest story of 1923 was that of Paul Strand and his teammates on the Salt Lake Bees. Though the team could do no better than fourth place, they hit with such ferocity that 70 years later many of their records still remain. For the season the ballclub hit .327, knocked out 2,395 hits, including 1,693 singles, and totaled 3,648 total bases—all Pacific Coast League records. The league records for runs (1,416), doubles (556), and runs batted in (1,294) are held by the 1924 Bees. In addition, the ballclub set several hitting records for games and series. The celebrated sluggers were part of two of the more famous games in Coast League history.

The first was their 35–11 loss to Vernon at Bonneville Park on May 11, 1923, a ballgame that set still-standing records for total runs and home runs (11). Vernon set records for runs scored, runs batted in (34), home runs (9) and total bases (67). And if that was not enough, Vernon right-fielder Pete Schneider set seven individual records: at-bats (8), runs scored (6), home runs (5), grandslams (2), total bases (22) and runs batted in (14).

Vernon first baseman Dallas Locker, standing at first base after singling, recalls that Schneider's sixth blast came within six inches of going out of the park. He further recalls, "Pete couldn't hit right-handers very well, but he murdered lefties. And he was very fast. He easily won a match race against Jigger Statz."

On August 18, Salt Lake exacted revenge for the shellacking by pounding Vernon 25–12. The Bees collected 25 hits, with every player in the lineup hitting safely except for the three men who shared the shortstop position; the three players filling that role went a collective 0 for 4.

The ballgame was proceeding innocently enough (at least for a Salt Lake game), with Vernon holding a 10–5 lead going into the bottom of the sixth inning. The first batter up for the Bees—a shortstop—made an out, then pitcher Pudgy Gould singled. Gould singled again before making the inning's final out in his third time up. The three at-bats remain a record for an inning and came against three different pitchers—Jakey May, Cecil Cruz and Al Carson. In all, the Bees scored 16 runs during that eventful sixth inning, which also remains a Coast League record for runs in one inning.

Though these two games were unusual, high-scoring games were a common occurrence at Bonneville Park, which hosted its first Pacific Coast League game in 1915 with the arrival of the city's new Coast League franchise. Bonneville's dimensions were a major reason for the hitting bonanzas; the 325 feet down both foul lines was about average, but center field was only 360 feet away, with power alleys that were also short. Add the 4,330-foot altitude of Salt Lake City and it is easy to understand why the team led the Coast League in home runs nine of the 11 seasons they played in Bonneville, while seven individual home run titles were won by Salt Lake players. They also led the league in hitting for eight of their 11 seasons: 1915, 1916, 1917, 1919, 1920, 1923, 1924 and 1925, producing batting champions Morrie Rath (1917), Bill Rumler (1919), Earl Sheely (1920), Paul Strand (1922 and 1923), and Duffy Lewis (1924).

Without question, Bonneville Park inflated the statistics of Salt Lake hitters. In 1923, the ballclub hit an astonishing .369 at home—more than eighty points better than their road batting average of .285. Bonneville's edge notwithstanding, the Bees, year in and year out, featured one of the best offensive lineups in the league.

The standard bearer for this hitting legion was Paul Strand. Winner of the batting championship in 1922 and triple crown in 1923, the six-foot,

Paul Strand (Don Hazelwood)

182-pounder was another in a long line of PCL sluggers such as Lefty O'Doul, Paul Waner, Buzz Arlett and Smead Jolley who began their careers as pitchers. Strand's pitching was decent enough to achieve a 42-32 minor league record and earn three brief appearances (1913–15) with the Boston Braves. It was not until 1919, at the age of 25, that Strand began concentrating on his batting. That year he hit .299 as a pitcher-outfielder for Peoria of the Three-I League. The following year he hit a league-leading .339 for Yakima of the Pacific International League and then .314 with nine home runs and 95 runs batted in in his first year at Salt Lake in 1921.

Respectable as his offensive numbers were, they hardly suggested the success that soon came. In 1922 Strand won the PCL's batting crown by hitting .384 with 28 home runs and 138 runs batted in. Along the way he hit safely in 35 consecutive games. He also set the organized baseball record for hits in a season with 289. Seven years removed from the major leagues, the ex-pitcher now began to draw attention from scouts for his hitting.

A left-handed batter and thrower, Strand was described as an awkward outfielder, though by 1923 some newspaper accounts suggested that he had become capable defensively. He played center field and batted fourth in the lineup in 1923, a season that would become one of the greatest offensive performances in league history. He won the triple crown (.394, 43 HR, 187 RBI) and broke his record for hits with 325. This mark will likely never be broken, especially since 200-game seasons do not appear to be making a comeback.

Strand's 325 hits came in 194 games; the outfielder sat out five late-season contests after he had broken his previous record. Not surprisingly, an examination of Strand's 1923 season reveals a picture of remarkable consistency. On the year, he hit safely in 168 ballgames and compiled hitting streaks of 19, 17, 12 (4 times), 11, and 10 (twice) games.

Perhaps nothing speaks better to Strand's stature as a hitter than the Oakland–Salt Lake game of April 28. Leading 5–3 with the bases loaded and two out in the bottom of the ninth, Oakland manager Ivon Howard ordered pitcher Harry Krause to walk Strand intentionally, making the score 5–4 and putting the tying run on third base. The unconventional strategy worked; the next batter, Joe Wilhoit, a .360 hitter, flied out to end the game. To put the move even more into perspective, consider that Wilhoit set the organized baseball record for hitting in consecutive games in 1919 when he hit in 69 straight games for Wichita in the Western League.

While hardly a week went by without Strand performing heroically at the plate, two ballgames stand out. The first came on June 9, when he led Salt Lake to an 11–10 win over Oakland by hitting for the cycle. In another tight ballgame on August 26, the Bees trailed Seattle 18–17 in the bottom of the ninth until Strand popped a game-winning two-run homer. Significantly, the blast was Strand's thirty-fourth of the year, breaking the Pacific Coast League record of 33 set by former Bees Bunny Brief in 1916 and Earl Sheely in 1920.

Strand's record-breaking season earned him another chance in the major leagues. Connie Mack paid Bees owner Bill Lane $35,000 and gave him pitchers Harry O'Neil and Hank Hulvey along with second baseman Clark Pittinger for the rights to Strand. Though the penurious Mack had paid dearly for Strand, he did not give him much of a chance with his Philadelphia Athletics. He optioned the 30-year-old outfielder to Toledo of the American Association after just 47 games, in which he hit .228, 0 HR and 13 RBI in 167 at-bats. Strand never returned to the major leagues, staying in the minors until he retired after the 1928 season. Though he started late as a hitter, Strand still managed to amass 1,956 hits in the minors, good enough for a career average of .334.

With Strand as their star, the 1923 Bees starting lineup was very impressive: Les Sheehan, 2b (.338, 36 HR, 130 RBI); Oscar Vitt, 3b (.337, 19, 112); Johnny Frederick, rf (.328, 16, 82); Paul Strand, cf (.394, 43, 187); Joe Wilhoit, lf (.360, 8, 86); Roy Leslie, 1b (.340, 15, 140); Walter Pearce, ss (.233, 2, 31); and John Peters, c (.338, 11, 74). Duffy Lewis also played in 128 games, mainly in left field, hitting .358 with 28 home runs and 118 runs batted in.

Just as hitters posted monstrous numbers thanks to Bonneville's forgiving confines, so did the pitchers. Rudy Kallio led the Bees staff with a 4.73 earned run average and 14-9 record, statistics that looked downright stellar compared to those of his moundmates. Richard McCabe (14-16, 4.97), Pudgy Gould (16-21, 5.98), Fred Coumbe (13-12, 5.99), Elmer Myers (11-16, 6.00), Sheriff John Singleton (15-15, 6.25) and Jim Duchalsky (1-3, 7.90). The staff managed just one shutout, that by Myers.

"Pitching has fallen into such a condition that a lead of eight or ten runs is absolutely worthless," wrote Salt Lake beat writer Les Coates in the *Sporting News*. "The Bees are two pitchers short in quantity and at least four minus in quality."

Another problem was at shortstop, where the midseason loss of Walter Pearce created a void at the critical position. Coates claimed that no fewer than 17 games were lost because of poor play at shortstop. Not until Tony Lazzeri was called up from Peoria was the position again in capable hands. Playing in 39 games, Lazzeri fielded less than spectacularly (.924), but hit well (.354, 7 HR, 21 RBI), displaying the power that would ultimately produce record numbers in 1925. Lazzeri, however, could do little to help the ballclub in 1923, as they finished in fifth place with a 94-105 record.

For player-manager Duffy Lewis, the season did not even live up to the modest preseason hopes he shared with reporters. "I really believe we've got a chance to better our fourth place position of last season," he told the writers. "But we're not talking about winning the pennant. We're just going to go out there and hustle for every game."

Lewis displayed aggressiveness at the plate and in the field. He had earned a reputation throughout organized baseball for his hitting and fielding skills, as well as his knowledge of the game. He joined the Salt Lake ballclub midway in 1921 after a successful 11-year major league career in which he had a .284 lifetime average and appeared in the World Series for the Boston Red Sox in 1912, 1915 and 1916. In 105 games for the Bees in 1921 he hit .403. The following year the 34-year-old was named player-manager, a role he filled for three seasons. The three-year stint was a record during the 11-year existence of the Salt Lake Bees. Third baseman Oscar Vitt took over as manager in 1925, moved with the franchise to Hollywood and managed the ballclub another 10 years.

During Lewis' tenure, the club never managed to finish higher than fourth place. Bill Lane fired Lewis following the 1924 season, stating that the

Pudgy Gould, left, and Tony Lazzeri (George E. Outland)

manager failed to condition and handle his players properly. Failure to gain a pennant could not be pinned entirely on the manager, or for that matter on any of the nine managers who failed to win a Pacific Coast League pennant for Salt Lake City.

Part of the blame must go to majority stockholder Bill Lane, whose abrasive and tightfisted ways failed to win friends or build baseball teams. An ex–Indian fighter, Alaskan gold miner and Utah politician, Lane was independent and spoke his mind. After buying the original San Francisco Missions franchise in 1915, he moved the club to a town that he thought craved baseball. But cold weather at the beginning and end of the seasons, along with the Bees' mediocre ballclubs, kept the fans away. Lane's fellow owners complained every year about the cost and time involved to travel to Salt Lake, the league's most remote city.

Duffy Lewis (George E. Outland)

Every year Lane denied rumors of his club's imminent move. Vancouver businessman Bob Brown made several overtures for the ballclub during the early 1920s, but Lane repeatedly refused them. In 1923, Fresno was rumored to be the new home of the Bees. This time Lane could be blamed for starting the rumors. Not only did he conduct the ballclub's spring training there, but he announced they would play their first two "home" series in the central California city. Lane did not deny that he might be experimenting with the site for a possible future there. If it was an experiment, it turned out badly.

A city of fewer than 60,000 residents, Fresno was smaller than both Salt Lake City and the league's least populated city, Sacramento. The city had once been home to a Pacific Coast League ballclub (1906) and supposedly loved baseball, for years serving as gracious host to PCL and major league clubs during spring training. On opening day in 1923, fewer than 2,000 Fresnoans turned out to watch their potential adoptees play Seattle. Rain cancelled three games, and crowds dwindled into the hundreds as the series wore on. Meanwhile in Salt Lake City, where the opener was often played in several inches of snow, blue skies and warm weather prevailed as the ballpark sat empty. Cutting his experiment short, Lane cancelled the second week of games in Fresno and returned home to Utah to host the Portland Beavers before much larger crowds than those in Fresno.

Angered by lackluster attendance, Lane vowed in 1924 to leave Salt Lake City and nearly moved to Long Beach in 1925. The move was blocked by Oakland's Cal Ewing, who foresaw that the Vernon ballclub would shift to San Francisco as a result, thereby diluting the Bay Area baseball market. Lane did fulfill his California dreams when he moved the ballclub to Los Angeles in 1926. But in 1923 the team remained in Utah. Lane may have lived in the geographic hinterland of the PCL, but that did not stop him from being in the middle of the most heated battle yet among Pacific Coast League owners and the league's president.

Civil War

Two warring factions squared off—one centered in San Francisco, the other in Los Angeles—spilling bad blood up and down the coast. Writing in the *Sporting News*, Matt Gallagher called it "Civil War." In one camp was President William McCarthy and the owners of the San Francisco, Sacramento, Seattle and Vernon franchises. Standing in opposition, ready to fight till the end over the future course of the league and McCarthy's autocratic rule, stood the Salt Lake, Los Angeles, Portland and Oakland franchises.

Trouble had been simmering for years. Oakland's Cal Ewing probably held the longest grudge, opposing McCarthy's appointment prior to the 1920 season because he feared an all-too-cozy relationship between the Seals' owners and San Francisco businessman McCarthy. In the intervening years, Ewing and McCarthy rarely saw eye to eye.

Ewing had as many allies as McCarthy had enemies. Bill Lane never forgave the president for banning Bill Rumler for his role in the 1919 betting scandal, seeing McCarthy's action as sanctimonious and a deliberate attempt to hurt his ballclub. Portland's Bill Klepper held the president in similar disregard for his failure to help him fight the lifetime ban handed down by Judge Landis in the Kenworthy tampering case of 1922. The ban forced Klepper to the background, but it did little to keep him from running the club. Throughout the 1923 season, Klepper ran his ballclub from behind the scenes, shooting public barbs at McCarthy as often as he could. Wrigley aligned himself with this troika and soon took the leadership role to oust the president.

McCarthy's tenure had been fraught with controversy and even violence. Betting scandals, tampering, player eligibility rulings, and debates over policies such as the draft were the difficult issues that confronted him during his three years on the job. At the January 1923 league meeting held in Portland, two issues widened the schism, putting McCarthy and four franchises on one side and the remaining four franchises on the other.

The draft, once again, was the first issue. As he did the year before, Ewing stood as the only owner in favor of subjecting PCL players to a major league draft. However, in 1921 Judge Landis made a ruling that forced Wrigley, Lane and Klepper to reconsider their original anti-draft stances. Basically, Landis ruled that the majors had the right to nullify a section of the agreement between the major and minor leagues and put 15 players out on option instead of eight as spelled out in the original provision. More importantly, Landis ruled that if a player had been on a major league roster and was subsequently sold or traded to the minors, he was automatically subject to the draft, even if that league declared itself draft-exempt. A PCL team that acquired a former major league player for a season, would risk losing him the following year for the draft price of $5,000. Players who had never appeared on a major league roster were exempt from the rule.

Landis wanted to promote upward mobility of players who did not stick during an earlier stint in the big leagues. McCarthy saw the action as a way to coerce the PCL into accepting the draft. He steadfastly refused to subject his league to the draft in any shape or form. San Francisco's Strub moved that the league stay draft-exempt and that no PCL team should use players who were draftable under the new rule. He further moved that any team using such a player would be fined $500 for each game wherein the offending player appeared and that the team forfeit every game in which the draft-eligible player participated.

Sacramento, Vernon and Seattle voted in favor of Strub's motion, while the other four teams opposed it. Essentially banning former major league players from their ranks, the opposing four maintained, not only reduced the overall quality of play in the league, but limited teams from improving themselves by acquiring proven veterans who had major league experience.

Oakland, Salt Lake, Portland and Los Angeles then proposed calling a special meeting of the National Association so that the minors could establish a more acceptable middle ground. The proposal clearly established a draft and anti-draft division among the league owners. The anti-draft faction won out. McCarthy cast the tie-breaking vote, as was his right under existing league bylaws. Ewing protested that McCarthy should not have the right to decide such an important issue affecting owners' pocketbooks. Yet McCarthy held firm.

The next order of business at the meeting came when Sacramento's Lew Moreing proposed raising roster limits from 18 to 25 players, with five roster spots designated for rookies without class AA experience. Cultivating younger players, Moreing advocated, would help wean the league from reliance on major league talent while developing future stars. Once again, a four-four split occurred. And once again McCarthy cast the tiebreaker in favor of expanding the roster.

Tempers heated and nearly boiled over into violence with Strub's next motion: to grant Vernon equal territorial rights as Los Angeles, a point of contention between the two Southern California franchises since 1909. Wrigley exploded. McCarthy and his allies had gone too far. Loss of territorial rights meant the Angels could no longer collect money from Vernon for use of Washington Park; from now on both clubs had equal rights to the ballpark. Though both ballclubs equally split the lease to Washington Park, Vernon paid a premium and the lease expired in 1925. With territorial rights, the Angels could negotiate even more favorable lease terms. Or, if they went through with Wrigley's plan to build a new ballpark (which they would), the Angels could charge the Tigers a hefty sum to use the facility. But even as Wrigley protested, McCarthy cast another tiebreaking vote, this time stripping the Angels of a right they had held for 14 years.

Incensed by the day's proceedings, Cal Ewing stormed out. Wrigley, Klepper and Lane publicly declared that McCarthy should be drummed out of office, if not immediately, at least when his contract expired in November. Wrigley, however, did not want to wait that long to turn the tables. To do that he would need to burst the bloc of four that supported McCarthy. Luring any of his opponents to his side seemed out of the question; emotions ran too deeply. However, it had become common knowledge among the owners that Seattle's Jim Boldt had become financially strapped and was eager to unload the ballclub. Control of the Seattle vote would shift the balance of power in favor of the Wrigley faction.

Within a month of the January meeting, Angel executive Charles Lockhardt and manager Red Killefer resigned from the Los Angeles ballclub and purchased controlling interest in the Seattle franchise. To no one's surprise, the ex–Wrigley employees indicated that they sided with Wrigley in the current dispute. Suddenly the minority had become "The Big Five."

Immediately Doc Strub and Vernon's Ed Maier charged that Wrigley had hatched the scheme. "Syndicate baseball," they called it—an allegation Wrigley denied. McCarthy stepped in and demanded to see correspondence between the new Seattle owners and Wrigley, as well as their bank statements and financial records of the transaction. When they refused to let McCarthy investigate, he refused to recognize the new owners and threatened further action.

"I consider syndicate baseball a greater harm to the national game than the activities of gamblers, crooked ballplayers and other irregularities," he proclaimed. "I want to serve notice now that this investigation will go on if I have to take it up with the National Board of Arbitration with a view to having Wrigley banned from baseball."

Wrigley, Lockhardt and Killefer charged that a spiteful McCarthy once again acted unfairly and autocratically to quash his opponents. Lockhardt refuted the notion that Wrigley's money bought the Seattle franchise, claiming that he had accumulated the cash from the sale (to Wrigley) of a glass-bottom boat business on Catalina Island as well as disposing of real estate in Los Angeles County. Later, he acknowledged that Wrigley had loaned him $125,000, but only until a bank loan could be secured to complete the Seattle deal.

To bypass the league president and gain their voting status on the Pacific Coast League Board of Directors, Lockhardt and Killefer filed a motion in civil court. The motion, however, was dismissed by a Los Angeles County judge, who refused to listen to arguments until all avenues of appeal within organized baseball had been exhausted.

A meeting of the league's directors took place on May 15 to review the draft issue. Lane stated that many of his veteran players—their bargaining powers enhanced because Lane could no longer acquire major leaguers—had leveraged their positions to extract higher salaries. Add the expanded roster to the equation, Lane said, and his ballclub stood to lose $20,000 for the season. Ewing, whose Oakland team was in last place, said he could not build a competitive team without drafting relations with the majors.

San Francisco's Charlie Graham scoffed at Ewing, citing that with or without relations with the majors, Oakland had not been in the first division for seven years. Lockhardt rose to add his opinion to the debate.

"You are not allowed to speak at this meeting," McCarthy said before Lockhardt could speak. And with that McCarthy had effectively undercut the uprising, preserving the narrow majority that opposed the draft, the same narrow majority that kept him in office.

For the rest of the season this majority held sway. Lockhardt's appeal to the National Board went unheard as the season ended in November. Meanwhile, politicking continued in both camps. Wrigley told reporters that the Big Five might withdraw from the Pacific Coast League and form a new league. But then, Wrigley and Maier appeared to be settling their differences, attending ballgames together at Washington Park and lunching in downtown eateries. In July, Sam Agnew, the Seals' catcher, made an offer to buy the Salt Lake franchise, doubtlessly with the encouragement if not financial backing of the Seals. Lane refused even to entertain the offer.

At the end of September, McCarthy so upset Lew Moreing that it appeared the Sacramento owner might withdraw his support. Prior to the crucial San Francisco–Sacramento series at the end of September, Moreing sent a letter to the league office asking that umpire Bill Byron not work the series. Byron's alleged ineptitude and attitude had incited a riot the year before in Sacramento. With emotions running high in the capital city because of its team's rare chance for a pennant, Moreing did not want to risk another incident.

McCarthy refused Moreing's request. Sure enough, near the end of the second game between the Seals and Senators, a questionable Byron call cost the home team the ballgame. His subsequent arrogance then started a riot that continued for more than an hour after the game ended.

When informed of the melee, McCarthy threatened to move the series to San Francisco. "To hell with McCarthy!" shouted a livid Lew Moreing, pounding a fist on the desk as reporters looked on. "I won't stand for it and hereafter he can fight his own battles." Later Moreing softened and reaffirmed his support, albeit weakly, for McCarthy.

With the November league meetings coming up, the old alliances seemed less certain. Suddenly the league owners, who loved to air their squabbles publicly, grew silent, though both the Big Five and the Little Three, as the two sides came to be known, indicated that they had set their strategies for the November 12 meeting, a meeting later dubbed "The Battle of Avalon."

The Battle of Avalon

The Monday morning meeting was to take place in the billiard room of the St. Catherine Hotel in the tiny town of Avalon on Santa Catalina Island, a site selected by league vote one year before. The Big Five rode out on Wrigley's boat on Sunday morning, gathering at the home of a Los Angeles attorney to review their strategy and, it was later revealed, to rehearse their plan for the Monday morning meeting. According to an account written by *Los Angeles Times* sportswriter Harry Williams, the group periodically broke from their rehearsal to look through binoculars for the arrival of the Little Three, who had rejected Wrigley's invitation to ride aboard his boat and had instead rented a yacht.

At nightfall, former Chicago sportswriter Oscar Reichow, now an employee of the Angels, shouted, "It looks like a boat. It looks like a boat. It *is* a boat!"

Indeed, the rival faction had arrived at the island. After some difficulty finding the dock, McCarthy and representatives of the Seals, Tigers and Senators came ashore, abandoned their plans to eat and sleep aboard the yacht, and registered at the St. Catherine where they were immediately met by a horde of sportswriters.

Posturing on both sides took place that night. McCarthy was steadfast in affirming his future as president and in denying Seattle a seat on the PCL Board of Directors. McCarthy's opponents kept the throng of sportswriters busy by floating the names of McCarthy's potential replacement. Ewing advocated former PCL President Allan Baum, while Lane claimed he supported either ex–Portland Beaver owner Judge McCredie or perhaps former Pittsburgh Pirate outfielder Fred Clarke, who was on hand for the meeting. Of course, Ewing and Lane had no intention of nominating any of these three men. Their plan had already been well-orchestrated, as became evident the morning of November 12.

Williams, who played a key part in the Monday proceeding, chronicled what took place for the Helms Athletic Foundation's *Pacific Coast League Record*. Following is an excerpt from his article "The Battle of Avalon":

> The meeting place was crowded — there being more than a hundred persons in the rather small room. It matters not that one prominent sportswriter attended, clad only in his bathrobe. This was to be the most democratic of meetings — not to mention the most dramatic. Everyone was seated, with President McCarthy at a table — slightly to the right side of the room. No one happened to notice an identical table at the left side of the room, which was partly obscured because Charley Lockhardt was sitting upon it, nonchalantly reading a newspaper. McCarthy and the three club owners supporting him overlooked all of this.
>
> Came the fatal moment.... It was time to call the meeting to order. Meantime, Harry Williams and [Oakland Oaks executive] Del Howard had stationed themselves at the head of the short stairway leading to the billiard room, and could hear every word said. Just as McCarthy started to call the meeting to order, Williams and Howard descended the stairs and Williams seated himself, gavel in hand, at the table on the left side of the room. Naturally, McCarthy and his followers were amazed. Williams, paying no attention to McCarthy, proceeded to call the meeting to order — while McCarthy was doing the same thing.
>
> "You are an interloper — you can't do that!" McCarthy shouted at Williams.
>
> "You are out of order, Mr. McCarthy!" Williams bellowed back.
>
> Completely dumbfounded, McCarthy and his followers lapsed into absolute silence. Williams and his supporters held their meeting, and elected Harry Williams president of the Pacific Coast League for a five-year term.

Once they elected Williams, the Big Five rescinded his power to vote on league matters as had been McCarthy's right. They then voted to re-establish drafting relations with the majors, dropped the roster limit back to 18, and reinstated the Los Angeles Angels' territorial rights.

Following this meeting, on the advice of Pacific Coast League attorney Harry Stafford, McCarthy and the other three club owners conducted their meeting. They re-elected McCarthy and reinstated a $20,000 purse for the top seven finishers in the 1924 season.

Two weeks of confusion reigned after the meeting. McCarthy attempted to conduct business as usual in San Francisco, even as Williams did in Los Angeles. McCarthy had the advantage, having access to all league records and funds.

Williams, operating on a fund established from a $200 assessment of each club, did not feel secure enough to quit his job with the *Times*, taking instead a two-month leave of absence. He struck a conciliatory tone, trying to mend the fences. "There will be no Big Five or Little Three so far as I am concerned. I am going to give everyone the same kind of deal." But when he wired the San Francisco Seals to collect their $200 assessment, he received a curt wire back: "Try and get it."

Soon John Farrell, secretary of the National Association of Professional Baseball Leagues, stepped in to run the league until the National Board of Arbitration decided who was the rightful president. At the end of December, the National Board announced its decision. Though it reprimanded Wrigley, Lockhardt and Killefer for "indiscreet and censurable conduct," the board found no evidence of syndicate baseball. As such, Seattle's vote was valid and Williams was indeed the new Pacific Coast League president.

"The gems were stolen; the burglar reprimanded, the policeman commended, and then the gems were returned to the burglar," said PCL attorney Stafford, criticizing the decision.

McCarthy took the decision better. "My only wish is that the Pacific Coast League will enjoy one of its greatest years in 1924. I'll always have a warm spot in my heart for baseball," he said. Surprisingly upbeat, the former president then attended a dinner in his honor at the Olympic Club in San Francisco before attending a mock wake the following day to celebrate his "demise."

Meanwhile, the office of the league president, which for 21 years had resided in San Francisco, was moved to Los Angeles. President Williams took over a league that remained badly divided, but at least now had a clear majority. The balance of power had shifted. The faction headed by Strub, with its strong-willed desires for PCL independence, was out; the Wrigley-Lane coalition, with its more moderate stance toward independence, was in.

1923 Final Standings

	W	L	Pct.
San Francisco	124	77	.617
Sacramento	112	87	.563
Portland	107	89	.546
Seattle	99	97	.505
Salt Lake	94	105	.472
Los Angeles	93	109	.460
Oakland	91	111	.450
Vernon	77	122	.387

Team batting leaders

Average:	Salt Lake — .327
Runs:	Salt Lake — 1,303
HRs:	Salt Lake — 204

Individual batting leaders

At-bats:	Merlin Kopp, Sacramento — 829
	Gene Valla, San Francisco — 829
Average:	Paul Strand, Salt Lake — .394
Runs:	Paul Strand, Seattle — 180
Hits:	Paul Strand, Salt Lake — 325
2B:	Les Sheehan, Salt Lake — 72
3B:	Pete Schneider, Vernon — 23
HR:	Paul Strand, Salt Lake — 43
RBI:	Paul Strand, Salt Lake — 187
Total bases:	Paul Strand, Salt Lake — 546
Stolen bases:	Merlin Kopp, Sacramento — 80

Individual pitching leaders

Winning percentage:	Harry Courtney, San Francisco — .760 (19-6)
Games won:	Ray Kremer, Oakland — 25
Games lost:	Jakey May, Vernon — 22
Most games:	Pudgy Gould, Salt Lake — 56
Most shutouts:	Walter Mails, Oakland — 5
	Vean Gregg, Seattle — 5
	Bill Prough, Sacramento — 5
Most complete games:	Ray Kremer, Oakland — 35
Most innings:	Ray Kremer, Oakland — 357
ERA:	Vean Gregg, Seattle — 2.75

Chapter 6

1924 – The Great
Six-Day Bicycle Race

The 1924 season marked a return to normalcy – at least by Pacific Coast League standards – with baseball overshadowing politics. Not that off-field squabbles did not continue, because there were plenty of those, but the hottest pennant race of the decade stole the spotlight.

A snapshot of the standings through August 18 portrays the season to that point. Atop the league, San Francisco was expected to win its third straight pennant. Its everyday lineup, virtually the same as the year before, was acknowledged as the league's best even by the most avid Seal-haters. The outfield featured two of the better youngsters in the league in center fielder Gene Valla and right fielder Paul Waner. Major league veteran Tim Hendryx and Joe Kelly shared left field chores. And there simply was no better infield in the minor leagues than third baseman Eddie Mulligan (.306, 13 HR), shortstop Hal Rhyne (.298, 2 HR), second baseman Pete Kilduff (.294, 13 HR) and first baseman Bert Ellison (.381, 33 HR). As they would for several years, good friends Archie Yelle and Sam Agnew shared the catching duties.

Many of these players were a year away from their best minor league seasons, yet they performed well enough through the summer of 1924 to keep the team in the pennant race. The problem proved to be pitching. Gone in a deal with the Chicago White Sox were Harry Courtney and Doug McWeeny, who spurred the winning 1923 pennant drive.

Just two games back, the second-place Seattle Indians, after an extensive offseason makeover, dogged the Seals through the summer and appeared ready to mount an assault on first as the summer wound down. Red Killefer moved from the front office to the on-field managerial role where he belonged. He and club president Charles Lockhardt then obtained pitchers George Stueland and Percy Jones from the Cubs and Harry "Suds" Sutherland from Portland. First baseman Elmari Bowman and part-time outfielder Frank Osborne were obtained from the Eastern League for second baseman Clyde Mearkle and cash.

Suds Sutherland (George E. Outland)

"You can tell the Seattle fans for me that the Indians will be right up there running one, two, three when the curtain falls next fall on the Coast League race," Killefer gushed in a letter to Lockhardt shortly after closing the deal for Bowman.

But Killefer had only begun to deal. Within weeks of the season opener, he obtained touted International League second baseman Cliff Brady, whose skills around the bag were counted on to steady brilliant but erratic shortstop Sam Crane. A seven-year major league veteran, Crane was named captain of the club prior to training camp. The outfield rivaled that of the Seals with returnees Brick Eldred, Bill Lane and Home Run Ray Rohwer.

Ross C. "Brick" Eldred played right field and batted fourth for the Indians, though he was hardly the prototypical cleanup hitter. Standing just five-feet-six-and-a-half inches and weighing 162 pounds, Eldred hit only 80 home runs in a minor league career that began in 1916 at Salt Lake City and ended in 1930 at Sacramento. While he might have lacked home run power, he could drive the ball, averaging 64 doubles a season for six years, 1920–1925. The capable-fielding outfielder played nine full seasons (1920–1928) with Seattle. Eldred turned 31 during the 1924 season and enjoyed one of his best seasons ever.

Also enjoying one of his best years was 32-year-old Bill Lane. The tiny (five-foot-six, 145 pounds) outfielder gathered 201 hits and 49 doubles on his way to a career-high .336 average. For the fourth time in his career, Lane led the PCL in stolen bases. He eventually achieved 468 lifetime thefts in the PCL, a league record.

Unlike Lane and Eldred, Ray Rohwer more closely fit the mold of a PCL outfielder. At five-foot-ten and 155 pounds he was not big, but the left-handed hitter mustered enough power to hit 196 home runs during a nine-year Coast League career. He, too, had one of the best years of his career in 1924.

Eldred, Lane and Rohwer were joined in the outfield by young Jim Welsh. He proved to be the surprise of the season, hitting .342 with 16 home runs. During one stretch in April, Welsh hit five home runs in five games, lifting the spirits if not the status of the last-place Indians.

Most often the Indians lined up like this during the 1924 season (statistics for the 1924 season are in parentheses): Bill Lane, cf (.336, 1 HR, 45 stolen bases); Cliff Brady, 2b (.261, 4 HR); Sam Crane, ss (.269, 1 HR); Brick Eldred, rf (.351, 7 HR); Elmari Bowman, 1b (.301, 10 HR); Ray Rohwer, lf (.325, 33 HR); Ted Baldwin, 3b (.299, 6 HR); and Red Baldwin, c (.282, 3 HR).

Overall, the changes to Seattle's lineup earned favorable comments from most Coast League writers, though preseason expectations did not include a Seattle run for the pennant. Seattle's *Sporting News* correspondent, Royal Broughm, summed up the prevailing view of the Seattle franchise: "A stronger outfield, a better infield combination and a slightly improved catching staff, but who's going to pitch?"

It was a valid question. The ace, Vean Gregg, was 39 years old. And the club's only 20-game winners from the year before, Harry Gardner and Elmer Jacobs, were gone; veterans Bill Plummer and Suds Sutherland suffered off years. With Gregg putting together nine straight wins en route to a 25-11, 2.90 ERA season, and with Stueland (18-13, 4.55 ERA), Jim Bagby (16-10, 4.76 ERA) and Percy Jones (13-11, 4.37 ERA) winning in the clutch, the Indians somehow found themselves running with the PCL's elite.

In third place on August 18, with a record of 74-69, the Oakland Oaks were vying for only their second winning season in 12 years. His pitching arm shot, Buzz Arlett (.328, 33 HR) now led the Oaks as a power-hitting outfielder. George "Frenchy" Lafayette and Ray Brubaker were also enjoying fine years at the plate. Veteran pitchers George Foster, Duster Mails, Earl Kunz, George Boehler and Harry Krause carried the ballclub with 135 complete games on the year.

Angered by his team's last-place performance the year before, Vernon's Ed Maier undertook an off-season makeover of the ballclub. When he was through he had assembled the youngest team in the league, and one which found itself in the first division for most of the year. Veteran pitchers Jakey May and Wieser Dell were sent packing, leaving Frank Shellenback as the only

Brick Eldred (George E. Outland)

holdover on a staff that included Eddie Bryan, Jim Christian, Ken Penner, and Claude Thomas. Two new outfielders cracked the lineup, with newcomers Michael Menosky and Jim Blakesley displacing veterans Hugh High and Ping Bodie. Similarly, Jim McDowell took over for Dan Murphy at first base, while second base duties were assumed by Wes Griffin, who gave the Tigers their first regular at the position in more than a year. Though not spectacular, the revamped Vernon Tigers were an improvement over the 1923 vintage.

No doubt pleased by their second-place finish in 1923, the Sacramento Senators returned virtually the same lineup in 1924. Whether it was bad luck or a sudden change in chemistry, the 1924 Senators fell short of their performance of the year before. The best fielding club of 1923 now found themselves booting balls right and left, finishing the season as the worst fielding team in the circuit. Their malaise spilled over into their offensive production as well, with the club batting average tumbling from .298 in 1923 to .283 in 1924 — again, last in the league. Art Koehler, one of the league's best catchers year-in and year-out, led the ballclub, hitting .341 with nine home runs.

The suddenly ineffective pitching of Moses Yellowhorse compounded the ballclub's problems, as did lack of depth on the staff as a whole. Only Bill Hughes, with a 20-19, 4.28 ERA, won more games than he lost. The decision to let pitcher Ken Penner go for the waiver price proved especially vexing when Penner turned in a sparkling 24-13, 4.00 ERA, performance for Vernon. Before the season ended, owner Lew Moreing fired manager Charlie Pick and replaced him with Buddy Ryan.

Adding Lefty O'Doul to the roster was supposed to enhance the pitching of sixth-place Salt Lake. But by August, arm trouble rendered him useless on the mound. Making the most of the situation, the Bees converted O'Doul to an everyday outfielder, where he fielded poorly but soon became one of the greatest hitters on the West Coast. O'Doul and manager Duffy Lewis staged a battle for the league batting title that was not decided until the final day of the season; Lewis won by the barest of margins, hitting .39204 to O'Doul's .39182. One more hit or one fewer at-bat and O'Doul would have eked out the PCL batting title.

Led by Lewis, O'Doul, Johnny Frederick (.353, 28 HR), Leslie Sheehan (.346, 22 HR), Roy Leslie (.339, 18 HR), Howard Lindimore (.339, 11 HR), and Oscar Vitt (.333, 15 HR), the 1924 Bees again led the league with a team batting average of .327. Despite the addition of six new pitchers prior to the season, poor pitching once again hindered the team, though that was not its only problem. The ballclub was doubtlessly distracted by owner Bill Lane's threat to abandon Salt Lake at midyear. Players also grew discontented with Lewis, and Lane publicly pilloried the manager for not conditioning the club properly and for not instilling discipline in the players. By fall, the friction erupted into clubhouse fisticuffs on several occasions, including one in which pitcher Harry O'Neil decked Lewis with a punch to the eye.

Seventh place Portland had its share of distractions as well. Reinstated manager Duke Kenworthy replaced the popular James Middleton but failed to generate the support from his players that Middleton enjoyed. As a result, Kenworthy was fired during the summer and replaced on an interim basis by slugger Frank Brazill. Though the team hit well (.310), it lacked pitching and defense. Dick Cox (.356, 25 HR), James Poole (.353, 38 HR) and Brazill (.351, 36 HR) starred offensively for the Beavers.

Trailing the pack in last place were the Angels, a preseason pennant favorite. Prior to the season, the team replaced half their infield, keeping middle fielders Jim McAuley and player-manager Marty Krug, and installing new players Ray Jacobs at third base and Walter Golvin at first. "We have added youth, speed and hitting power to our club," Krug said of the changes. "Ray Jacobs is destined to develop into one of the greatest third sackers the Coast League has ever had, not alone in fielding, but also in hitting."

With returnees Wally Hood (.338, 22 HR) in left field and Babe Twombley (.312, 2 HR) in right, along with center fielder Cedric Durst (.342,

Bill Lane (George E. Outland)

17 HR), who was obtained from the St. Louis Browns, the Angels fielded one of the better hitting outfields in the league. For a last place team, Los Angeles had surprisingly good pitching: a mix of veteran hurlers—Doc Crandall, Elmer Myers and Nick Dumovich—and promising rookies—George Payne and Charlie Root.

Despite its talent, the team had a difficult time winning. To add spark to the lineup two hitters were added during the summer—Walton Cruise, a fourth outfielder who was expected to provide power, and Ray Grimes, obtained from the Chicago Cubs to replace the disappointing Golvin. The ballclub also obtained catcher Joe Jenkins from Salt Lake City in June, shoring up its deficiencies in that department.

Cruise looked bad early, prompting club president Joe Patrick to chide business manager Oscar Reichow, who had made the $15,000 deal for the outfielder. "Oscar, are you sure this is the man you bought? Are you certain those Eastern fellows didn't switch players on you?" he asked. Cruise soon rounded into form to hit .318 on the year, but it was Grimes who proved the late-season catalyst.

From first to last, only 14 games separated the eight teams on August 18. It was still anyone's pennant.

The Harry Williams regime begins

The presidency foisted upon him in the stormiest session in league history, Harry Williams presided over a pennant race that promised high drama and attendance that was on a pace to shatter league records. From the outset his reign seemed blessed. Following his first meeting as undisputed president, a meeting in which the eight teams voted unanimously on seven agenda items, Williams declared, "It seemed just like the good old days."

The veteran sportswriter had been covering the PCL for seven years, mainly for the *Los Angeles Times* and as a correspondent to the *Sporting News*. Shortly after losing a bid for the league presidency to William McCarthy prior to the 1920 season, Williams left California to take a position with the *New York Globe*. Less than a year later, however, he returned to the West, assuming sportswriting duties once again for the *Times*, where he remained until the December 1923 Battle of Avalon.

Except for the usual and frequent suspension of players for fighting among themselves and with umpires, Williams did not have to deal with much controversy during the 1924 season. As a writer, he had been a longtime advocate for umpires; as president, Williams sought to reduce the violence against them. First, he fired the umpires who tended to inspire the least respect and cause the most problems, most notably Bill Byron. Then he instituted stiff suspensions instead of fines against players who engaged in fights or especially unseemly arguments with umpires. McCarthy had enjoyed limited success with a suspension-only policy, but Williams felt that longer suspensions would be a strong deterrent to umpire abuse. To further support the men in blue, Williams got league owners to fund $3 a day in meal money for half the season and to allow new umpires to be trained by using a rookie as a third umpire in many late-season games.

While deftly handling the routine chores of the job, Williams soon felt a shift in the league's balance of power. Owners of no fewer than five teams were threatening to either sell their franchises or relocate to another city. Any change whatsoever could have disrupted the delicate 5–3 majority that favored Williams.

When Bill Klepper sold his franchise to Tom Turner and John Shibe of the Philadelphia Athletics after the season, not only did Portland become the second franchise in the league with a direct link to a major league ballclub, but the so-called Big Five contingent of owners was put in jeopardy. Next came an announcement in November that PCL icon Cal Ewing had sold his Oakland ballclub to Washington Senators pitcher Walter "Big Train" Johnson and partner George Weiss for a price near $400,000. But just two weeks later the sale fell through when Johnson's financial support crumbled.

Earlier in the season, the Salt Lake City Bees left town for a lengthy road trip, after which owner Bill Lane promised his ballclub would not return; instead, he said, the team would finish out its "home" schedule in Vancouver, where longtime Bees suitor Bob Brown promised the local ballpark would be ready and filled with fans. Lane, however, relented when a group of Salt Lake businesses ponied up enough money to guarantee visiting teams their fair share of receipts for playing in Bonneville Park.

This mollified Lane for the time being, but in late August he and the Angels' William Wrigley hatched a plan to move the team to Long Beach in 1925. The plan called for the Bees to play in the new spring-training ballpark Wrigley had built in Long Beach or to share Washington Park until the new Wrigley Field was built. Anticipating opposition, Lane and Wrigley succeeded in changing the league by-laws that required unanimous approval of any franchise move; now only a simple majority was required.

If the Bees moved, Vernon's Ed Maier vowed to relocate his team to San Francisco, resurrecting the old Mission team and giving San Francisco continuous baseball at Recreation Park. Continuous baseball in San Francisco would have hurt Ewing's Oakland Oaks, who not only played some of their games at Recreation Park, but also counted on San Francisco fans ferrying across the bay to view Pacific Coast League action when the Seals were on the road. Ewing maintained that the Bay Area could not support three Coast League ballclubs, and his fear of that eventuality was at least partially behind his attempted sale of the franchise to Johnson and Weiss.

In November when the vote came up for Lane to transfer his club to Long Beach, Ewing lobbied enough votes to block it. But both Wrigley and Lane made it clear that they *would* succeed in moving the franchise for the 1926 season.

Williams stayed safely out of the fray, allowing the owners to settle matters on their own. He had learned from McCarthy's ouster that a heavy-handed president could be assured a short reign. And in the constantly changing world of PCL politics, Williams could not afford to upset anyone.

Ironically, Williams also faced the threat of a gambling scandal. Here, too, he decided not to overstep his bounds. While McCarthy made a blood-enemy of Bill Lane and irritated other owners for his much-publicized handling of the 1919 PCL betting scandal, Williams took a low-key approach.

Charges were raised by American League president Ban Johnson that the Coast League was soft on gamblers and that the illegal activity flourished at Coast League ballparks, particularly at Los Angeles' Washington Park. Coast

League officials were already sensitive about such charges, both from the earlier scandal and the news that former Seals phenom and New York Giant outfielder Jimmy O'Connell had attempted to bribe Philadelphia's Heinie Sand prior to a game in 1924. Though slightly more subdued than in its pre-scandal heyday, gambling continued openly in Coast League ballparks. The Coast League, Johnson intimated, was a breeding ground of corruption.

Wrigley flew into a rage, demanding that Johnson either prove or retract his allegations. Williams echoed the demand. From his offices in Chicago, Wrigley told Angels management to clean up any traces of gambling. Soon after, Angels business manager Oscar Reichow warned visiting teams to stay clear of their usual lodging site, the Barbara Hotel, because notorious Chicago gambler Nick "The Greek" Dandalos had taken residence there. In August, 70 suspected gamblers were thrown out of Washington Park.

Johnson launched his own investigation, violating protocol that he act through Commissioner Landis or simply let the PCL handle its own affairs. Landis was enraged. Wrigley, a longtime Landis ally, and Salt Lake's Bill Lane excoriated the American League chief and tried to rally support for a censure by the entire National Association.

Johnson defended his action: "I am not so much interested in Coast League gambling in itself, but these gamblers are so strongly entrenched and have so much money, they can reach their slimy fingers right into the American League."

Johnson and Landis had been feuding as far back as 1914. As a federal judge, Landis had presided over a case involving the legitimacy of the Federal League, which threatened organized baseball's reserve clause. Johnson called Landis a showboat for the way he handled the case, even though the judge's delayed ruling allowed the Federal League to crumble, thereby benefitting organized baseball. Landis was named baseball's first commissioner in 1919 to deal with the Black Sox scandal. The commissioner replaced the National Commission, which had been dominated by Johnson since 1903.

A committee of American League owners was formed to look into Johnson's action on this and other disputes with Landis. Ultimately, they sided with the judge, censuring Johnson for exceeding his authority in the PCL gambling issue. No further investigations were announced and the issue died.

Crowded at the top

As August came to a close, the *San Francisco Chronicle*'s Ed Hughes wrote: "It is too late for the Los Angeles club to do anything except make trouble for the other clubs. The club was wrecked last fall and has not made much of a showing this year." He went on to say that it was "anyone's pennant."

Hughes' assessment was shared by the rest of the league's beat writers. Last place Los Angeles had shown little all year, and the rest of the league was the most balanced in memory.

Except for the thirteenth week of the season, when it dipped into second place, San Francisco held firmly to first place. Seattle had climbed from last place after two weeks of play to second by the ninth week of the season, elbowing its way into first for a few days during the thirteenth week.

Oakland, Vernon, Sacramento, Salt Lake City and Portland hovered in and around third place, waiting for Seattle to fall. A non–California team had not won the pennant in 10 years and the Indians did not seem destined to break the dry spell. But they continued to apply the pressure. As September came and went, they remained in second place, losing some ground, but still within 4½ games of the league-leading Seals.

Almost without notice, the written-off Angels clawed their way out of the cellar and into third place, just a half-game back of the Indians. Oakland and Salt Lake trailed by just another game, meaning that five clubs had a legitimate shot at the pennant. With two weeks remaining in the season, the race shaped up like this:

	W-L	Pct.
San Francisco	102-84	.559
Seattle	97-88	.524
Los Angeles	96-90	.516
Oakland	95-91	.511
Salt Lake	94-91	.508
Vernon	93-94	.497
Portland	86-99	.465
Sacramento	80-106	.430

Los Angeles had plunged into the thick of the race by playing the best ball in the league over the previous nine weeks, compiling a 43-23 record. Their torrid play included five straight over Seattle in their series the first week of October, bringing the Angels within one win of the second place Indians. The series in Seattle concluded on a sour note for the Indians. Not only did they lose 3-1, but they gave the game away by committing five errors, allowing two unearned runs to score. With but two series left to play, Seattle appeared rattled and braced for an inevitable fall. Two of the club's better players—outfielders Jim Welsh and Bill Lane—were injured and lost for the season. The Associated Press wire report from Seattle characterized the team's mood: "The Seals are scheduled to open a seven-game series here tomorrow with Seattle's chances for the 1924 pennant gloomy."

Seattle's chances brightened somewhat on Tuesday, October 7, when Vean Gregg shut out San Francisco, 8-0. Sylveanus Augustus Gregg had started his major league career in 1911, playing three years for the Cleveland

Indians in which he went 23-7, 20-13 and 20-13. The following year he was traded to the Boston Red Sox at mid-year and compiled a 12-7 record for the two teams on the year. From there his pitching career floundered, as he went 4-2 in 1915 and 2-5 the following year. In 1918 for the Philadelphia Athletics, his record fell to 9-14. Gregg found himself out of the major leagues even though he had compiled a 90-61 record and his earned run average had never climbed above 3.44 in a single season.

The six-foot-one, 185-pound left-hander longed for a return trip to the majors. When the Yankees made inquiries for the aging pitcher in 1924, Gregg became furious with Lockhardt when the Indian president nixed a deal that would have sent Gregg to New York in time for the American League pennant drive. As it was, Lockhardt dealt Gregg to the Washington Senators. Ironically Washington had beaten out the Yankees for the 1924 American League pennant and had gone on to win the World Series. Gregg, however, would not share in those heroics; Lockhardt's deal called for him to join the Senators at the conclusion of the PCL season. Gregg did just that, ending his major league career in 1925 with a 2-2, 4.14 ERA, season.

Hardly disheartened by their defeat on Tuesday, the Seals rebounded on Wednesday to win an 8–6 cliffhanger and restore their 4½ game lead. Down to their last out in the ninth, San Francisco used back-to-back doubles by Ellison and Waner to knot the score at five. The teams traded a run in the twelfth before Waner's bases-loaded single in the thirteenth produced the winning margin. The only good news for Seattle came when they learned that the Angels had been rained out in Portland for the second game in a row, thus preserving Seattle's two-win margin over the southlanders for second place.

Even this good news was dashed the next day. Bad weather cancelled the San Francisco–Seattle game, but did nothing to stop Los Angeles from beating Portland. Five games remained in their important series with San Francisco; nothing less than a sweep would allow Seattle to overtake San Francisco and stave off the Angels.

Friday, October 10, dawned with threatening skies over Seattle. As game time approached intermittent blue skies shone through and a sparse crowd prepared for the series' pivotal game. Though doubleheaders would follow on Saturday and Sunday, the game at hand meant a two-game swing in the standings: a Seattle win would bring them to within 3½ games of the leaders, a loss would drop them 5½ back.

By this time of year, McClellan and Rainier Streets were perpetually muddy, and fans had to slop their way into nearby Dugdale Park. Also known as Rainier Valley Park, the 15,000-capacity ballpark was named after D.E. Dugdale, who owned the Seattle franchise for several years before selling out. Dugdale still owned the stadium, leasing it to the Indians and local high schools and colleges for football games, which left the baseball playing surface as rutted and treacherous as McClellan Street. The ballpark met a fiery demise following a July 4 fireworks show in 1932, but on October 10, 1924, it was a happier place—at least for the locals.

Scoring five runs in the bottom of the eighth inning, Seattle beat the Seals, 5–3, spoiling an outstanding game by young San Francisco pitcher Davey Crockett. Veteran Suds Sutherland earned the win. The big blow for Seattle came when, with a runner on second base, Frank Emmer hit a ball that bounced into the left field stands—a home run under the rules at the time. Despite the win, Seattle fell to third place when Los Angeles swept a doubleheader in Portland.

The following day, Seattle's pitchers dominated the Seals. Fred Fussell threw a three-hit shutout, leading to a 5–0 win. In the second game, George Stueland limited the Seals to four hits for a 6–2 victory. Suddenly, San Francisco led the Angels by just one game, and Seattle by 1½.

Seattle's chances, which only a week earlier had seemed quashed, were now restored. Their pitchers for Sunday—Vean Gregg and Percy Jones—had been throwing well. In the 10-inning first game, Gregg pitched to form in going the distance for a 5–4 win. The veteran helped his cause with a two-run single in the second inning. A half-game behind in the standings, Seattle had San Francisco hitters on the ropes. In the second game, Jones powered through the lineup time after time, allowing just three hits. Seattle won the nightcap, 3–0, and this, coupled with the Angels' doubleheader rainout in Portland, vaulted the league's northernmost team into first place.

For the Seals the trip had been a nightmare. They had dropped six of seven games and fallen into third place. Almost as bad, they earned only $1,126.14 as their share of the series. To put that in perspective, a visiting team could expect to earn far more than that from a typical weekend game in Recreation Park. Bad weather, college football and the long PCL schedule had limited crowds for the critical series. Despite the disappointing turnout, Seattle had enjoyed their best season for attendance. On August 1, they surpassed their previous record set in 1923. Furthermore, the franchise that had been the center of controversy the year before now appeared stable.

Now the ballclub could concentrate on baseball, a luxury lacking since the franchise was readmitted into the league in 1919. Seattle first suffered through the bombastic days of William Klepper before having to endure the well-meaning but misguided management of majority owner Jim Boldt, a baseball tyro. The year 1923 was one of adjustment for the new club management, the players and the fans alike. But by 1924 things looked to be clicking, and despite the late-season drop-off in attendance, the team announced net earnings of $70,000 for the year. Two years later when the team was for sale, the team claimed net earnings of only $3,000 for the 1924 season.

Boarding the train Monday morning, October 13, the Seattle ballclub were especially ebullient: They led the league and they were to play seven games against the Portland Beavers, a team in disarray. Down south, Los

Angeles manager Marty Krug openly voiced his anger that his club's two rained-out games in Portland could not be replayed. Had they won both—a real possibility considering they had already beaten the Beavers 12 straight and 22 of 26 times—the Angels would have entered their season-ending series with Vernon in first place. Even so, Los Angeles' chances were considerably better than the slumping Seals', who had to hope both Seattle and Los Angeles lost, while they battled their tough Bay Area rivals, the Oakland Oaks.

With seven games to play, the top four teams were clustered within 3½ games:

Seattle	103-90	.534
Los Angeles	102-90	.531
San Francisco	103-91	.531
Oakland	101-94	.518

The Six-Day bicycle race

With the race so close, and the teams hotly jockeying for the top spots, the *Los Angeles Times* dubbed the last week of the season the "Six-Day Bicycle Race." The final week opened on Tuesday with the Angels still en route home to play Vernon, while rains cancelled the Seattle-Portland opener. Suddenly, there was a new competitor in the pennant race—rain. A real possibility arose that inclement weather could cancel the entire series in Portland. And should Los Angeles, San Francisco or Oakland surpass the idle Indians, one of these teams would claim the pennant; there were no provisions in the PCL's marathon schedule to make up rainouts once a series had concluded. A rained-out series would have cost Seattle the pennant. Seattle President Lockhardt proposed moving their series to Washington. Joe Patrick, the Angels' president, agreed to such a move, but Harry Williams negated the decision, knowing Seattle hardly promised tropical conditions.

Adding to the drama of the final week, Patrick announced that he would give his ballclub a $5,000 bonus should they win the pennant. Demonstrating that his was not an idle offer, he gave each player on the roster a $100 bill prior to the concluding series.

Even though they did not play a single inning on Tuesday, the Indian and Angel fortunes improved when the Seals dropped the first game of their series to Oakland. The Seals effectively put themselves out of the game—and the pennant race—after just five Oakland batters had come to the plate. Joe Bratcher and Ray Brubaker opened the game with singles. Frenchy Lafayette then bounced a ball to the first base side of the mound, which Oliver Mitchell misplayed into a single. Ted Cather's single scored Bratcher, bringing Buzz Arlett to the plate. The switch-hitting Arlett defied convention, opting to bat left-handed against the southpaw Mitchell. Arlett sent the pitcher's first offering over the fence for a grand slam. A large contingent of Oakland fans celebrated for several minutes after the former pitcher crossed home plate, and then they stood by as Oakland held on to win, 6–1.

The next day San Francisco won, while the Indians beat the Beavers twice. The badly demoralized Portland ballclub put up a struggle in the first game, leading 6–3 in the ninth. Brick Eldred led off the frame with a pinch-hit single, which was followed by Frank Osborne's single to right. Clancey Cutshaw pinch-hit, lofting a deep flyball to score Eldred, who tagged up at third base. Ray Rohwer followed with a home run to tie the game, before Bowman's blast to left put the Indians ahead to stay.

The second game of the doubleheader also saw the Indians rally for the win. Despite Rohwer's third home run of the day, Seattle trailed 4–3 in the eighth. Then Portland pitcher Rube Yarrison fell apart. This is how the correspondent to the *San Francisco Chronicle* described the eighth inning: "Pick out any chapter of recent war history that tells of terrific artillery work and you have an accurate description of what happened this afternoon. Rohwer opened the frame with his last homer of the day, and four singles, two walks and an error counted six more." Seattle won 10–6.

When Vernon first baseman Jim McDowell belted two home runs to beat Los Angeles 4–2, dropping the Angels three games back in the win column with five games to go, *Los Angeles Times* writer Robert Ray sounded a dour note. "It's not all over yet," he wrote, "but it might just as well be." Ray and *Chronicle* writer Ed Hughes both blasted Portland for not giving their best against Seattle. "You might as well give half the pennant to the Beavers," Hughes wrote.

Seattle, Los Angeles and San Francisco all won on Thursday, and again on Friday, but with time running out on the season, Ray again summoned up his pessimism: "The Indians haven't clinched the pennant yet, but the Angels and Seals have a much better chance of changing the verdict of the recent World War."

Seattle continued to dominate Portland to win its tenth consecutive game on a dreary Oregon Saturday. The game began at 10:30 A.M. so that the University of Southern California–Oregon Aggie football game could be played at the ballpark that afternoon. Sixty-five fans and one umpire turned out to watch the teams. One umpire overslept, forcing Portland outfielder Charles High to umpire the bases while the other umpire called balls and strikes. The Beavers scored first, on two walks and a base hit by Babe Thomas off Percy Jones. Jones soon settled down, holding the Beavers in check for a 6–3 win. Rohwer's two-run double in the fifth put Seattle ahead for good.

Both San Francisco and Los Angeles swept their doubleheaders. But the half-game they both picked up still left them with formidable odds to overcome. Entering Sunday's doubleheaders, Los Angeles had to win both their games while Seattle lost both for the Angels to claim the title. The Seals could win only if they swept the doubleheader, Seattle lost two games, and Los Angeles lost one.

Recreation Park was filled to capacity for the Sunday morning game between the Seals and Oaks. It did not take long for fans to witness the Seals' elimination from the pennant race, when the Oaks pounded Marty Griffin and Marvin Moudy for 12 hits in an 11–3 romp. Though the Seals won the nightcap 7–6, it was too late.

In Washington Park, 15,000 fans watched as Angel Charlie Root outdueled Vernon ace Eddie Bryan for a 4–1 victory, keeping the club's pennant hopes alive. However, moments later the crowd groaned when the final score of the Seattle-Portland game was posted: Seattle 12, Portland 4.

The Seattle Indians had clinched the pennant. And they did so with an exclamation point, battering pitcher Clyde Schroeder and Rube Yarrison for 16 hits. The Indians had won their eleventh straight game, and might have extended their streak to 12 had the nightcap not turned into a farce. Several non-pitchers on both clubs took the mound, and Indian manager Red Killefer caught the entire game, as other players exchanged positions willy-nilly. The frivolity may have been what Portland needed all along, as they won their first game in two weeks by gathering 18 hits en route to a 15–1 victory.

The loss did not, of course, detract from Seattle's accomplishment. Arguably, the San Francisco Seals were the best team on paper. And over the last two months no team played better than the Angels. But no team performed more consistently than Seattle during the course of the year.

Vean Gregg, Ray Rohwer, Brick Eldred and Bill Lane earned their due among the elite of the league. And though Killefer's skill as a manager was well-known, his work during the 1924 season was a greater accomplishment than the pennant he earned as manager of the 1921 Angels. The red-headed manager had taken a team that in 1923 threatened to strike if he assumed the managerial duties and molded it into a harmonious unit. For his success, Killefer may have been the best paid manager on the coast, if not in all of baseball. In salary and dividends on his stock as part-owner, Killefer claimed that he earned $25,000 for the 1924 season.

There is no arguing that the Indians were not the most dominant champion of the decade—their .545 winning percentage remained the lowest by a PCL champion until 1963—but their flag had been well earned. The Indians managed to stay with the front-running Seals all season, beat them in head-to-head competition when it counted most, and withstand the challenges of both San Francisco and Los Angeles during a pressure-packed final week.

Any chance Seattle had to further establish their place in history was literally washed away by the ubiquitous Northwest rains. A planned Junior World Series to be played in Seattle against American Association champion St. Paul was cancelled due to rain after a first-game win by the visitors. With the washout, the season came to an end.

Ownership changes, gambling accusations, and threats to shift franchises did little to overshadow an exciting season of Coast League baseball. Atten-

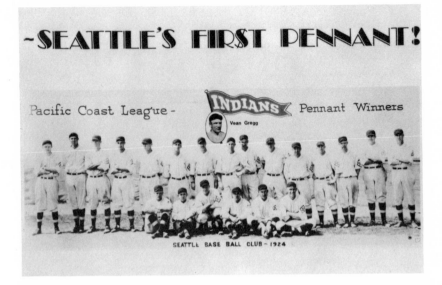

~SEATTLE'S FIRST PENNANT!

Pacific Coast League - **INDIANS** Pennant Winners
Vean Gregg

SEATTLE BASE BALL CLUB - 1924

1924 Seattle Indians (Tony Pirak, courtesy Museum of History & Industry, Seattle WA)

dance hit a new record high of 2,235,510, breaking the previous record of 1,825,916 set in 1923.

"As late as last fall it was a question whether the Coast League would continue to exist as such," President Harry Williams said at year's end. "It apparently had been torn so completely asunder that it seemed in the throes of dissolution. But the circuit pulled itself together, and the season for the most part has been one of constructive cooperation. The club owners are entitled to the highest commendation. Baseball politics has been buried so deep under prosperity that it is hoped it can never be resurrected."

1924 Final Standings

	W	L	Pct.
Seattle	109	91	.545
Los Angeles	107	92	.538
San Francisco	108	93	.537
Oakland	103	99	.510
Salt Lake	101	100	.502
Vernon	97	104	.483
Portland	88	110	.444
Sacramento	88	112	.440

Team batting leaders

Average:	Salt Lake—.327
Runs:	Salt Lake—1,416
HRs:	Salt Lake—194

Individual batting leaders

At-bats:	Eddie Mulligan, San Francisco—820
Average:	Duffy Lewis, Salt Lake—.392
Runs:	Howard Lindimore, Salt Lake—183
Hits:	Bert Ellison, San Francisco—307
2B:	Roy Leslie, Salt Lake—73
3B:	Buzz Arlett, Oakland—19
HR:	Jim Poole, Portland—38
RBI:	Bert Ellison, San Francisco—188
Total bases:	Bert Ellison, San Francisco—496
Stolen bases:	Bill Lane, Seattle—45

Individual pitching leaders

Winning percentage:	Ed Bryan, Vernon—.722 (13-5)
Games won:	Oliver Mitchell, San Francisco—28
Games lost:	Walter Mails, Oakland—22
	Jim Christian, Vernon—22
Most games:	Walter Mails, Oakland—56
	John Singleton, Salt Lake—56
	Phil Mulcahy, Salt Lake—56
Most shutouts:	Not Available
Most complete games:	George Boehler, Oakland—30
	Ken Penner, Vernon—30
Most innings:	George Boehler, Oakland—396
ERA:	Doc Crandall, Los Angeles—2.71

Chapter 7

1925 — Team of the Decade

Tuesday, April 7, 1925, brought baseball weather San Francisco style — cold, gray and misty. Recreation Park was filled to capacity, with a good part of the legion comprised of U.S. Navy seamen from the Pacific Fleet, which had invaded San Francisco for a week's shore leave. At 15th and Valencia Streets they found a dilapidated bandbox that locals called "Old Rec" and which had its share of oddities. The right field wall stood an inviting 235 feet away, though a looming 50-foot screen atop the wall knocked down even the most vicious line drives, turning potential extra base hits into singles. Experienced right fielders played against the wall for big hitters, often taking a carom off the wall and throwing out an unwary hitter who tried to stretch a single into a double.

Rec Park had other quirks as well. None were quirkier than the Booze Cage, field level seats protected by chicken wire that separated players from San Francisco's rowdiest and — often — drunkest fans. The Booze Cage was eight rows high, consisting of wooden benches that ran from first base to home and around to third base. Prior to prohibition, 75 cents bought a Booze Cage ticket and a shot of whiskey. In 1925, the booze was not legal, but it flowed just as freely. The liquor fueled the emotions of Booze Cage denizens — hardcore fans who berated home and visiting players alike with such ferocity that only the chicken wire prevented full-scale riots.

The base lines were only 15 feet or so from the Booze Cage, and sometimes the walk to the plate was an exercise in self-control for players. "Suhr, you're a bum, they'd yell," former Seal Gus Suhr recalled many years later. "What's a matter? You been out drinking all night!" The rough language, hard drinking and rough-hewn manners of the regulars usually kept women from entering the tight Booze Cage quarters.

The Booze Cage hardcores took surreptitious pulls on their flasks and looked with guarded optimism at the gray April sky. With the 1925 season about to begin, they looked at their Seals with similar restraint. To believe the words of manager–first baseman Bert Ellison, the Seals were a shoo-in for the 1925 Pacific Coast League pennant. Then again, they were a shoo-in in

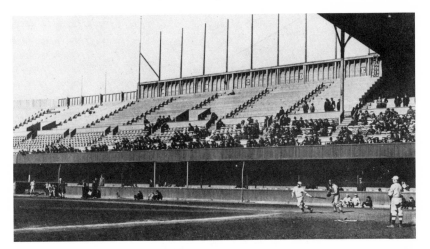

Recreation Park (John E. Spalding)

1924, too, when a late season pitching collapse ruined their hopes for a third straight pennant.

To shore up their pitching, the Seals brought in two ex–major leaguers: 10-year National League veteran Jeff Pfeffer (not to be confused with his older brother, Big Jeff Pfeffer) and 29-year-old Doug McWeeny, who had won 20 games for the Seals in 1923 and who had just been dropped by the Cleveland Indians.

The boys in the Booze Cage tucked away their flasks, bundled up in their overcoats and settled into their field-level seats to await McWeeny's 1925 debut. They were not disappointed. McWeeny performed as billed in winning the opener 6–4. Another off-season acquisition, right fielder Frank Brower, led the offense with two homers, the second a game-winning, two-run blast in the bottom of the tenth.

Perhaps the Seals really did have the players to return to championship form. And for San Francisco fans of the 1920s, nothing but a pennant would do.

"No fuss is made here over a pennant winner," wrote *San Francisco Chronicle* sportswriter Ed Hughes in 1925. "In some towns the fans get all hopped up, buy the players gold thing-a-majigs, put them up at exclusive clubs, and in many ways make them feel that they have done something worthwhile. If an Oakland club should win the pennant, the members of that team would be given the freedom of the city, with all that that implies. But here in San Francisco the fans are used to good teams. They want the Seals to win, of course, but they do not run around making little yipping cries of delight when the Seals win a flag. In other words the fans are blasé."

Even for stoic San Franciscans, it was difficult not to get excited about the

Doug McWeeny (George E. Outland)

1925 Seals. Seals owners Alfie Putnam, Dr. Charles Strub and Charlie Graham believed they had their best team ever. With the additions of Pfeffer, McWeeny and Brower, the team looked like this (1925 statistics in parentheses): Bert Ellison, 1b (.325, 22 HR, 160 RBI); Pete Kilduff, 2b (.306, 20 HR, 126 RBI); Hal Rhyne, ss (.315, 3 HR, 97 RBI); Eddie Mulligan, 3b (.286, 10 HR, 77 RBI); Paul Waner, lf (.401, 11 HR, 130 RBI); Gene Valla, cf (.333, 6 HR, 72 RBI); Frank Brower, rf (.362, 36 HR, 163 RBI); Sam Agnew, c (.325, 20 HR, 85 RBI); Archie Yelle, c (.267, 1 HR, 21 RBI); and Pete Ritchie, c (.315, 1 HR, 26 RBI).

The four infielders had played together for three years and were considered the best in the league individually and collectively. The *Sporting News* wrote: "It is a better infield than Boston or Philadelphia in the National and one or two clubs in the American." Waner and Valla were the two best young outfielders in the league. Brower had played for Cleveland the year before; for $7,500 the Seals received a lifetime .284 major leaguer with a cannon arm. With the possible exception of Art Koehler and Merv Shea of Sacramento, Agnew and Yelle formed the best tandem of catchers on the West Coast.

The basic five-man pitching rotation—Guy Williams, Doug McWeeny, Oliver Mitchell, Bob Geary and Marty Griffin—was *expected* to win a hundred games. Another addition, young Marvin Moudy, was counted on for added depth.

Bert Ellison (George E. Outland)

Fourteen in a row

The 1925 Seals started slowly; their 5-4 record trailed both Salt Lake and Los Angeles. A season-opening split with defending champion Seattle did not portend a pennant.

Then the team came alive to take the last four games of a seven-game series with Oakland. They followed that with seven straight over Sacramento, Pfeffer getting two of the wins and McWeeny a shutout.

The 11-game surge put the Seals in a first place tie with Salt Lake, setting the stage for the first of three exciting series with the Bees. In 1924, the two teams stood toe-to-toe, producing some memorable offensive numbers. A May series in Salt Lake saw the two teams amass 264 hits and 38 home runs in seven games; the Saturday game in that memorable series produced 54 hits and 99 total bases. The Seals' Bert Ellison led all hitters with a 25 for 37 performance that included 10 home runs. While the season-long series with the Bees in 1925 would not produce such monstrous numbers, it would showcase the year's most exciting baseball. Their first showdown of the year came in San Francisco on April 28.

Salt Lake's reputation for slugging had reached mythic proportions. They had virtually rewritten the PCL's record books in 1923 and 1924. The 1925 team was equally awesome. Three San Francisco natives led the Bees' attack: third baseman–manager Oscar Vitt, shortstop Tony Lazzeri and first baseman Lefty O'Doul. Coming into the series, the trio sported .400-plus batting averages. Though the three had their share of hits, their team lost its first three games against the Seals as the San Francisco winning streak reached 14.

In Friday's game, the Bees snapped the Seals' winning streak, reviving their hopes for taking the series and assuming first place in the league. Game five featured a duel between Pfeffer and Dick McCabe. Tied 2–2 going into the top of the ninth, Salt Lake pushed across the go-ahead run.

In the bottom of the inning, 34-year-old Tim Hendryx pinch-hit for reliever Guy Williams and worked a walk. The tying run was on first with nobody out and leadoff hitter Gene Valla at bat. At third Vitt crept up closer, expecting the bunt. The first baseman held the runner and readied to break toward home, while second baseman Howard Lindimore cheated over to cover first. The Bees were prepared to keep the tying run off second if Valla bunted. Instead Valla swung away, sending a sinking liner to center. Johnny Frederick came in hard but missed and the ball bounded cleanly past him. By the time he caught up with the ball and threw it home, Hendryx and Valla had scored the tying and winning runs. Mulligan led the charge of Seals greeting Valla as he crossed the plate; the hometown assemblage looked on, stunned by the bang-bang turn of events. Not only had Valla's inside-the-park home run won the game, it broke the Bees' hopes for a series win.

The Seals took the doubleheader the next day to win the series five games to two, putting them three games up on Salt Lake in the pennant race. The following week, however, the Seals split a six-game series with last-place Vernon before regaining form by winning the next three series against Sacramento, Vernon and Portland.

The Angels come to town

A two-week homestand in June followed, starting with seven games against the Angels. Trailing San Francisco by 12½ games, Los Angeles needed this series to climb back into the race. Compared to the summer of 1924, their current third-place standing was cause for optimism. The year before they were in last place as late as July 15 before rallying to make a serious run for first. A 107-92 finish placed them second, a percentage point ahead of San Francisco. Even more galling to the Seals was the Angels' winning seven of eight games during a crucial September series, sabotaging the Seals' pennant hopes.

The 1925 Angels featured much the same cast, though star Jigger Statz did not return to the team from Chicago until late June, and the team featured a new second baseman and catcher. Future Chicago star Charlie Root won 25 games for Los Angeles in 1925. Hard-hitting left fielder Wally Hood provided power all year.

In the first game, the Seals entered the eighth inning down 8–5. Five straight hits later, the score stood 10–8 and the Seals never looked back. The key blow of the inning was a three-run, bases-loaded double by reserve infielder Nobby Paynter, playing because Hal Rhyne had been spiked on the hand earlier in the series.

In the afternoon game, the Seals overcame the Angels' six runs with a 10-run sixth inning. During the inning catcher Pete Ritchie, in an infrequent start, banged one off the Lucky Wedding Ring sign in right field to earn $20 from a local jeweler. San Francisco held on to win, taking five games from the Angels and leaving the visitors clinging to third by a half-game over Seattle.

Salt Lake's revenge

By the time the Seals arrived in Salt Lake City on June 23 they were like a marathon runner who had found his pace, moving ahead, steadily and inexorably. They followed the Los Angeles series by taking four of seven from Portland. Thus far, they had not lost a series.

Nothing San Francisco baseball fans read in the *San Francisco Chronicle*'s Sporting Green on the morning of June 24 diminished their enthusiasm for Bert Ellison's surging team; in the first game of the seven-game showdown with second place Salt Lake—this one in Utah—San Francisco prevailed 9–7 on the strength of a three-run homer by Pete Kilduff.

The next day the Seals lost 10–9, with Marty Griffin blowing a six-run lead in a disastrous sixth inning in which Rhyne's throwing error allowed the tying run to score. A Bee run in the seventh stood up to win the game and tie the series at one apiece.

Thursday's game conjured up images of the day before. This time Salt Lake overcame a four-run deficit, scoring five runs in the seventh inning off a reeling Jeff Pfeffer. Leslie Sheehan's grand slam tied the score, and this time Mulligan's throwing error allowed the winning run home.

On Friday a trio of Seals pitchers were responsible for the team's collapse, holding out until the ninth before doing so. In the eighth inning, his team behind 5–2, Tony Lazzeri blasted one over the right field screen off Oliver Mitchell. Davey Crockett came in to relieve Mitchell and immediately exacerbated the situation, yielding two hits and a run, leaving the Seals clinging to a 5–4 lead.

In the ninth Crockett continued to struggle, surrendering a single and a walk to start the inning. Geary came in to allow a base hit to Sheehan. The score was tied, with nobody out.

O'Doul then walked to load the bases. For San Francisco the situation looked dire. And if any hope remained, the PCL's Mr. Everything in 1925, Tony Lazzeri, dashed it by lashing a single to drive in the game-winning run.

The 1925 season was Tony Lazzeri's first—and last—full season in the Pacific Coast League. Lazzeri had a career year for the Bees, hastening his departure to the majors. Bill Lane sold Lazzeri to the Yankees for $35,000 and five players of Lane's choosing. Lazzeri went on to a stellar 14-year career with the Yankees and earn induction into the Hall of Fame.

Here's what the native of the Butchertown district of San Francisco did in 1925: hit 60 home runs, drive in 222 runs, score an organized baseball record 202 runs, and collect 512 total bases—all statistics that led the league. In becoming the first player in organized baseball to hit 60 home runs, Lazzeri also hit for average, with a mark of .355. Of his 60 home runs, 39 came at Bonneville Park.

Thanks largely to Lazzeri, the Seals had now lost three straight games. And Lazzeri was not finished. The next day he hit three home runs and a triple to drive in eight runs, powering the Bees to an 11–7 win. Again Salt Lake had come from behind; again Seals pitching fell apart. Reprising his role of the day before, Geary gave up 19 hits in a complete game loss.

The devout citizens of Salt Lake went to church on Sunday, June 28, 1925. Everybody else went to Bonneville Park to see if the Bees could extend their winning streak. Bill Lane, who had already announced plans to leave Salt Lake mainly because of poor attendance, faced a problem of a different sort at the start of the doubleheader—the biggest crowd Salt Lake had seen in years. The throng of 12,000 spilled onto the field before the game, requiring added security officers to pack them back into the stands. "Not in years has Salt Lake been worked up to such a baseball fever," came the report from the *Chronicle*'s Salt Lake correspondent.

But Speed Geary did not give the local fans much to cheer about, scattering seven hits and three runs through seven innings. Meanwhile, home runs by Valla and Waner led a battering of Salt Lake pitchers Elmer Ponder, Sheriff Singleton and Hank Hulvey. At the end of seven the score stood 9–3 in favor of the Seals.

The crowd began stirring in the bottom of the eighth when the Bees closed the gap to 9–6 on a three-run homer by Tony Lazzeri. In the ninth inning, down by three with two out, O'Doul came to the plate, with Sheehan and Hulvey aboard. Seconds later, the crowd erupted: O'Doul's dramatic home run to right had tied the score. Jeff Pfeffer had again blown the lead and the crowd was going crazy with Lazzeri coming to bat representing the winning run.

When Lazzeri sent Pfeffer's pitch out of the park, the fans could not contain themselves, throwing money at Tony as he circled the bases. As the *Chronicle* put it, "When they (throw money) at Salt Lake it means something."

The *Sporting News* described the scene: "Twelve thousand people rushed out on the field that day and threw dollars and halves at the fence busters. They went simply daffy over Tony."

In the nightcap of the doubleheader, the Seals halted their five-game losing streak, winning an abbreviated game 8–6. The Seals left town shaking their heads with their first series loss of the season and deep concerns about the collapse of their pitching.

With the series, Salt Lake closed to within 6½ games of San Francisco, and evened the season's record against the league leaders at seven games apiece. Clearly, they could play with the Seals; for the seven-game series, the Bees hit .381 en route to 58 runs.

Return of Salt Lake

In August, hot off their second series sweep of last-place Sacramento, the Seals led Salt Lake by 7½ games. When the Bees' train rolled into town on Monday, August 10, they were looking for a sweep to tighten the race and to prove that the previous series was not a Bonneville Park fluke.

The Bees were playing at a .599 clip, including a recent five to two series win over Oakland. Salt Lake's hitters were hot and looked forward to another chance at San Francisco's pitchers, who were injured, tired and sore. McWeeny had pitched only two innings since feeling a pop in his shoulder in July, and Marty Griffin's arm was responding slowly to treatments. With their two aces questionable, the Seals could not even rely on their number three man, Guy Williams. He, too, was struggling to overcome a sore arm.

Knowing how badly he was needed, McWeeny gutted through six innings in game one, a twisted ankle sending him to the showers. Bob Geary finished up and the Seals coasted to a 5–2 win. The next day fireworks came from the Seals' bats. Salt Lake's Rudy Kallio's famed drop ball did not drop and the Seals jumped all over him for 19 hits on the way to a 17–7 win.

Salt Lake rallied in the seventh to win the Thursday game, 4–2, and then pushed four runs across in the top of the ninth in the Friday game to register a dramatic 10–9 win. Umpire Jack Carroll was handed an assist by Seals fans for a questionable ninth-inning call. In what would have been a game-ending double play, Carroll was too busy making the call at second to get a good look at the play at first.

"Safe!" he ruled, though the fans in Rec Park saw otherwise. Manager Ellison held his temper in check, but Carroll had not endeared himself to the locals. If Carroll had any doubts, a shower of seat cushions and game programs confirmed the fans' opinion.

"The umpiring this year in the Coast League is absolutely the worst seen in the Coast League in many, many seasons," wrote the *Chronicle*'s Ed Hughes, who had been covering the league since its 1903 inception.

Salt Lake center fielder Joe Connolly and Seals third baseman Ed Mulligan apparently agreed with the *Chronicle* sportswriter. The following day Carroll sent them packing for arguing balls and strikes. Mulligan argued so vehemently that he was suspended by PCL President Harry Williams. Mulligan would overcome this brush with authority, later becoming president of the class A California League, a post he held for 20 years. Today the Edward Mulligan Award honors the California League's rookie of the year.

By Sunday's doubleheader, trailing in the series three games to two, the Bees were fed up with Carroll. When the eighth inning of the first game rolled around, Vitt had already been banished to the clubhouse. Yet the writers in the pressbox could spot him peeking around the clubhouse door in center field to view the action.

The score knotted at 6–6, Lazzeri opened the eighth against McWeeny with a double to left, giving the Bees three cracks at scoring the potential winning run. McWeeny took the sign from catcher Sam Agnew, stretched and set. But instead of pitching to the next batter, first baseman Fred Coumbe, McWeeny stepped off the rubber and lobbed the ball to Ellison at first base. Out.

Carroll ruled that Lazzeri had missed first en route to his double. Vitt sprinted from center and looked ready to fight. Bees catcher John Peters stepped in to prevent his manager from physically abusing the umpire. As it was Vitt set an unofficial PCL record by getting tossed twice from the same game.

Lazzeri, too, was ejected. When order was restored and Coumbe popped out, he could not help giving Carroll a word or two as he returned to the dugout. Carroll told him to keep on moving, banishing him to the clubhouse as well.

Though Salt Lake scored a run in the eighth, they had lost three-fourths of their starting infield to Carroll's iron hand. The Seals rallied for four in the bottom of the eighth and held on for the win. They took the nightcap as well and Salt Lake left town muttering about the injustice of the men in blue. Vitt was suspended after Carroll reported that the Bees' manager had threatened him with bodily harm; Lazzeri drew a $25 fine for his role in the Sunday ruckus.

Following the series with Salt Lake, Ellison's men travelled across the bay to Oakland where they split a six-game series. Los Angeles came next, the fourth-place Angels still harboring hopes of unseating the Seals. The Seals took the series, and one game illustrates how the Seals always found a way to win.

Trailing 2–1 in the Thursday game of August 27, the Seals were down to their last out in the ninth. They had outhit Los Angeles 12–2 but left seven men stranded. McWeeny was overpowering, striking out seven with his powerful fastball. Still it looked like San Francisco had squandered too many chances to win.

Things looked particularly bleak because on the bench sat tiny Ray Flashkamper, a five-foot-seven utilityman who had gone two for 11 on the year. With Kilduff on second, Flashkamper pushed the pitch from Los Angeles's Tom Hughes into center to score the tying run.

In extra innings a barehanded stop by Kilduff behind second base and a flashy doubleplay started by Rhyne preserved the tie until the bottom of the eleventh. Brower led off, hitting one so hard off the screen in right that he had to settle for a single. Hendryx bunted him to second. Kilduff's drive to right hit high off the screen. By the time the ball dropped to the ground Brower had scored the winning run.

What is remarkable about the win — in addition to Flashkamper's cameo heroics — is that the Seals did it with a patchwork lineup. Valla, Waner and Ellison all sat out the game with injuries. This was nothing new. Though never devastated by injuries, the team had its share of aches and pains, requiring some creative lineup adjustments by Ellison. At various times throughout the year, Ellison played first, short and third. Waner played left and right fields as well as first base on occasion. Infielder Nobby Paynter and outfielder Lloyd Waner would step in occasionally, while Hendryx hit .303 in his 330 at-bats. Brower also moved around the outfield and played a little first base as well.

During the game just described, third string catcher Pete Ritchie had to step in at first base. Later in a series against Portland, Ritchie had to pinch-umpire for an ailing Bill Phyle. He pinch-hit later in the same game before resuming his umpiring duties.

The homestretch

Seven weeks remained and each team in the league had one more crack at the Seals. At eight games back, only Salt Lake had a realistic shot at first place. Seattle's hopes of defending their championship dimmed with each day; at 14 games back they needed a complete San Francisco collapse. Fourth place Los Angeles — 15 back — could set their sights on Seattle, and maybe Salt Lake, but not even the Coast League had enough games for them to catch San Francisco.

The Seals' homestretch would begin with 17 games in the treacherous Northwest. In 1924 late season trips to Portland and Seattle had dropped San Francisco out of first and paved the way for Seattle's eventual pennant. With Valla, Ellison and Waner injured and questionable, a race to the finish remained possible.

Despite losing the concluding doubleheader in Portland, the Seals hung on to win seven out of ten in the series. The gem of the series was a three-hitter by Pfeffer in the Friday game that raised the team's record to 100-53.

A long train ride to Seattle followed. The Indians needed a sweep to entertain even a fantasy of first; instead they managed to win only two of seven games. Now trailing by 17½ games, Seattle's pennant hopes were dead.

Meanwhile, down in Southern California, the Salt Lake Bees were splitting eight games with the Vernon Tigers. By the time San Francisco arrived in Salt Lake on September 23, they led the Bees by 11 games, but bitter memories remained from their last visit to Bonneville Park.

Smead Jolley (National Baseball Library and Archive, Cooperstown, NY)

This time the memories would be sweeter—four wins, two losses and a tie. Most memorable of all was the emergence of Smead Jolley, one of the greatest hitters in the history of minor league baseball. During this series with Salt Lake, Jolley went 13 for 23, with four home runs and five doubles. In the series' first three games he drove in nine runs.

Jolley's acquisition reflected how the Seals did business in the 1920s. Charles Putnam, knowing full well that he had a bundle coming for Rhyne and Waner, decided to purchase Jolley from Corsicana of the class D Texas Association, outbidding a host of other teams, including Seattle. According to the *Sporting News* Seattle had already closed a deal for Jolley. A pennant almost assured, Putnam did not want the team to rest on their laurels.

Brought aboard for pitching support, Jolley won only one game that year. When Valla's mother was severely injured in an auto accident, Jolley stepped in to play right field on September 19 and quickly won over the fans and local sportswriters, smashing four hits in five at-bats. Even Valla's .333 average that year would pale to Jolley's .447, 12 home runs and 16 doubles in just 132 at-bats.

Slow afoot and clumsy afield, Jolley's liabilities limited him to 473 games for American League teams Chicago and Boston. He did, however, finish with a .305 lifetime average in the majors, including two full seasons wherein he hit over .300 and belted double-digit homers and batted in more than a hundred runs. If ever a player could have benefitted from the designated hitter rule, Jolley was it. A left-handed batter, he made a minor league career of banging line drives over and off the short right field fence at Rec Park, his drives so powerful that they were said to splinter the wooden fence and tear through the chicken wire screen. The major leagues' loss was the minor leagues' gain; during his minor league career Jolley hit .366, third best in minor league history.

The Seals clinched the pennant on October 9, a day when Bob Geary earned his twentieth win, a 2–1, 12-inning decision over Vernon, and Hal Rhyne set a PCL record with 18 fielding chances. Following that game, the Seals coasted to six wins and four losses to end their regular season. Next up: the Junior World Series.

The "sort of" October classic

The American Association's Louisville Colonels had clinched the championship on September 11 and staked their claim to the mantle of best minor league club in the land. But Jack Dunn's Baltimore Orioles, still riding an unprecedented crest of success that began in 1918, knocked off the Kentuckians four games to three in a post-season series. In so doing, Dunn took the luster off the nine-game Louisville–San Francisco series that was to start Thursday, October 22, in San Francisco. Since Dunn could not be persuaded to play the Seals — no doubt due to the modest financial rewards of a series played so far away — the Junior World Series failed to generate much enthusiasm.

The Seals found themselves in a no-win situation. A loss to Louisville meant they would be viewed as no better than the third best minor league team in the land; a win would only give them arguing rights to first — and Dunn's reputation could counter that claim as far as eastern writers were concerned.

Interest was further dampened by the Seals' success. They had led by so much all year and clinched the PCL so early that people stopped paying much attention. The *Chronicle*'s coverage of the Seals shrank; baseball had run its course as far as San Franciscans were concerned.

Meanwhile, college football fever raged. Talk was of Pop Warner, Ernie Nevers and company down the peninsula at Stanford, and of a surprisingly strong Cal team across the bay. Yet, the Junior World Series went on.

The loss to Baltimore notwithstanding, Louisville featured several outstanding players managed by Joe McCarthy, already named manager of the Chicago Cubs for 1926. Center fielder Ty Tyson played for the New York Giants the next year, while first baseman Harvey Cotter had just returned from the Cubs. Pitchers included once or future major leaguers Ed Holley, Ben Tincup and Nick Cullop, a late season addition from Atlanta of the Southern Association. Right fielder Joe Guyon followed in the footsteps of Jim Thorpe, starring in football for Pop Warner at Carlisle and later at Georgia Tech. The fleet, 200-pound Chippewa Indian drew a lot of attention from scouts but never landed in the majors.

In game one before a half-filled Rec Park, the Colonels embarrassed the Seals. Tincup, also of Indian descent, six-hit Ellison's men en route to a 7–0 win. He was helped by Tyson, who in addition to running down nine fly balls, hit a single, double, and home run to drive in three runs. McWeeny had been blasted by Louisville and many players openly derided the Seals, saying the team's "ace" was not even good enough to make an American Association roster.

But the Seals bounced back. They won the second game 9–2, with Guy Williams getting the win and Paul Waner's five for six providing the punch. Game three evoked images of the Seals versus Salt Lake as San Francisco rallied for five runs in the bottom of the eighth to win 5–2.

McWeeny's revenge came in the first game of the Sunday doubleheader. His 9–0 shutout over Tincup and company upped the San Francisco advantage to three games to one and silenced the taunts from the Louisville bench. Geary, with help from Griffin, pitched the win in the nightcap to bring San Francisco to within one of a series victory.

Strub, Graham and Putnam no doubt viewed a swift resolution with mixed emotions. On one hand, a decisive win would add credence to their claim that they had assembled the best minor league team in the land. On the other hand, every game short of nine the two teams played meant thousands of dollars in lost revenues. As it was, after five games the Seals' owners were losing money for the series. Attendance averaged less than 6,000 a game—not nearly enough for a profit in a shortened series.

The Junior World Series took place only because San Francisco's owners took a gamble. They lured Louisville west with a no-lose offer, guaranteeing to pay all the visitors' travel, lodging and meal expenses for the trip—an outlay of about $9,000. On top of that, the team paid their own players' expenses, as well as the travelling expenses and $500 salary of one of the two umpires. Louisville picked up the $500 tab and expenses of the second umpire.

Through the first five games, $19,190.80 had been collected from ticket sales—of which $13,433.60 would go to the players (split 60/40 between the winners and losers). Of the $5,757.20 left after the players' cut, half would go to Louisville's owners. Adding in Louisville's $9,000 travel costs and the

$500 umpire fee, the Seals organization had commitments to pay about $29,500 and had received only $19,190.80 — a loss of about $10,000. Concession sales added to receipts, but after deducting expenses for vendors, ticket takers, security and other employees, the sale of food and a few programs would not make up the shortfall.

On Tuesday, October 27, game six commenced with all the charm of a funeral. An autumn chill and morbid interest enticed few fans to the ballpark to witness the Colonels' interment. The corpse resurrected itself, however, scoring five late runs off McWeeny in relief to win 11–9. Three San Francisco errors — two by Rhyne and one by Ellison — helped give Louisville new life. The Seals then lost again on Wednesday before a meager crowd. Nick Cullop earned the 6–2 win.

By game number eight, it looked as though neither team wanted to be there. Louisville won the 12–11 debacle in which there were 48 hits and eight errors (five by the Seals). With the Seals stranding 16 runners, Louisville managed to eke out the win.

Seals pitching had all but vanished and defensively the Seals played flat. Several Seals, including Paul Waner, made last second cancellations of their train reservations to stay for the eighth game. Physically the Seals were in San Francisco, but their minds were in their hometowns. The only bright spot was that a ninth game would help cut the financial losses.

Artistically, the deciding game of the series improved only slightly on the game eight abomination. Crockett and Williams yielded eight Louisville runs. However, the Seals kept pace, with Ellison scoring on Sam Agnew's bloop single to center in the eighth to secure a 9–8 win. McWeeny earned the win with 2⅓ innings of relief.

The Seals' place in history

The Junior World Series win solidified San Francisco's claim to best in the minors, though their lackluster series play hardly added an exclamation mark to the assertion. Yet a look at the ballclub makes it clear how good the 1925 team really was:

- Seventeen players played or would go on to play in the majors.
- The team included two future Hall of Famers, including one — Lloyd Waner — who could not crack the lineup even though he was just two years away from hitting .355 for the National League champion Pittsburgh Pirates.
- The team batted .315 for the season — seven of eight regulars averaged over .300, and the other, Eddie Mulligan, hit .286.
- They had a league-leading fielding percentage of .968.
- Four pitchers (McWeeny, Williams, Mitchell and Geary) won 20 games or more; three others (Griffin, Crocket and Pfeffer) won 12 or more. McWeeny (20-5) and Griffin (16-4) led the league with an .800 winning percentage; McWeeny's 2.70 earned run average also topped the league.

- The all–Pacific Coast League all star team announced in the *Sporting News* listed six Seals on the first team (Kilduff, Mulligan, Rhyne, Waner, Yelle and McWeeny) and four on the second (Ellison, Valla, Agnew and Geary).
- They lost only three of the 27 series they played in 1925.
- Their winning percentage of .643 was the league's highest since 1906.

No doubt the team dominated 1925 and were the strongest of the four pennant-winning Seals teams of the 1920s. Further, they were clearly the best team of the decade in the PCL.

The argument can be made that the Seals were the best PCL ballclub of all time, though fans of the 1934 Los Angeles Angels would claim otherwise. It is true the latter club had superior pitching, but it is hard to ignore the Seals. In either case, the two ballclubs rank with any of the Baltimore Oriole teams of 1919 to 1925, and the 1937 Newark Bears—the ballclubs generally hailed as the best minor league clubs of all time.

Waner's quest for .400

With his team powering its way to the PCL title, Paul Waner was in his third season in the PCL, and as far as he was concerned it was one too many. Waner thought his 1924 season, in which he batted .356, should have earned him a job in the majors, but scouts remained wary because of his slight build. Though listed at 5-foot-8½ inches, 153 pounds, Waner admitted that he never weighed more than 140 pounds with the Seals. Waner reported that Joe Devine, a scout for the Pirates, told him that he would need to hit .400 before the Pirates would sign him.

Waner, Seattle's Frank Brazill and Salt Lake's Lefty O'Doul paced PCL hitters all season long. From June on, the three exchanged the batting lead nine times; O'Doul commanded the top spot the longest, from July 25 through September 19.

Waner's hopes for .400 and a batting title took a severe blow at the end of August when he was stricken with nausea and dizziness. Vowing to play despite his condition, Waner could not muster the strength for a single at-bat in the 10-game series against Portland. After missing the first two games against Seattle, Waner finally returned with a three for 12 performance in a doubleheader.

While Waner and the Seals fretted over his condition, the cause of his problem surfaced. Waner had been shot in the face in an off-season hunting accident that had left a load of leadshot in his jaw. A doctor in Portland removed the birdshot poisoning Waner's system, and he could once again set his sights on PCL pitchers.

On August 1, O'Doul led the league with a whopping .429 average. In one series against Vernon he went 19 for 21, including 11 consecutive hits. By

Paul Waner (John E. Spalding)

August 24 he still was hitting .420 — 22 points above Waner. But his average dropped steadily the last months of the season and he finished at .373.

Brazill and Waner continued to toy with the .400 mark. Seven months and 197 games into the season, the two men stacked up so:

	hits	at-bats	avg.
Waner	278	695	.400
Brazill	278	703	.395

Waner could sit out the final doubleheader of the year. He would have reached his goal of .400, and short of a minor miracle in Seattle, he would

Frank Brazill (Tony Pirak)

have won his PCL batting title. Brazill would need to go six for six in his
doubleheader against Portland to take the title — an achievement that would
catapult him to .4005, slightly ahead of Waner.

But Waner decided to risk his .400 dream season. In the morning game
at Rec Park, Oakland pitcher George Foster retired Waner in his first at-bat,
dropping the hitter's average under .400. Whatever panic Waner might have
felt did not show. In his next three trips to the plate, he picked up two
hits.

Up north, Brazill went one for four in the first game of a doubleheader.
At last content that he had beaten all comers, Waner called it a year at .401,
the first .400 average in PCL history.

Waner and Rhyne were sold to the Pittsburgh Pirates in a package deal
for $95,000. According to reports, Waner's value was about $35,000 of this
amount; again, Waner's size entered into the argument. The irony, of course,
is that Rhyne enjoyed only a mediocre major league career, while Waner went
on to play 20 years and earn a berth in the Hall of Fame.

Waner's PCL achievements were an indicator of his major league success.
Just a year after his .401 PCL season, he hit .336 for Pittsburgh, which would
have won the National League batting crown under the at-bat criteria used
today. In 1927 Waner hit a career high .380, leading the league in triples, total
bases, hits and runs batted in.

1925 Final Standings

	W	L	Pct.
San Francisco	128	71	.643
Salt Lake	116	84	.580
Seattle	103	91	.531
Los Angeles	105	93	.530
Portland	92	104	.469
Oakland	88	112	.440
Sacramento	82	119	.408
Vernon	80	120	.400

Team batting leaders

Average:	Salt Lake—.321
Runs:	Salt Lake—1,377
HRs:	Salt Lake—197

Individual batting leaders

At-bats:	Lefty O'Doul, Salt Lake—825
Average:	Paul Waner, San Francisco—.401
Runs:	Tony Lazzeri, Salt Lake—202
Hits:	Lefty O'Doul, Salt Lake—309
2B:	Paul Waner, San Francisco—75
3B:	Lefty O'Doul, Salt Lake—17
HR:	Tony Lazzeri, Salt Lake—60
RBI:	Tony Lazzeri, Salt Lake—222
Total bases:	Tony Lazzeri, Salt Lake—512
Stolen bases:	William Hunnefield, Portland—42

Individual pitching leaders

Winning percentage:	Doug McWeeny, San Fran.—.800 (20-5)
	Marty Griffin, San Fran.—.800 (16-4)
Games won:	Clyde Barfoot, Vernon—26
Games lost:	Herman Pillette, Vernon—26
Most games:	George Boehler, Oakland—58
Most shutouts:	Not Available
Most complete games:	George Boehler, Oakland—34
Most innings:	George Boehler, Oakland—417
ERA:	Doug McWeeny, San Francisco—2.70

Chapter 8

1926 — One for the Angels

William Wrigley, Jr., was a man accustomed to success. In 1891 he started a company to sell soap, offering baking soda as an incentive. Before long customers came calling for the baking soda, ignoring the soap. Figuring that people needed a nudge to keep buying baking soda, Wrigley began including a pack of chewing gum with each box. Once again, the sales premium soon became more popular than the product. And so a chewing gum empire was born. In 1893, Wrigley introduced Wrigley's Juicy Fruit and Wrigley's Spearmint gum. By 1925, his company earned profits of $10 million a year. His chewing gum legacy continues to this day, with the Wrigley Company annually grossing more than $1 billion.

William Wrigley entered baseball with a keen desire to match his success in the business world. After buying the National League Chicago Cubs in 1921, Wrigley turned around and bought the Los Angeles Angels a few months later for more than $100,000. In the Angels, he inherited a team that went on to win the Pacific Coast League championship just a few weeks later. However, 1922 came and went without a PCL flag. The next year brought a sixth-place finish for the Angels. The following year the Angels bounced back to come within a whisker of winning the PCL title, but in 1925 they slid back down to fourth. Meanwhile, the Cubs languished in the second division, bottoming out in 1925 with a 68-86 record, dead last in the National League. Despite these disappointments, Wrigley enjoyed at least one high note in 1925: the dedication of his new ballpark at Forty-first and South Park in Los Angeles.

The place that Wrigley built

Eighteen thousand fans—the most ever to see a baseball game in Los Angeles since the deciding game of the 1919 series between the Angels and Vernon Tigers—waited expectantly under glorious September skies. It was not the baseball game that brought out this many fans on a Tuesday afternoon, September 29, 1925. No, the hometown Los Angeles Angels were a hopeless 22 games behind their opponents, the San Francisco Seals. The attraction on

Wrigley Field, 1925 (Vic Pallos)

this day was not baseball so much as it was a baseball park—Wrigley Field, the place Coast League President Harry Williams called "the latest in stadium architecture." William Wrigley presided over the opening, which included a flag-raising ceremony and the throwing of the first pitch by Los Angeles Mayor George Cryer, with U.S. Marshall Al Sittel and Harry Williams acting as umpires. In January 1926 the ballpark was officially dedicated to the memory of the dead of World War I in a ceremony conducted by Baseball Commissioner Kenesaw Mountain Landis.

Compared to the other Coast League ballparks, and indeed some major league parks, Wrigley Field was a sight to behold. The double-decked structure spared no luxury for its day. Chicago architect Zachary T. Davis (who also designed Wrigley Field and Comiskey Park in Chicago) created a park that was as comfortable for the players and fans as it was for club executives. A 150-foot clocktower, with its four 15-foot clocks, could be seen from miles away. Inside the tower were eight floors of offices, including showers for Angels officials and for visiting club representatives. A double column of windows afforded plenty of natural light, while an observation tower atop the structure provided clear views of the nearby San Gabriel Mountains and the Pacific Ocean. Though impressed with the new ballpark, *Los Angeles Daily Times* writer Bill Henry described the rectilinear tower as "a package of chewing gum standing on end."

The players' comfort was an obvious concern, with relatively plush clubhouse accommodations that featured six showers and a spacious locker room. Not to be left out, fans who had endured dilapidated Washington Park found a clean, spacious place to watch a baseball game. A 72-foot-long scoreboard dominated the right field area, standing five stories high and providing enough space for inning-by-inning scores of the other PCL games being played.

The double-decked stands ran from foul pole to foul pole, and a single level of bleachers was situated in right field. A home run down the left field line would have to travel 340 feet and clear a 15-foot brick wall; a similar shot to right would have to travel 339 feet, while a drive to dead center needed to soar 412 feet. These dimensions appeared challenging; however, the 345 feet to both power alleys were not, especially since a prevailing outbound wind served as a jetstream for flyballs. Though hardly a bandbox, Wrigley Field would fit in nicely with the generous spirit of Coast League parks.

On the ballpark's opening day, the hitters found the ballpark to their liking, the Seals and Angels combining for 29 hits and 18 runs. The Angels won 10–8, with Doc Crandall picking up Wrigley Field's christening win. Paul Waner hit the park's first home run, though Jigger Statz stole the future Hall of Famer's thunder by hitting for the cycle.

Some press accounts speculated that Wrigley had spent too much on Wrigley Field—reportedly $1.3 million—and that its 21,000 seats were too many for a minor league field. Not only did Wrigley have to listen to these rumblings, but there were the nagging problems that had to be dealt with: adding clay to the infield dirt, replacing the wire mesh behind home plate because it was too thick for good viewing, and enduring batters' complaints that it was difficult to see the ball in Wrigley's creation. But these problems were minor and eventually solved. What concerned Wrigley most as he looked ahead to the 1926 season was achieving the goal that had proven so elusive—winning the PCL pennant.

"Now you have the park," he told his staff. "Go out and get a pennant winner. Spare no expense." And with that Wrigley said publicly he would spend a million dollars to assemble the best PCL team of 1926.

Building the 1926 Angels

Wrigley did not have to spend a million dollars, but Angels executives haggled, bartered for and bought a team that fulfilled Wrigley's command.

When Wrigley bought the Angels in 1921 it established the first direct relationship between a major league team and a Coast League team, even though Wrigley—and not the Cubs—owned the Angels. While Branch Rickey was developing an extensive farm system for the St. Louis Cardinals, Wrigley's Angels never operated as training grounds for the Cubs, promising from day one to keep the two entities separate. Players did head in good numbers from the Angels to the Cubs, and vice versa, but it was not a farm system. Rather, as one might expect, the two clubs enjoyed extraordinary knowledge of one another's personnel and a willingness to cooperate that comes when two entities serve the same master.

This willingness was not always in evidence, as pointed out in the *Sporting News*: "While Wrigley owns the Cubs and Angels, relations between the two teams have not been as harmonious as many persons thought." The main reason for this was that each club operated in its own self-interest. Minority stockholders William Veeck and Joseph Patrick disagreed about how close the Cubs and Angels should work. Veeck felt the Angels should act as a training ground for the Cubs; Patrick favored more independence. The dispute was eventually resolved when Veeck sold his interest in the Angels to return exclusively to his executive role with the Cubs. Thereafter, with few exceptions, the Angels bought and sold players to serve their needs and not to bring aboard future Cubs.

Club President Patrick, a longtime friend of Wrigley's, and Business Manager Oscar Reichow, a former Chicago sportswriter, were charged with running the Angels. They knew that in 1926 Wrigley expected nothing less than a pennant. Also on the hot seat was player-manager Marty Krug, who would need to help build the team as well as manage it.

The outlook for 1926 was not bright. After all, the Angels had finished fourth in 1925, 22½ games in back of San Francisco. Preseason newspaper reports characterized the team's pitching prospects as weak with the departure of staff ace Charlie Root to the Cubs. With the Cubs taking second baseman Clyde Beck in a trade, the infield's strongest player was missing. In the outfield, left fielder Wally Hood was a holdout, leaving only Jigger Statz in center as a sure thing. The catching corps was mediocre at best.

Patrick, Reichow and Krug had their work cut out for them. Good news came at the end of March with the arrival of outfielder Art Jahn as part of the Beck trade. As a 29-year-old rookie for the Cubs, Jahn had hit .301 in 226 at-bats. Though he lacked power, Jahn could play a steady left field. Another outfielder who came as part of the Beck deal was 23-year-old Art Weis. He, too, was a sure-handed outfielder who had accumulated 341 at-bats and a .270 average in four years at Chicago. If not spectacular, the outfield was at least set.

To shore up the catching, the Angels traded pitcher George Payne for James Harrison "Truck" Hannah along with a pitcher, Rube Yarrison. Hannah was a 36-year-old career minor leaguer who still had plenty of years ahead of him, though he was clearly on the downside of his career. At six-foot-one and 190 pounds, Hannah was still strong enough to throw out opposing runners without rising from his catcher's crouch. During the off-season he made his own catcher's gloves, conditioning them with a carefully created concoction that included tobacco juice.

The biggest question mark appeared to be the infield. Veteran Cub shortstop Johnny Mitchell came down from the Cubs to alleviate some of the uncertainty, displacing incumbent Ray Jacobs, who moved to first base, a new position for him. Rookie Gale Staley won the second base job, while ex–Vernon infielder Ed Hemingway joined the club to play third. As it turned out, however, Hemingway played 160 games at second and none at third, and Staley appeared in 82 games at second.

Conspicuously missing from this lineup was power. Not a single Angel could be counted on for the long ball. This fact was not lost on the Angel brass who turned their attention northward, where rumblings could be heard from the troubled Seattle franchise.

Star third baseman Frank Brazill threatened to sit out the entire season unless granted more money. Coming off his best year ever — in which he just missed hitting .400 and winning the PCL batting crown — Brazill held fast to his demands. He nixed a trade to Minneapolis of the American Association and rejected every Seattle offer.

Seattle manager Red Killefer grew nervous and increasingly convinced that Brazill would not report. With the season opener just a few days away, majority owner Charles Lockhardt decided to act, selling Brazill for $10,000 to the Angels. The sum was called the highest ever for a "non-prospect player." As an ex–major leaguer, Brazill was eligible for the major league draft, and if drafted the Angels would receive just $5,000 in compensation.

The Angels did not care, preferring a slugger to an investment. Wrigley had the money and his team needed a slugger. And since the Angels held a $10,000 note owed by Seattle, Brazill was sent packing to Los Angeles and the note was torn up. Happy to be home, the native Southern Californian came through as expected in 1926 and proved to be the key offensive addition to the ballclub. Another player who came through was left-hander Earl Hamilton, another offseason acquisition, who proved to be the big winner of a surprisingly strong pitching staff.

The season begins — finally

Pitcher Elmer Jacobs earned opening day honors, though he would have to wait four days while the heaviest April rains in 43 years delayed the start of the season. Ironically, the first-ever home opener in traditionally rainy Portland went off without a hitch; it was the clubs in normally sunny California that had to defer to the elements.

When his chance finally came on Saturday, April 10, Jacobs made the most of it, shutting out Oakland with help from Yarrison, 4–0. Left fielder Wally Hood ended his holdout in time to contribute a single, while Statz popped two triples, and Brazill a home run. The new-look Angels were off to a strong start.

After 10 games they stood at 7-3, good enough for first place. By the third week in May they held tenuously to their lead; the early race was one of the

Truck Hannah (George E. Outland)

tightest in history, with only Seattle and San Francisco more than four games back. In the early stages of the season it looked as though all eight teams would be in the hunt. The Angels, it seemed, were not the only ballclub tired of finishing behind San Francisco; many clubs had made wholesale changes to their lineups. But the biggest changes were made by Salt Lake and Vernon, which picked up stakes and moved to Hollywood and San Francisco, respectively, before the season began.

The move gave San Francisco continuous baseball at Recreation Park. When the Seals hit the road, the "Mission Bears," as they were called in 1926, stepped in to play. Similarly, Los Angeles and Hollywood shared the modern confines of Wrigley Field. Under new owners William McCarthy and Stanley Dollar, the Mission Bears went through three managers: Walter McCredie resigned for health reasons and former Pittsburgh Pirates catcher Walter Schmidt was fired after a brief stint, giving way to Bill Leard, who had been managing in the Utah-Idaho League. This upheaval did not deter the ballclub from achieving third place — a major accomplishment considering they finished dead last in 1925. Leading the way were pitchers Bert Cole (29-12) and Herman Pillette (21-16), right fielder Ike Boone (.380, 32 HR, 137 RBI) and center fielder Evar Swanson, who hit .316 and led base stealers with 43 thefts.

Down in Hollywood, the former Salt Lake Bees were not enjoying the success of the Missions. Now known as the Stars or the Sheiks, the heavy-hitting former Bees suddenly became anemic at the plate. Their team batting average dropped to .266, 55 points less than the year before. In just one season, the ballclub went from the best-hitting team in the league to the worst. The loss of Tony Lazzeri definitely hurt the club's offense. So did leaving the thin air and cozy confines of Salt Lake's Bonneville Park, which seemed to hurt hitting throughout the league. The overall drop in team averages also raised speculation that the ball had been deadened or that the 1926 pitchers were a stronger lot than the year before. But almost assuredly, the drop from 1925 to 1926 in the league batting average — from .288 to .280 — and in runs — from 8,345 to 7,252 — came because the Bees left Bonneville.

Hollywood's Lefty O'Doul, cut in preseason by Chicago Cubs manager Joe McCarthy for supposedly being a poor fielder with a weak arm, once again led his club with a .338 average, 20 home runs and 116 runs batted in. The decision to release O'Doul looked especially foolish when in a preseason game between the Cubs and Stars, O'Doul made two circus catches and threw a runner out at third as his ballclub defeated McCarthy's. Despite O'Doul's strong year, Hollywood's lack of offense relegated the team to a sixth place finish.

The Angels' first test

The Angels entered the season braced for a fight with the San Francisco Seals. But with the Seals reeling in last place — largely from the loss of stars Paul Waner, Hal Rhyne and Doug McWeeny — Los Angeles looked for different opponents to conquer. On the strength of a 13-game winning streak on the road, the Angels held a firm grasp on first place as June began. Their lineup, which had come together just days before the season opener, was now meshing smoothly. This was the lineup manager Marty Krug presented most days: Jigger Statz, cf (.354, 4 HR, 59 RBI); Ed Hemingway, 2b (.278, 0 HR, 64 RBI); Frank Brazill, 3b (.336, 19 HR, 111 RBI); Ray Jacobs, 1b (.255, 21 HR, 102 RBI); Art Weis, rf (.317, 7 HR, 80 RBI) or Wally Hood, rf (.301, 13 HR, 82 RBI); Art Jahn, lf (.337, 8 HR, 118 RBI); Johnny Mitchell, ss (.264, 0 HR, 83 RBI); and Truck Hannah, c (.237, 4 HR, 55 RBI).

Only Mitchell, Jacobs and Hannah were hitting less than .300 during the first months of the season. At the same time, the Los Angeles pitching staff emerged as the best on the coast. Beginning June 29 the club faced its first big test: a nine-game series at Wrigley Field against Sacramento, which trailed the Angels by five games.

Coming off a seven-game series against the Seals in which they pounded 92 hits and averaged seven runs a game, Sacramento was hot. Their dismantling of Seals pitching contributed to the stress Seal manager Bert Ellison felt over his team's collapse. A few days after the Sacramento series, Ellison resigned, saying, "I saw Jack Miller worry himself into the grave and I came to the conclusion that I had better take a rest."

With the Angels within reach, Sacramento felt confident about their chances going into the series. First baseman Wilbur Davis (.308, 12 HR, 93 RBI), catcher Art Koehler (.301, 10 HR, 98 RBI) and second baseman Johnny Monroe (.295, 13 HR, 97 RBI) led the Solons' hitting attack. The pitching staff of Elmer "Specs" Shea (15-11), Speed Martin (14-12), Rudy Kallio (18-16), Ray Keating (14-14) and Lauri Vinci (15-21) was considered among the top three in the league.

They were not, however, enough to stop the Angels, who took six of the nine games. Vinci provided the Solons a bright spot with a 12-inning shutout win. Other than that, Jigger Statz stole the show, mainly with his glove. Sacramento owner Lew Moreing credited Statz with robbing Sacramento of four games with his fielding.

Jigger Statz

Arnold John Statz received the nickname Jigger after a term referring to an iron golf club. Indeed, Statz was one of the better golfers in the Pacific Coast League, finishing second to Speed Martin of Sacramento in the 1926 Professional Baseball Association's golf championship. His qualifying round of 80 led all entries, trouncing Judge Landis who came in at an even 100. It was on the ballfield, however, that Statz became a Coast League institution. Perhaps the best fielding outfielder in league history, the five-foot-seven-inch, 150-pound Statz covered center field like a graceful gazelle.

During his 18 years with the Angels—a minor league record for longevity with one club—Statz recorded 6,872 putouts, a Coast League record. He was the defensive standard by which the league's center fielders in the 1920s and 1930s were measured. This fielding capability, along with his line-drive hitting skills, earned him several chances in the major leagues. Of the eight different seasons he made major league appearances, his best by far came from 1922 through 1924. During this stretch with the Cubs, he hit .297 in 462 at-bats in 1922, .319 in 655 at-bats in 1923, and .277 in 549 at-bats in 1924. Lack of power contributed to Statz's limited major league career, as he hit only 14 home runs during that three-year stretch.

He did not show much power in the Coast League either; instead, he displayed a remarkable consistency in compiling a minor league lifetime average of .315, which included 12 seasons of .300 or better for the Angels. The Pacific Coast League record book testifies to Statz's prowess. His lifetime records include most years with one club; most games played, 2,790; most

Jigger Statz (Don Hazelwood)

times at bat, 10,657; most runs scored, 1,996; most hits, 3,356; most total bases, 4,405; most one-base hits, 2,564; most two-base hits, 595; most three-base hits, 137; most putouts by an outfielder, lifetime, 6,872; most assists by an outfielder, lifetime, 263; and most chances accepted by an outfielder, lifetime, 7,135. In addition, Statz holds the PCL record for most home runs in an inning (two) and most stolen bases in a game (six).

Another record he set was in 1926, when he tied Art Weis for the highest fielding percentage by an outfielder (150 games or more), committing just two errors in his 604 chances. Right fielder Art Weis handled 322 chances in 1926 and committed just one error.

Statz's fielding performance during the 1926 season rounded out a sensational year in which he hit .354 and led the league with 291 hits, 823 at-bats, 68 doubles and 18 triples. The performance earned him two years with the Brooklyn Robins in the National League before his return for good to the PCL.

Oakland's final shot

Behind Statz's all-around play, the Angels continued to breeze along comfortably through the dog days of summer and into September. With 32 games remaining only second place Oakland, at 10 games back, had a chance. The season would boil down to an 11-game series between the two teams beginning Tuesday, September 21, with a doubleheader. After a disappointing 1925 season in which they finished in sixth place and 24 games under .500, the Oaks surprised everyone with their performance in 1926.

The 1926 season had started poorly for Oakland owner Cal Ewing, who now had to compete with both the Seals and the Mission Bears for the Bay Area baseball dollar. With baseball every day in San Francisco, Ewing had little hope of drawing fans from the city or the peninsula—fans had all they could handle on their side of the bay. Ewing had to establish a strong base of support in the East Bay if the team was going to succeed. To do that, Ewing needed a contender.

In Buzz Arlett, the Oaks had one of the greatest stars in the history of the Coast League; he was about to enjoy the best season of his career in 1926 (.382, 35 HR, 140 RBI). Arlett was not the only excitement in Oakland. Two slick-fielding middle infielders had the Bay Area and the rest of the Pacific Coast League talking. Shortstop Lyn Lary and second baseman Jimmy Reese displayed the flash, poise and talent to supplant the Seals' Pete Kilduff and the departed Hal Rhyne as the best doubleplay combination in the circuit. To protect his investment in the two youngsters, Ewing took out $100,000 insurance policies on each. With Leo Dickerman (12-5), Hub Pruett (22-13), Arthur Delaney (21-13) and Harry Krause (19-12), only the Angels would prove to have a better pitching staff.

Going into the series-opening doubleheader on September 22, the Oaks appeared to match up pretty well with the talented Angels, having the speed and pitching to stay in tight ballgames and Arlett's power to counter that of Frank Brazill. This notion, however, was quickly dispelled when the Angels took the first game of the doubleheader 14–4. Statz and Mitchell, with four hits apiece, led the attack against Oakland pitcher Joe Oescheger, who had been obtained from the Missions and was given the starting assignment even though he was on his way to a meager 5-14 record for the year.

The second game of the doubleheader contrasted markedly from the first, featuring a pitcher's duel between Doc Crandall and Howard Craghead. Craghead went the seven-inning distance, yielding only five hits and one run along the way. Crandall did better than that, firing a three-hit shutout to win

Art Weis (Don Hazelwood)

1–0. Craghead's undoing proved to be a fourth inning single by Frank Brazill followed by an RBI double by Wally Hood.

Two games into the crucial series and Oakland now stood 12 games down with 30 to go. Prospects were dim. Still, nine games remained in the series. Winning eight of nine could cut the lead to five—close enough to make the last few weeks of the season interesting. The next day again offered up a doubleheader—a chance for the Oaks to wipe out the Angels' victories of the day before.

Rube Yarrison would have no part of the Oaks' resurrection, throwing a three-hit shutout. Not an Oak reached second base in the 4–0 loss. Though hindered by the absence of the injured Arlett, who missed both ends of the doubleheader, the Oaks were not in the same class as the Angels. Cal Ewing's club was able to salvage some respect with a 4–2 win in the nightcap against Elmer Jacobs. However, the Oaks could not stop Statz, who enjoyed another outstanding day. Statz collected six hits in seven at-bats, which followed his Tuesday performance of four-for-eight.

In Thursday's single game, Los Angeles jumped out to a 5–0 lead and coasted along until the eighth inning, when Oakland strung together six straight hits to tie the game. Suddenly awakened, the Angels responded in the home half of the eighth. The inning started with relief pitcher Pudgy Gould walking Frank Brazill, who then moved to second on Hood's single to left. Johnny Mitchell sacrificed both runners along. Brazill scored the go-ahead run on Truck Hannah's sacrifice fly to left fielder Joe Bratcher. Alertly, Hood tagged up at second and headed for third, advancing home when short-stop Lyn Lary's relay to third missed the mark. The Oaks collected two singles in the ninth, putting the tying run on base. Krug brought in workhorse pitcher Earl Hamilton (279 innings pitched), who induced pinch-hitter Ray Brubacker to ground into a fielder's choice and then struck out pinch-hitter Ralph Shinners to end the game.

The loss effectively put the final nail in Oakland's coffin. When the series ended Oakland had won just three of the 11 games, leaving them a hopeless 15 ½ games back with only 21 games to play.

In the end, Oakland came up with another pitcher, a powerful outfielder and a little luck short of a pennant. Still, their second-place finish was cause for Ewing to celebrate, especially since his club drew more than 400,000 fans during the season, second to the Seals, who drew only a few thousand more. Indeed, the PCL as a whole seemed to thrive under the new configuration as more than 1.9 million fans paid to see games during the season. The attendance mark exceeded 1925's and was the third best in league history.

For the Angels, the season ended four years of frustration. The 1926 flag was an organizational achievement, with credit going to William Wrigley for his commitment—and his pocketbook—as well as to the front office led by Joseph Patrick and Oscar Reichow. Contributing to the personnel decisions and managing the club day-to-day, Marty Krug took a brand new team and led them all the way. On the field, the ballclub led the league in fielding (.971 pct.) and pitching, where they had standout years from Earl Hamilton (24-8, 2.48 ERA), Wayne Wright (19-7, 3.08 ERA), Doc Crandall (20-8, 2.20 ERA), Elmer Jacobs (20-12, 2.20 ERA), and Rube Yarrison (13-8, 4.09 ERA).

For Crandall the year was especially memorable, marking his twenty-first season in organized baseball and tenth with the Angels. Ten thousand fans came out for a July ballgame to honor Crandall, showering him with flowers, gifts and money. The popular 38-year-old right hander responded by pitching a 4-3, 10-inning win over the Missions for his 200th win in the Pacific Coast

Doc Crandall (George E. Outland)

League. He retired after the 1929 season, ending a remarkable career that began in 1906 with Cedar Rapids and included a six-year stint with John Mc-
Graw's New York Giants from 1908 to 1913. It was at New York where Crandall earned his nickname, when famed writer Damon Runyon dubbed him
"the doctor of sick baseball" for the pitcher's relief abilities. Soon Otis Crandall became Doc Crandall. His outstanding statistical legacy includes 101 wins
against 62 losses in the majors, with an impressive 2.92 earned run average.
His minor league statistics are equally impressive: 249 wins, 163 losses and a
2.96 ERA. Crandall also hit well, playing some infield in the majors, where he
hit .285 in 887 at-bats.

The hitters were paced by Statz, who, as already mentioned, had a typical
superstar season. While the lineup did not offer the sock of the 1925 Seals,
it did manage a highly respectable .289 team batting average. Even manager
Krug contributed with the bat (.390, 2 HR, 29 RBI in 131 at-bats), playing a
little infield now and again.

The 1926 version of the Angels proved to be their strongest of the decade.

Their 121-81 record (.599 pct.), while not quite as impressive as the Seals' pennant-winning records, dominated the season. Just as San Francisco collapsed after their highwater year of 1926, so would the Angels, who dropped to last in 1927 with an 80-116 performance. Wrigley had to wait until 1933 for his next Coast League pennant, enduring several frustrating seasons along the way. Nevertheless, Wrigley's 1926 team demonstrated Wrigley's commitment to making the Angels a winning entity in their own right.

1926 Final Standings

	W	L	Pct.
Los Angeles	121	81	.599
Oakland	111	92	.547
Missions	106	94	.530
Portland	100	101	.498
Sacramento	99	102	.493
Hollywood	94	107	.468
Seattle	89	111	.445
San Francisco	84	116	.420

Team batting leaders

Average:	Missions—.290
Runs:	Los Angeles—978
HRs:	Portland—156

Individual batting leaders

At-bats:	Jigger Statz, Los Angeles—823
Average:	Bill Bagwell, Portland—.391
Runs:	Evar Swanson, Missions—157
Hits:	Jigger Statz, Los Angeles—291
2B:	Jigger Statz, Los Angeles—68
3B:	Jigger Statz, Los Angeles—18
HR:	Elmer Smith, Portland—46
RBI:	Buzz Arlett, Oakland—140
Total bases:	Buzz Arlett, Oakland—444
Stolen bases:	Evar Swanson, Missions—43

Individual pitching leaders

Winning percentage: Earl Hamilton, Los Angeles — .750 (24-8)
Games won: Bert Cole, Missions — 29
Games lost: Marvin Moudy, San Francisco — 22
Most games: Marvin Moudy, San Francisco — 64
Most complete games: James Elliott, Seattle — 37
Most innings: James Elliott, Seattle — 367
ERA: Elmer Jacobs, Los Angeles — 2.20
                     Doc Crandall, Los Angeles — 2.20

All Stars of 1926

(One asterisk indicates players were selected by a vote of the league's managers in August. Two asterisks indicate the year-end selection by D.E. Dugdale in the *Sporting News*.)

Catcher

Art Koehler (Sac)* ** and
Truck Hannah (LA)* **

First base

Ray Jacobs (LA)* and
Jim McDowell (Missions)**

Second base

Johnny Monroe (Sac)* **

Shortstop

Johnny Mitchell (LA)* ** and
Lyn Lary (Oak)*

Third base

Eddie Mulligan (SF)* and
Doc Prothro (Port)**

Utility

Ike Caveney (Sea-Oak)* **;
Ed Hemingway (LA)*; and
Brick Eldred (Sea) **

Outfield

Ike Boone (Missions)*;
Jigger Statz (LA)* **;
Buzz Arlett (Oak)* **; and
Art Jahn (LA)* **

Pitchers

Bert Cole (Missions) *;
Rudy Kallio (Sac) *;
Frank Shellenback (Holly) *;
Elmer Jacobs (LA) * **;
Wayne Wright (LA) *;
Doc Crandall (LA) **; and
Jim Elliott (Sea) **

Chapter 9

1927 — A Buzz in Oakland

Shortly after New Year's Day, the Oakland Oaks virtually wrapped up the 1927 pennant, at least according to several baseball writers. Spring training had yet to be held, and the season still needed to be played, but when George Boehler was released by the Brooklyn Robins to the Oaks, he became the final cog needed in the Oakland machine that already had the best pitching, the finest infield and, in Buzz Arlett, possibly the greatest Pacific Coast League player of all time.

The 35-year-old Boehler had pitched nine years in the majors with little success, yet in the Coast League he overpowered hitters, winning 26 games in 1924 and 23 in 1925, leading the league in strikeouts both years. Oaks owner Cal Ewing expected nothing short of 20 wins from the veteran, and Boehler delivered. His 22 wins in 1927 led the league, as did his 160 strikeouts.

The team took over first place on May 1 and never surrendered it, showing remarkable poise for a club that had not won a pennant since 1912 — and which would not win another until 1948.

The rest of the pack

To win the pennant, the Oaks had to withstand the surprisingly strong challenge of the San Francisco Seals, a young ballclub held in little regard prior to the season. The Seals featured 1927 batting champion Smead Jolley, as well as four youngsters who were fast approaching successful major league careers — Gus Suhr, Earl Averill, Roy Johnson and Dolph Camilli. The impact player for the Seals, however, proved to be Lefty O'Doul, who won the first-ever PCL Most Valuable Player Award. Voted by the league's beat writers, the award earned O'Doul a $1,000 check and a certain amount of revenge on Hollywood Stars owner Bill Lane.

Prior to the season, apparently in a fit of anger, Lane sold O'Doul to San Francisco for $7,500, claiming that the outfielder did not show enough hustle on the field. The move turned out to be one of the worst in PCL history, and not only because O'Doul was voted the league's most valuable player. The popular O'Doul helped the Seals lead the league in attendance. While the

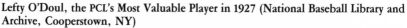

Lefty O'Doul, the PCL's Most Valuable Player in 1927 (National Baseball Library and Archive, Cooperstown, NY)

young, hustling Seals had gained a considerable following, they lacked a marquee player, with the arguable exception of Jolley. O'Doul, however, was a PCL star who drew his hometown followers to the park week in and week out. While he may not have been a similar attraction in Southern California, he nevertheless could have helped Hollywood both at the plate and at the gate. As if to show Lane of his folly right off the bat, O'Doul started the 1927 season by hitting safely in his first 19 games, compiling a batting average over .500.

The Seals had a pretty good idea what they were getting with O'Doul. They first plucked O'Doul off a San Francisco sandlot in the fall of 1916 when they were impressed by his pitching. By his own admission, the 19-year-old O'Doul was too thin and weak to play at the PCL level. After a year in Des Moines, O'Doul returned to the Seals in 1918, where he went 12-8 before World War I called him away for a year. A failed year with the Yankees followed, after which the six-foot, 180-pound pitcher was sent back to the Seals. In 1921 O'Doul enjoyed his best year ever as a pitcher, compiling an outstanding 25-9 record, with seven shutouts and a 2.39 ERA.

Soon enough the Yankees exercised their option and took O'Doul back in 1923, but soon sent him to the Red Sox. By now O'Doul had developed a sore arm and did not last long in Boston. He reappeared in the Coast League—this time with Salt Lake City in 1924. He came to Salt Lake as a pitcher, but before the season ended he had developed into one of the league's most feared hitters. For the 1924 season he hit .329, then followed that with .375 and .338 in 1925 and 1926, respectively.

By now O'Doul had the measure of PCL pitching, and his 1927 numbers proved it—a .378 average, 33 home runs, 158 RBI, and league-leading totals for total bases (428) and runs scored (164). His performance earned O'Doul yet another trip to the big leagues, when the New York Giants drafted him at the end of the season. So began O'Doul's six-year outfield career. In that time he won two National League batting titles—1929 for the Philadelphia Phillies, where he came within a whisker of hitting .400, finishing at .398; and in 1932 with Brooklyn, where he hit .368. Lifetime, O'Doul hit .349 in 11 major league seasons. These numbers—along with his contributions to the game as a PCL player and manager and as a baseball ambassador to Japan—have inspired many to call for reconsidering O'Doul for the Hall of Fame.

Another popular figure added to the team was Ping Bodie, who also helped boost attendance, particularly from San Francisco's considerable Italian community. Born Francesco Stephano Pezzolo, the 39-year-old Bodie had enjoyed a colorful career that began in the California League in 1905 and included four stints in the Coast League—1908 through 1910, 1915 through 1916, 1922 through 1923, and 1927 through 1928. In 1910 Bodie led all minor leaguers in home runs with 30—a considerable number in that dead ball era. During his career, Bodie played nine years in the majors with the Chicago White Sox, Philadelphia A's and New York Yankees, compiling a .275 lifetime average in 1,050 games. In the minors he performed even better—a .308 lifetime average in 1,781 games.

However, not much was expected of him in 1927. Yet he turned out to be a key addition to the Seals by playing in 109 games, filling in ably at first base and in the outfield. On the season "Pudgy Ping," as the *Chronicle*'s Ed Hughes called the player during his waning days, hit .324 with 12 home runs and 80 runs batted in.

Led by O'Doul (.378, 33 HR, 158 RBI and 40 stolen bases) and Jolley (.397, 33 HR, 163 RBI), San Francisco challenged the Oaks for much of the year before falling off the last two months to finish 14½ games behind. For want of a couple of pitchers to help Marvin Moudy (19-11, 3.46 ERA), Herb May (20-16, 3.74 ERA) and Oliver Mitchell (17-13, 4.68 ERA), the Seals might have come closer.

The same could not be said of the Bay Area's other team, now called the Mission Bells. This was a team that lacked both pitching and hitting. Though they would finish next to last, the ballclub did attract the third largest crowds in the league. At least part of the reason was Harry Hooper, the future Hall of Famer who had ended his 17-year major league career in 1925, retiring to Capitola, California.

After retiring, Hooper had hopes of managing in the majors or high minors. But when the 1927 season started and no job offers were forthcoming, it appeared he might have to wait at least one more year. Little could Hooper have anticipated that just three weeks into the PCL season, Missions owner Bill McCarthy would fire his manager, "Wild Bill" Leard, for breaking training rules.

Leard it seemed had been on quite a bender, missing a Wednesday game in Seattle, then showing up in such bad shape on Thursday that the players locked him in the clubhouse and played the game without him. Leard was McCarthy's third manager in just over a year. Veteran skipper Walter McCredie resigned because of failing health and pressures of the job. He was replaced by Walter Schmidt, who was subsequently fired and replaced by Leard for the last few weeks of the 1926 season.

A Bay Area native, Hooper broke into professional baseball in 1907 with Oakland of the outlaw California State League. Charlie Graham owned part of the Sacramento franchise in that circuit and was attracted to Hooper one afternoon when the youngster bounced a routine groundball to second baseman Doc Strub and easily beat the throw to first. Graham offered $25 for Hooper, Oakland agreed, and Hooper came to Sacramento, where he worked as both a ballplayer and a civil engineer. The next year Graham sold Hooper to the Boston Red Sox for $2,000. Before his career ended, Hooper had played in four World Series and formed one of baseball's best outfields with Tris Speaker and Duffy Lewis. By 1927, the 40-year-old manager could still play the outfield, appearing in 78 games while hitting .284 in 218 at-bats.

Those were the last numbers Hooper posted in professional baseball. Prior to the 1928 season, McCarthy fired his player-manager — when Seattle manager Red Killefer became available — and Hooper's professional career was over.

While Hooper's career neared its end, another Mission player's was just beginning. Twenty-three-year-old second baseman Neal "Mickey" Finn was a fan favorite, winning a late-season vote for the title of "most popular Mission," for which he received a silver trophy. Finn was rumored to be highly sought-after by several major league clubs, but a late-season injury hurt his marketability. As it was, he started his four-year major league career in 1930. Teaming with Gordon "Oskie" Slade at shortstop, Finn was part of a slick-fielding infield combination that helped the Missions rank second in team fielding.

Another team that could field well but do little else was sixth-place Hollywood. Like the Missions, the ballclub featured a formidable doubleplay combination in second baseman Johnny Kerr and shortstop Dudley Lee. Yet the Stars still were trying to adjust to Wrigley Field, their new home since moving from Salt Lake after the 1925 season. In the absence of Bonneville Park's forgivingly short fences and high altitude, the Stars' batting averages fell like autumn leaves in 1926. The once-feared Bees, who led the league in hitting with a .321 mark in 1925, posted the worst average on the coast at .270 in 1926.

O'Doul's loss hurt the ballclub, as did the decision by manager–third baseman Oscar Vitt to confine his activities to the dugout. In an effort to find the right combination, Lane and Vitt shuttled players on and off the roster all preseason and for much of the early going, settling somewhat on a lineup by early summer when the team began to play respectable baseball. Only three regular Stars hit above .300: outfielders John Frederick (.305), Babe Twombley (.309), and Pat McNulty, whose .312 average came in only 106 games. None of the three hit with any power, and slugging honors went to Kerr, who led the team with 18 home runs en route to a .276 batting average and team-leading 41 stolen bases. Despite this offensive anemia, pitchers Hank Hulvey (17-14, 2.97 ERA), Frank Shellenback (19-12, 3.05 ERA) and Bill Murphy (14-8, 3.39 ERA) enjoyed good years on the mound.

For the Stars, there was little good news in 1927. When the season ended, Lane announced losses of $30,000 for the year—twice the amount he had lost in his Hollywood honeymoon season of 1926.

Hollywood was not the only team hemorrhaging red ink. Outside the Bay Area, attendance slid measurably in PCL cities, thanks mainly to Oakland's anticlimactic dominance of the rest of the league. Third place Seattle, a team that perennially had a hard time attracting fans, suffered financially worst of all. The 1927 Indians showed fans lots of offense (second in team batting with a .305 average), but they tended to kick the ball around a bit (last in team fielding at .956). Pitchers Johnny Miljus (13-5, 2.36 ERA), Little Joe Edwards (20-17, 3.36 ERA), Kyle Graham (13-10, 3.64 ERA) and Ed Brandt (19-11, 3.96 ERA) enjoyed fine seasons. Outfielder Everett "Pid" Purdy, the 23-year-old from the White Sox, was one of the PCL's most pleasant surprises, hitting .366, with eight home runs and 76 runs batted in. Marty Callaghan, Pelham Ballenger and Brick Eldred also produced at the plate. Callaghan broke Art Weis's league record of 150 consecutive games without an error. At the end of the year, both Callaghan and Purdy were sold to Cincinnati.

Even with such talent, the Seattle team failed to attract fans. As early as July, the ballclub was forced to borrow money from the league to make its payroll. Part of the reason was simply that Seattle was not as wild about baseball as the Bay Area. Another reason cited in some *Sporting News* accounts blamed fans' animosity towards Charles Lockhardt and Red Killefer, the out-of-towners who bought the team under dubious circumstances and who never ingratiated themselves to the locals, despite winning a pennant in 1924.

Portland did better at the box office than Seattle, but worse on the field. The Beavers finished in fifth place even though they hit for the league's highest average. Before the season started owner Tom Turner expressed concern about his team's pitching. But his efforts to swing deals with a major league or minor league ballclub proved fruitless. To make matters worse, the club's best pitcher, Ray Lingrel, who had gone 13-6 the year before, was lost for the year with a circulation problem in his pitching arm. Johnny Couch and Ed Tomlin were the only two Portland pitchers in 1927 to win more games than they lost with records of 18-15 and 16-9, respectively.

At the plate, the Beavers were a different story. Former major leaguer Elmer Smith, who had led the league in home runs the year before, repeated the trick in 1927, clouting 40 roundtrippers. Smith also hit .368 and drove in 141 runs to pace an attack that included former Coast League triple crown winner Paul Strand (.355, 18 HR, 105 RBI), Frank Sigafoos (.335, 10 HR, 76 RBI) and Doc Prothro (.330, 10 HR, 100 RBI). As impressive as these players were, they ultimately took a back seat to 23-year-old shortstop William "Bill" Cissell. Though his numbers—.323, 5 HR, 64 RBI—did not match up with the other Beavers', his potential did.

Cissell was one of the fastest men in the league, once timed circling the bases in 14.2 seconds and in the 100 yard dash in 10.2 seconds—both times coming while in full uniform and while wearing baseball spikes. Though he led the league's shortstops in errors with 76, Cissell's range and instincts outweighed his mistakes, most of which were attributed to inexperience. Turner had purchased Cissell two years before for $13,000—a princely sum for a PCL owner to spend for a lower minor leaguer. As the season wore on, major league teams began seriously courting Turner for rights to his shortstop. Turner held firm, and when the season ended he maintained that he would keep Cissell for another year. Turner reported that he had received many offers for his player, but most were lacking in cash, offering several players instead. Like many of his fellow owners, Turner had become wary of the players received in trades with the majors. More often than not, the players did not perform as billed, and owners such as San Francisco's Graham, Oakland's Ewing, and Turner were increasingly demanding cash, not players.

A month after the season ended, Turner got his cash—$123,000 from the Chicago White Sox—as well as players Ike Boone and Bert Cole. Turner's $13,000 investment in his shortstop had paid off and Bill Cissell was on his way to a nine-year major league career.

After a fifth-place finish the year before, Sacramento did little in the offseason to improve their chances in 1927. The Senators did manage to win one more game than in 1926 to reach the 100-win plateau, finishing in fourth place at five games above .500. This slight improvement could largely be attributed to outfielder Ray Rohwer (.334, 14 HR, 95 RBI), who had been acquired late in 1926 from Portland. Sheriff Singleton (16-13, 3.25 ERA) and Max Rachac (15-14, 3.99 ERA) led the pitching staff.

While the Sacramento Senators did little to distinguish themselves from the previous year, the Los Angeles Angels made it very clear they were not the same team as in 1926. Unfortunately, they did so by turning the pennant-winning team of 1926 into the doormats of 1927. Jigger Statz's departure to the Brooklyn Robins hurt most. Dick Cox came to Los Angeles in the Statz deal and he filled in admirably at the plate (.345, 13 HR, 90 RBI), but lacked Statz's class in the outfield.

George Boehler was to have come in the deal for Statz, but Commissioner Landis overruled it. Boehler had been drafted from the Oaks by the Brooklyn Robins in 1925 for $5,000. Landis ruled that Boehler must either stay with Brooklyn or be returned to the Oaks, which he subsequently was for $10,000. It is not certain that Brooklyn and Los Angeles were intending to pull a fast one on the Oaks by drafting Boehler into the major leagues and then essentially giving him to another PCL team in a sweetheart deal. Nevertheless, such transactions were common in the 1920s and that was the basis for Landis's ruling. So Boehler (22–12, 3.10 ERA) went to the Oaks.

That was not the last indignity suffered by Los Angeles. The ballclub also lost two of their best pitchers when 39-year-old Doc Crandall left the team, opting to own, manage and pitch for Wichita of the Western League. Elmer Jacobs had been sold to the White Sox, leaving only Earl Hamilton and Doc Wright as starting pitchers. Veteran Bill Piercy was added along with two youngsters to fill the pitching void, and as the season began the Angels and Oaks were co-favorites for the PCL title. The team hit well, led by Cox, Art Jahn (.343, 17 HR, 146 RBI) and Frank Brazill (.327, 21 HR, 76 RBI), but the new pitching staff performed abysmally, and the team finished a woeful 40½ games behind Oakland.

As if they needed more headaches, the Angels also found themselves embroiled in the league's biggest controversy during the season. In a raucous April game between Los Angeles and Oakland, the Oaks' Buzz Arlett and the Angels' Johnny Mitchell, Ed Hemingway and Frank Brazill were ejected by umpire Crooke. A police officer was needed to escort Brazill from the field, the hot-headed third baseman being more interested in assaulting Crooke than in taking a shower.

A few days later, Angel manager Marty Krug jumped umpire Mal Eason after a disputed foul ball call. The manager was ejected, but the following day Brazill sought to avenge his manager's ejection when he knocked Eason down and slugged him at least twice, according to a report in the *Sporting News*.

League President Harry Williams handed down fines and indefinite suspensions to both Krug and Brazill. However, the matter was not over. Fearing

George Boehler (Don Hazelwood)

an upsurge in violence against them, the umpires went over Williams' head and appealed to Judge Landis to investigate the "sinister influences" at work. Umpires Crooke, Eason and Fred Westerveldt were involved in most of the incidents that year. Crooke was allegedly choked by Oaks manager Ivon Howard and was later hit by a bat that slipped from Doc Prothro's hand, "flooring Crooke like a poled ox." Westerveldt was involved in a violent confrontation with Seals pitcher Walter Mails, in which several Seals were ejected and the pitcher was suspended for a week.

At Landis' behest, Mike Sexton of the National Association interviewed Brazill, Krug and Angel President Joe Patrick, as well as umpires Eason and Westerveldt. Several sportswriters called for Williams to fire the entire lot of umpires for going over his head in the dispute. Williams remained oddly silent, sparking speculation that he had urged the umpires to bypass him for political reasons. According to this theory, Williams owed his hiring — and job security — to the Angels, and to come down harshly against the club's manager and star player would have been self-destructive.

Several weeks passed before Landis acted on Sexton's investigation, and all the while Brazill remained suspended. Finally, the first week of June, Landis wired Williams with his decision: "Notify Krug and Brazill and all managers and players that hereafter personal assaults on umpires will be immediately followed by suspensions or ineligibility of offenders for periods of from 90 days to one year."

Later Eason was fired by Williams and replaced by George Magerkurth, a big, no-nonsense umpire who was last seen in the American Association beating up an abusive Milwaukee Brewer. Eason responded by suing Brazill, Krug and the Angels for $85,000. A court ruled that Brazill owed the umpire $650, but that neither Krug nor the Angels owed any damages.

A Buzz in Oakland

Since its one and only pennant, won in 1912, the Oakland Oaks had finished above .500 three times and in the first division three times. As one of four charter members that had remained continuously in the league since 1903, Oakland had won the fewest pennants. Only intermittent charter members Seattle and Sacramento had done as poorly. The Oaks had much history, but little success. Then why was the ballclub suddenly one of the favorites to win the 1927 pennant?

Mainly because it returned virtually the same team that in 1926 finished second to Los Angeles by winning 111 games and losing 92. Owner Cal Ewing, it seemed, had finally put all the pieces together for a championship ballclub. And what better present for Ewing's sixtieth birthday could there be than the Pacific Coast League championship?

Born in the Sacramento River town of Suisun in 1867, Cal Ewing had spent virtually all of his life in baseball. As a youngster he played ball on the streets of Oakland. Though not much of a ballplayer, Ewing loved the game and quickly decided his future lay more in management. He played amateur ball until 1888 and then ran an athletic club in Oakland before buying the Oakland franchise of the California State League in 1898. Ewing's strong advocacy for expanding the California League provided the impetus that eventually established the Pacific Coast League in 1903.

In 1906 he almost singlehandedly saved the PCL, when the San Francisco earthquake and fire destroyed the original Recreation Park. Ewing stepped in and ordered the Seals to play games at Idora Park in Oakland. At the same time, Los Angeles was suffering financial difficulties and Ewing helped bail them out as well. For several years after that, Ewing owned both the Oakland

and San Francisco franchises. Though this smacked of syndicate baseball, Ewing's support enabled the ailing league to survive.

From 1907 through 1909 he served as league president. Under Ewing's presidency, the PCL began to flex its muscle, staving off an attack from the outlaw California State League (a different league than the one which evolved into the Pacific Coast League in 1903). As the preeminent West Coast baseball league, the Coast League forced the California League to become a part of organized baseball as a class C circuit — essentially a training ground for the PCL. The change in status eventually led to the demise of the California League in 1915.

During this time, Ewing had gained respect beyond the West Coast and was well-known among his National Association peers. Through all the political turmoil of the 1920s, Ewing remained the PCL's emissary to the National Association, representing the circuit on issues of major policy.

But the owner was not universally loved. Seals owner Charlie Graham and Ewing had locked horns at least as far back as 1909, during the battles between the California and Pacific Coast Leagues when Graham owned the California League's Sacramento franchise. And though his team jumped over to the Coast League, Graham rarely agreed with Ewing on matters of league policy. This held true during the 1920s, when the two owners often found themselves on different ends of the spectrum on various issues of major and minor importance.

Given Oakland's status as the poor stepchild in the Bay Area pecking order, the Seals' virtual dominance of the league in recent years, and Ewing and Graham's less-than blissful relationship, a pennant for the Oakland Oaks in 1927 would be a source of pride, revenge and fulfillment for Cal Ewing.

The ballclub Ewing fielded in 1927 featured youth and experience, speed and power. From top to bottom, the team showed little weakness, except perhaps at catcher, where the position was played by a committee of Addison Read, Al Bool and Del Baker. Ernie Lombardi joined the team late in the season and played in 16 games. Here is the lineup the Oaks presented most of the time: Tony Governor, cf (.325, 3 HR, 48 RBI); Jimmy Reese, 2b (.295, 2 HR, 83 RBI); Lyn Lary, ss (.293, 12 HR, 102 RBI); Joe Bratcher, lf (.321, 12 HR, 101 RBI); Buzz Arlett, rf (.351, 30 HR, 123 RBI); John Fenton, 1b (.278, 12 HR, 110 RBI); Ike Caveney, 3b (.279, 5 HR, 71 RBI); and Addison Read, c (.253, 1 HR, 24 RBI).

Boehler joined a pitching staff that was already the league's deepest. No fewer than seven pitchers reached double figures in wins: Art Delaney (14-10, 3.05 ERA), Boehler (22-12, 3.10 ERA), Wilbur Cooper (15-12, 3.35 ERA), Harry Krause (15-6, 3.56 ERA), Pudgy Gould (17-5, 3.61 ERA), Elmer Shea (13-8, 4.05 ERA) and Bob Hasty (12-11, 4.14 ERA). For the 40-year-old Krause, this was his twenty-first year in professional baseball, his eleventh with Oakland.

One former pitcher helped little on the mound, pitching and winning but a single game. Yet without Russell "Buzz" Arlett the Oaks would not have won the 1927 pennant. The most prolific power hitter in Pacific Coast League history, Arlett holds the league record for career home runs with 251 and runs batted in with 1,188. He is second in home runs and runs batted in among the 400,000 or so men who have played minor league baseball, accumulating 432 homers and 1,786 RBI in a minor league career spanning from 1918 to 1937. At six-foot-three and 225 pounds, Arlett could power the ball from either side of the plate, and his career minor league average of .341 is the best for all switch-hitters.

For the Oakland Oaks, Arlett was more than just a hitter; he was the heart and soul of the ballclub, a man who was as likeable as he was talented. He broke in with the club in 1918, when he accompanied his brother, infielder Alex "Pop" Arlett, to training camp. Before long Buzz was asked to do a little pitching and soon won a place on the roster. Arlett had a powerful fastball and an excellent spitball. Between 1919 and 1922, he compiled a 95-71 record, including a record of 29-17 with a 2.89 ERA in 1920.

Had not a sore arm ended his pitching career, Arlett would likely have been one of the PCL's greatest pitchers. However, the pitcher did not lament his fate for long. In 1923, he played 149 games—including 102 as an outfielder—hitting .330 with 19 HR and 101 RBI. The era of Buzz Arlett, pitcher, had ended, but the era of Buzz Arlett, slugger, had begun. Between 1923 and 1930 he averaged .355, with 30 home runs and 138 RBI. His 1927 numbers for average, home runs and runs batted in were, in typical Arlett fashion, among the league's top ten hitters. Although he is not particularly famous for his speed, 1927 was the fourth consecutive year in which he stole 20 or more bases. On May 15, the outfielder stole home against the Seals to beat them 3–2.

This remarkable consistency did not, however, earn him an invitation to the major leagues. Arlett could blame Cal Ewing for that. The Oakland owner reportedly demanded nothing less than $100,000 for his prize outfielder, a price no team was willing to pay for an outfielder with questionable defensive skills. And because he had never appeared in the majors, Arlett was not subject to the draft.

He did play one year in the majors, when Ewing eased his demands. For the 1931 Philadelphia Phillies, Arlett played in 121 games, hitting .313, with 18 HR and 72 RBI. For this performance, Arlett was released. Like Smead Jolley, his slugging counterpart across the bay, Arlett's defensive limitations often overshadowed his offensive skills. Because Arlett was 32 years old that year, the Phillies likely believed he would never become much of a fielder. Arlett played six more years in the minors after his release by the Phillies, logging time with Baltimore, Birmingham, Minneapolis and Syracuse.

Yet his name would always be synonymous with Oakland baseball, especially Oaks Ballpark. Sometimes referred to as Emeryville Ballpark because

it was located in that town south of Berkeley between Oakland and the bay, the ballpark was bounded by Park Avenue, San Pablo Avenue, 45th Street and Watts Street. During the Oaks' heyday, the area surrounding the ballpark was a popular place to be. Visiting players stayed at the nearby California Hotel and hung out in local restaurants. The hometown favorites also frequented the watering holes near the park, and Arlett was said to be one of the more generous and gregarious of the Oak players.

The ballpark was built in 1913 and torn down in 1957. Except for a 296-foot right field porch, the ballpark's dimensions (center field, 407 feet and left field, 335 feet) were on the spacious side for the PCL. A grandstand rimmed the field in all but left field, and the park could accommodate 11,000 fans. The stands behind home plate were partially covered by a small roof, topped by a modest press box.

For all the attention Arlett garnered in 1927, he actually took second stage to the ballclub's infield, especially the flashy doubleplay combination of second baseman Jimmy Reese and shortstop Lyn Lary. Ewing thought so highly of his infield that he insured first baseman Jack Fenton, third baseman Ike Caveney, Lary and Reese for $200,000 against death or career-ending injury.

Los Angeles Times writer Matt Gallagher praised the Oakland infield as the league's best: "Lyn Lary and Jimmy Reese, the keystone combination have been doing good work for some time, while Jack Fenton, the first baseman, looks like the best prospect on the club."

Fenton did demonstrate flashes of power, but Lary was the best prospect on the ballclub. The 21-year-old shortstop had been impressing opponents since entering the league on August 25, 1924, just a few weeks after his high school graduation. The youngster had all the tools for success and looked to be on his way to the majors following the 1927 season. But when Ewing could not swing a deal on the magnitude of Portland's Cissell transaction, Lary remained on the Oaks for another year. In 1929 Lary began a successful major league career, hitting .309 in 236 at-bats for the New York Yankees. He played four more years for the Yankees before being traded to the Boston Red Sox one game into the 1934 season. Lary played seven more years after that, logging time with six different teams. During his major league career, Lary hit .269 and had a fielding percentage of .955.

Ewing insisted on dealing Lary and Reese together, stating that the two players were a natural combination that should not be broken up. The New York Yankees apparently agreed, making a deal with Ewing in 1927 for the pair that allowed both players to stay with the Oaks for further seasoning. As noted earlier, Lary made the jump to the Yankees in 1929. Reese followed a year later. The reported sale price for the two players was $150,000.

Opposite: **Buzz Arlett accepts a new car on "Buzz Arlett Day." Jimmy Reese, in uniform, looks on. (Doug McWilliams)**

"OAKS" OF 1927

"OAKS" CHAMPIONS 1928

BACK ROW: LOMBARDI, MURPHY, HASTY, DICKERMAN, TRAINER BURKE, BOOL, CRAGHEAD, SHINNERS, LARY, BOATHER, DAGLIA.

MIDDLE ROW: REESE, GUSTO, COOPER, GOVERNOR, CAVENEY, DELANEY, KRAUSE, METZ, BRATCHER.

FRONT ROW: MACEDO, SPARKS, BAKER, FRAZIER, READ, BRUBAKER, GOULD, MANAGER HOWARD.

Though Reese played only three years in the majors, he, ironically, enjoyed more lasting fame than Lary. As a major leaguer, Reese was Babe Ruth's roommate on the Yankees, and the Bambino took a liking to him from the outset. This association with Ruth, and his longtime role as a coach with the American League California Angels organization, earned Reese lasting recognition. Reese also played second base for one of the greatest minor league teams of all time—the 1934 Los Angeles Angels.

Another player of note for the 1927 Oaks was utilityman Ray Brubaker. He played 15 consecutive years with the Oaks beginning in 1920. In 1927 he provided utility and pinch-hit support by hitting .323 in 155 at-bats.

The 1927 Oakland Oaks were not the most fearsome team of the decade. On the year, they scored 157 fewer runs than the San Francisco Seals. This statistic helps portray why the team won. As the *San Francisco Chronicle's* Ed Hughes wrote: "The Oaks have a strong pitching staff and a swift defense and sure defense, so the team does not need many runs to win."

And win they did. Maybe they would not be confused with the 1927 Yankees, but the 1927 Oaks were good enough to make Oakland fans forget—for a season at least—25 years of frustration.

Attendance woes

With most teams out of the running for the pennant during the waning days of the season, it was not uncommon for teams to suffer at the gate. In 1927, the Oaks led by so much for so long that attendance dropped even during the summer, prompting teams to try any way they could to draw fans.

The first attempt to bolster attendance actually occurred before the season began. Anticipating the traditional late-season slide in attendance, the Pacific Coast League cut its schedule by a week and opened the 1927 season on March 29 so that the season would end prior to the World Series in October. The decision backfired somewhat, when first-week games were cancelled and attendance was down because of rains. At the end of the season, crowds were low, World Series or not.

A frequent ploy to increase attendance was to have a "Day" in honor of a popular player. This was nothing new and was often sponsored not by the ballclub (though it certainly encouraged the practice), but by fans. Saturday, August 27, was "Ping Bodie Day" at Recreation Park, sponsored by members of San Francisco's Italian community. The player received a check for $1,500 and gifts that included "a big salmon, a little pig and fruits and vegetables of all kinds." Across the bay, Jimmy Reese may have fared even better on "Jimmy Reese Day," taking home a check for $1,000, a diamond ring and other assorted gifts. Lyn Lary also had a day in his honor, thrown by fans from his hometown of Visalia. Portland manager Ernie Johnson was honored by

Opposite: **The 1927 Oaks (Doug McWilliams)**

citizens from his off-season home in Laguna Beach, California, when they lavished him with gifts at Wrigley Field.

Lefty O'Doul probably had the most memorable day of all. On "Lefty O'Doul Day" he received $2,000 in cash and other gifts. Then to show his appreciation, the former pitcher took to the mound and threw a two-hit shutout over the Missions, winning 3–0.

The Angels attempted to lure fans to the park by broadcasting games on radio, the first reported time Coast League baseball hit the airwaves. But with their Angels hopelessly out of the running and the attractions of college football and the Southern California beaches, people stayed away in droves. This spurred Angels President Joe Patrick to lead the effort for a split-season schedule in 1928, despite opposition from the three Bay Area teams, who derided split seasons as "bush league." Not insignificantly, the three Bay Area teams—the Oaks, Seals and Missions—all did well at the gate in 1927.

The year's record attendance for a seven-game series came when the Seals and the Oaks squared off at Recreation Park. For the week, 72,878 fans turned out. The Sunday doubleheader drew 10,096 for the morning game and 17,946 in the afternoon, with several thousand fans reportedly turned away for the latter game.

Junior PCL

For the second year in a row, several Coast League owners decided to send their younger players to the Utah-Idaho League for development in 1927. Five teams announced working agreements with members of the class C league prior to 1927:

Oakland Oaks—Ogden Gunners
San Francisco Seals—Logan Collegians
Los Angeles Angels—Pocatello Bannocks
San Francisco Missions—Idaho Falls Spuds
Sacramento Senators—Twin Falls Bruins

The PCL had talked for years about developing a farm league to reduce reliance on the majors for castoff players. Not only were PCL owners tiring of getting retread major leaguers whose press notices exceeded their capabilities, but developing homegrown talent made better business sense as well. Under the draft rules then in existence, players without major league experience were not draftable, meaning a talented youngster could be developed and sold for a high price. Following the 1927 season the PCL owners underscored their commitment to developing their own talent, reducing the number of roster spots for veterans from 20 to 18, and increasing the number of rookies a team could carry from five to seven.

1927 Final Standings

	W	L	Pct.
Oakland	120	75	.615
San Francisco	106	90	.541
Seattle	98	92	.516
Sacramento	100	95	.513
Portland	95	95	.500
Hollywood	92	104	.469
Missions	86	110	.439
Los Angeles	80	116	.408

Team batting leaders

Average: Portland — .307
Runs: San Francisco — 1,123
HRs: San Francisco — 155

Individual batting leaders

At-bats: Lyn Lary, Oakland — 765
Average: Smead Jolley, San Francisco — .397
Runs: Lefty O'Doul, San Francisco — 164
Hits: Lefty O'Doul, San Francisco — 278
2B: Buzz Arlett, Oakland — 54
                Ed Rose, Missions — 54
3B: Jimmy Reese, Oakland — 17
HR: Elmer Smith, Portland — 40
RBI: Smead Jolley, San Francisco — 163
Total bases: Lefty O'Doul, San Francisco — 428
Stolen bases: John Kerr, Hollywood — 41

Individual pitching leaders

Winning percentage: Pudgy Gould, Oakland — .773 (17-5)
Games won: George Boehler, Oakland — 22
Games lost: William Piercy, Los Angeles — 20
                      Herman Pillette, Missions — 20
                      William Ludolph, Missions — 20
Most games: Herb May, San Francisco — 55

Most shutouts:	Not Available
Most complete games:	George Boehler, Oakland — 24
	Frank Shellenback, Hollywood — 24
	Ray Keating, Sacramento — 24
	Little Joe Edwards, Seattle — 24
	Earl Kunz, San Francisco — 24
Most innings:	Clyde Barfoot, Missions — 308
ERA:	Johnny Miljus, Seattle — 2.30

Chapter 10

1928 — No Tears Due or Justified

Sixty miles north of Sacramento, California, Judge Frank Fogalsong issued a judicial order barring Colusa resident Frank Nutter from the Sacramento Senators' three-game series with Seattle the first week of October, 1928. Neither a gambler nor a hooligan, Nutter was something worse. He was a jinx. Supposedly, every time Nutter attended a Senators game, they lost. In Fogalsong's view, the Senators, locked in a first-place tie with San Francisco for the PCL's second-half title, could ill afford to lose any of its last three games, especially because of a jinx. Fogalsong's order was tongue-in-cheek, but it demonstrated the interest and excitement the Senators had generated in the Sacramento and San Joaquin Valleys in 1928. As the season approached its end, California's capital city and the area as far south as Stockton and north to the Oregon border became consumed by pennant fever.

For the first time in its history, the Coast League had opted to divide the season into two halves. The idea was to maintain fan interest late in the season by avoiding the runaway pennant races that had occurred in recent years. A post-season, seven-game playoff series between the first- and second-half winners would also swell attendance, the reasoning went.

To keep the players hustling, team owners pooled money to create a $20,000 purse. The winner of the playoff between the first- and second-half champions received $9,000, the runnerup $6,000. The third and fourth place teams would then receive $3,000 and $2,000, respectively.

The new format and incentives helped stir excitement in Sacramento. After finishing third in the first-half race, the Senators ran neck-and-neck with first-half winner San Francisco and runner-up Hollywood for the second-half crown. In late summer and early fall afternoons in 1928, Moreing Field swarmed with activity, quite a contrast to previous years when the Senators had been eliminated from contention. Down at Charley Doyle's Cigar Stand at 730 K Street, where advance tickets could be purchased, long lines became common, and dozens of regulars congregated to discuss the Senators' chances. Over at the Sacramento Bee Building at 7th and I Streets, an "Electronic Diamond" told the story of Senators road games to hundreds and sometimes thousands of diehard fans. And in homes throughout the Sacramento area people huddled around their RCA Radiola, their Atwater Kent or Kolster radios to follow the hometown heroes. "These were not radio re-creations like those that came later," said sportswriter Bill Conlin, who remembers listening to the broadcasts as a young boy. "The announcer would read wire reports as they came in and sometimes there would be long pauses between the action. For example, the announcer would say, 'now batting French ... strike one.' Then several seconds, even a minute or so later, he'd say that French grounded out or whatever. You had to be a real fan like I was to listen to it."

With three games to go the Senators and Seals were deadlocked with 59-37 records. Sacramentans were unusually optimistic about their chances, mainly because the Seattle Indians were coming to town. The Senators had already beaten the last-place ballclub 20 of 25 times, most recently sweeping seven games. San Francisco had slightly more difficult opposition with the seventh-place Angels, whom they were to play in Los Angeles.

Win, lose or draw, the Sacramento Chamber of Commerce announced it would honor the beloved Senators with a banquet after the season. "The fight the boys have put up entitles them to an expression of appreciation," the *Sacramento Bee* reported. The chamber also placed collection boxes at its offices and at Moreing Field, encouraging fans to donate money to give to the players after the season.

A byproduct of the split season was a concluding three-game series, rather than the PCL's typical seven-game series. Sacramento opened their series by beating Seattle 9-4; San Francisco beat Los Angeles 7-3. The next day both teams won again, though Sacramento did so in dramatic fashion on Earl Sheely's solo home run in the ninth inning that finished off Seattle 5-4. Entering the last game of the season tied for first place, neither team left the decision to chance. Sheely again homered, leading a 20-hit Senators barrage and a 16-2 victory. Almost as emphatically, San Francisco routed Los Angeles 10-2. The season's second half had ended in a deadlock.

Earlier in the week, PCL President Harry Williams met with Senators owner Lew Moreing and the Seals' Charlie Graham to discuss a tiebreaker. They decided on a three-game playoff for the second-half title. If the Seals won the playoff, they would take the entire $15,000 first-place purse; if the Senators won, they would assure themselves of at least $6,000.

Improbable finalists

That the Senators were in the running for the PCL championship at all came as something of a shock. The 1928 team certainly had talent, and preseason predictions put them consistently in the first division, but Sacramento had never made the breakthrough from contender to champion. In the

Lew Moreing (Kay Roper)

previous nine years, the team had finished in the first division four times, climbing as high as second place in 1921 and 1923. Until 1928, those were the highwater marks for a mediocre franchise.

Sacramento replaced Portland in 1918, re-entering the Pacific Coast League after a four-year hiatus. The Sacramento team was called both the Senators and the Solons, though they did not officially assume the latter name until 1937, when the owners at that time—the St. Louis Cardinals—sought to avoid confusing the team's identity with that of the Washington Senators. In 1918 the ballclub was backed by the chamber of commerce, which sold shares in the club to several local businessmen. But by 1920, the chamber wanted to unload its burden, lacking the experience to run a baseball team either on or off the field. Charles and Lewis Moreing stepped in to buy the club for a post-war bargain of $14,000 in assumed debt.

The men were two of four baseball brothers from Stockton. Cy Moreing managed Stockton in the California State League earlier in the century, while his twin brother William played on the same ballclub. The two men became successful real estate developers in the Stockton area. Likewise, Charles and Lewis made substantial amounts of money in real estate and farming.

Several times in the 1920s, the Moreings had reportedly put the ballclub up for sale, citing financial woes that stemmed from the size of the Sacramento market. For most of the 1920s the Sacramento franchise, as compensation for their small population base, received an additional 5 percent of the cut on their games in visiting ballparks. The *Sporting News* reported in 1925 that "the Sacramento club may also be moved as the Moreing brothers, owners, have placed the franchise on the block with the declaration that baseball does not pay in that town and probably never will."

By 1928 Charley had died and Lew took over sole ownership of the ballclub. The 1928 season proved to be Moreing's best, both on the field and at the gate. A headline in the November 29, 1928, issue of the *Sporting News* asked and answered its own question: "The Country's Best Baseball City? Why, er—Sacramento!"

The publication based this bold declaration on per capita attendance, citing the Senators' 1928 attendance of 237,000 fans and its population of only 90,000. As a point of comparison, the *Sporting News* said that New York drew only one-eighth of its population and the Cubs drew one-third. And while the Senators attracted only the fourth most fans in the PCL, the *Sporting News* again emphasized that the city was the smallest by far in the circuit.

Part of Sacramento's attendance should have been credited to Lew Moreing's hometown of Stockton, where most of the morning games of the Sunday doubleheaders were played. The town that inspired the legendary poem "Casey at the Bat," Stockton was a hotbed for baseball. In 1929, Moreing promised the town every Sunday morning home game in exchange for a guarantee of a thousand "season tickets"; within 48 hours 600 tickets were sold, and shortly thereafter the magic 1,000 figure was achieved.

Eventually, things soured for Lew Moreing, not because of failure running his ballclub—because he did relatively well drawing fans and selling players—but from outside pursuits. A failed mining venture in 1933 eventually broke Moreing and a bank took over the ballclub, naming Earl McNeely as receiver and field manager.

One of the assets the bank took was Moreing Field. The corner of Riverside and Y Streets in Sacramento had been the site of Coast League baseball for years. The field was first known as Buffalo Park, but when the Moreings took over the ballclub the park became known as Moreing Field. In 1921 improvements were made to the park, creating a facility with 2,000 reserved seats and 8,000 grandstand seats. Several ballplayers were given off-season jobs to help with construction. Moreing Field maintained its name until the St. Louis Cardinals bought the franchise from the bank and the ballpark became known as Cardinal Field. Later it was named Doubleday Park, before becoming Edmonds Field in 1944. Edmonds Field was named after *Sacramento Union* sports editor Dick Edmonds, who was instrumental in the drive to keep the Solons from moving that year. In 1948 the ballpark burned to the ground, but it was resurrected once again as Edmonds Field, a steel and concrete structure.

Moreing Field (George E. Outland)

Edmonds Field hosted its last Pacific Coast League ball game in 1960, when the franchise moved to Hawaii.

Despite all its changes in name and ownership, the ballpark saw the likes of some of the PCL's greatest players, and some of its greatest games. In 1928, it saw one of Sacramento's best teams ever.

Three-game series

On the last day of the regular season, four Pacific Coast League ballplayers were drafted by major league teams. Among those selected was Sacramento first baseman Earl Sheely. Sheely's new team was the Pittsburgh Pirates, for whom he hit .293 in 1929. The next season Sheely ended his major league career, finishing with a .300 lifetime average in nine seasons. The trip to Pittsburgh would have to wait, however, as the six-foot-three-and-a-half right-handed slugger still had a few games to make Lew Moreing appreciate his preseason acquisition.

At 35, and with an ankle that had been badly set after a break, the gimpy Sheely nevertheless had a lot of hits left in "Black Betsy," the midnight black bat he swung. Moreing obtained him in a deal with the Chicago White Sox, who would receive in exchange the pick of Sacramento's players following the 1928 season. This turned out to be 25-year-old outfielder Clarence "Dutch" Hoffman.

Sheely was the only significant preseason addition to the lineup, and his presence turned the Senators into contenders. The right-handed slugger had already gained considerable fame in the Coast League, playing for Salt Lake where he won three consecutive home run crowns in 1918, 1919 and 1920, adding the batting title in 1920 with a .371 average. In his encore performance in the league, he starred from the beginning, setting a blazing pace on his way to a stellar season with a .381 average, 21 home runs and 128 runs batted in. His performance bettered the mark of his predecessors at first base — Frank McGee and Jack Knight — who hit a collective .262 with 11 home runs and 78 runs batted the year before. Thanks to Sheely, Sacramento jumped from sixth in hitting in 1927 to second in 1928, with their team batting average improving from .287 to .304 and their run production increasing from 959 to 1,045.

Another addition who contributed to the club's success was spitballer Pudgy Gould, whom Oakland released in June. Gould enjoyed a 13-8 campaign with a 3.01 earned run average. The staff aces, however, were a pair of Sacramento veterans: Ray Keating and Laurie Vinci. Keating reprised his outstanding 1927 season, in which he won 20 and lost 15, by streaking to a 27-10, 3.14 ERA season. With Vinci's 23-11, 3.57 ERA season, the two pitchers accounted for 50 of the 112 Senator wins. Doc Crandall (6-4), Max Rachac (9-8) and Rudy Kallio (12-11) also contributed winning seasons.

This staff was supported by the Coast League's best defense. In Ray French the Seals had a player who would set the minor league record for most games played at shortstop (2,736). And Jim McLaughlin turned in an all-star year at third base, both at bat and in the field. As a team, Sacramento stacked up very well against San Francisco, and Sacramento fans actually believed their team might have a chance against the mighty Seals. Of course the Senator fans of 1928 did not have the benefit of hindsight; if they had, they would have recognized just how formidable the 1928 Seals really were.

As they always did, owners Putnam, Strub and Graham led PCL teams in player development, recruiting vast numbers of younger players. If a player showed promise they would keep him around or ship him off to the Utah-Idaho or Western League for development. In spring training of 1928 the ballclub trooped 80 players to Monterey. The biggest surprise of camp was 18-year-old Frankie Crosetti, a local high schooler who had been tagged a prospect but who had been given little chance of making the ballclub. After all, the Seals had veteran Eddie Mulligan anchoring third base and had acquired major leaguer Babe Pinelli to back him up.

Crosetti stole the show. When he hit a grand slam in an exhibition game against the Pittsburgh Pirates, the Seals had seen enough and Mulligan was sent packing. *San Francisco Chronicle* writer Ed Hughes wrote about the decision: "Crosetti may falter later, but the way he worked in the exhibition games and the first week of the season it would take a wonder to replace him. He made some plays against Seattle that had the whole town talking. The Seattle pitchers took plenty of shots at his head, but they did not scare him a bit. He had his cuts and drove out many an extra base hit." Crosetti eventually gave way to Pinelli at third, but a storied professional playing career that would include seven World Series was launched.

Other key acquisitions for the Seals included young Joe Sprinz, a catcher obtained from Des Moines of the Western League; pitcher–first baseman

Earl Sheely (George E. Outland)

Hollis "Sloppy" Thurston from the Washington Senators; and shortstop Hal Rhyne, who returned to the Seals after Pittsburgh let him go. The two most important newcomers to San Francisco, however, were pitchers Elmer Jacobs and Walter "Dutch" Ruether. Former Yankee Ruether accepted a $5,000 signing bonus and a $5,000 salary from the Seals, making good on the deal by producing a 29-7, 3.03 ERA season. Jacobs returned to the Coast League after a year with the Chicago White Sox to post equally impressive numbers — 22-8, 2.56 ERA.

The Seals won the first-half championship with a 58-34 record, good enough to beat Hollywood by five games and Sacramento by eight. Featuring the league's best outfield and an infield that mixed veterans and youngsters, the Seals' lineup led all PCL clubs in hitting with a .308 average. This is the

Earl Averill (Don Hazelwood)

way they would line up for the three-game series with the Senators for the second-half championship: Roy Johnson, lf (.360, 22 HR, 76 RBI); Babe Pinelli, 3b (.310, 2 HR, 31 RBI) or Frank Crosetti, 3b (.248, 4 HR, 22 RBI); Earl Averill, cf (.354, 36 HR, 173 RBI); Gus Suhr, 2b (.314, 22 HR, 133 RBI); Smead Jolley, rf (.404, 45 HR, 188 RBI); Sloppy Thurston, 1b (.347, 24 HR, 98 RBI); Hal Rhyne, ss (.312, 6 HR, 106 RBI); and Joe Sprinz, c (.236, 4 HR, 49 RBI).

In Johnson, Averill and Jolley, the Seals had one of the greatest outfields in minor league history. Roy Johnson was sold after the season to the Detroit Tigers for $75,000, beginning a solid 10-year major league career. Similarly,

Earl Averill began his Hall of Fame career when he was traded to the Cleveland Indians at the end of the year. The Averill deal was reportedly consummated over a breakfast of spareribs and sauerkraut between Cleveland General Manager Billy Evans and Seals Vice President Charlie Graham. In exchange for Averill, the Seals received $35,000 cash and pitchers James Zinn and Johnny Miljus. In a travesty of justice, the third outfield member, Smead Jolley, was bypassed by the major leagues, his defensive liabilities again cited as the reason. Perhaps the best pure hitter ever to appear in the Pacific Coast League, Jolley broke Paul Waner's batting record by posting a .404 average for the 1928 season.

Anchored by Rhyne at shortstop, the 1928 Seals fielded nearly as well as their 1925 ballclub (.965 versus a league-leading .968 in 1925); yet they were only the sixth best fielding team in the league. Suhr, a first baseman by trade, was out of position at second, and Pinelli and Crosetti did not make fans forget Eddie Mulligan at third base.

As a group the Seals could slug, leading the league with 182 home runs. During one stretch in July, they homered in 18 straight games, clouting 36 during the streak.

The Senators fared better than most against this lineup, winning 11 of 24 encounters with the Seals on the year. Led by veterans Koehler, French and Sheely, the 1928 Senators demonstrated all year long that they could play with the best. Their starting lineup featured only two sub-.300 hitters: Ray French, ss (.287, 9 HR, 77 RBI); Johnny Monroe, 2b (.321, 10 HR, 94 RBI); Frank Osborne, rf (.316, 12 HR, 97 RBI); Earl Sheely, 1b (.381, 21 HR, 128 RBI); Clarence Hoffman, cf (.335, 11 HR, 96 RBI); Art Koehler, c (.305, 8 HR, 60 RBI); or Hank Severeid, c (.301, 10 HR, 59 RBI); Jim McLaughlin, 3b (.310, 10 HR, 81 RBI); and Ray Rohwer, lf (.289, 10 HR, 84 RBI).

When Sacramento fight promoter Fred Pearl walked out to Moreing Field at ten minutes to three on Saturday afternoon, October 6, to announce the batteries for the first game of the playoff for the second-half PCL title, an overflow of 10,000 fans erupted with a prolonged ovation when Sacramento pitcher Laurie Vinci and catcher Art Koehler were announced. The hometown fans maintained their enthusiasm during a satisfying 5-1 win. Vinci turned in a six-hitter, limiting the Seals to no hits after the fifth inning. Elmer Jacobs took the loss, leaving the ballgame for a pinch-hitter in the fifth inning, his team trailing 2–0.

San Francisco produced its only run in the fifth inning when Hal Rhyne tripled to center and then scored on a single. Sacramento, meanwhile, scored all the runs it needed in the second inning. Sheely led off with a walk; Hoffman singled him to second. Koehler bunted the two over to second and third, enabling them to score on McLaughlin's liner to center. The Senators added Hoffman's solo home run in the seventh and two more runs in the ninth to end the scoring.

Sunday morning the series moved to San Francisco's Recreation Park, where the Senators needed only to win one game in a doubleheader to take the second-half pennant. Sacramento came out slugging, drawing first blood on Sheely's RBI single in the first. Before the day was over, they punished pitchers Walter Mails, Val Glynn and Oliver Mitchell for 19 hits and 10 runs. Koehler, Monroe, Osborne and Sheely all homered. The majority of the 17,000 fans at Rec Park had little to cheer as the game entered the bottom of the ninth, with Sacramento leading 10–1. But then Pudgy Gould began to tire, surrendering four hits and a walk. Two errors aided San Francisco in the inning as the Seals scored six runs to climb back into the game. It was not until Doc Crandall relieved Gould to record the final two outs that the inning, the game and the season's second half were over. Sacramento had won its first baseball championship of any kind. An estimated 5,000 Sacramento fans had trekked to San Francisco. Many of them could be heard for blocks as their train pulled away for a joyous ride home to Sacramento.

For the players, the two-game sweep of the Seals meant that they could do no worse than a $6,000 bonus — the losers' share of the $15,000 first-place prize money. On the season, the Seals and Senators had beaten each other 13 times. The best-of-seven playoff series would break the tie and decide the 1928 Pacific Coast League championship.

The PCL title series

Ray Keating and Dutch Ruether — the league's two best pitchers — squared off in game one of the playoffs at Rec Park. But the game was far from a pitchers' duel. Sacramento pummelled Ruether for 18 hits, yet the veteran shut out the Senators for six innings. He finally fell apart in the seventh and eighth innings, when Sacramento touched him for 10 of their hits and all five runs. Every man in the Sacramento lineup, except for the pitcher's spot in the order and left fielder Les Sheehan, had two or more hits.

Unfortunately for Sacramento, Keating was even less effective. He lasted only 3⅔ innings, yielding seven runs. The Seals went on to score five more to win easily 12-5. Remarkably, neither team hit a home run in the slugfest. Jolley drove in three runs, while Thurston, Johnson, Averill and Suhr each drove in two.

The next day, Thursday, October 11, the two teams returned to Sacramento, and things turned ugly. San Francisco took a 1–0 lead into the bottom of the fourth, when Seals pitcher Elmer Jacobs began to struggle. Osborne doubled, advancing to third on Sheely's single. Hoffman walked, then Koehler singled to tie the score. When Jacobs fell behind on the count to McLaughlin, Jacobs and Manager Nick Williams protested home plate umpire Henry Fanning's strike zone.

After several minutes of wrangling, Fanning decided he had heard enough and ejected Williams. The umpire then pulled out his pocket watch, telling

Williams to leave the field in short order or his ballclub would forfeit. This incensed the Seals and incited the fans as the argument escalated. Seconds later Jacobs wheeled and fired a baseball at Fanning, striking him just above the knee hard enough to knock him to the ground.

Jacobs' act shocked the onlookers, which included PCL President Harry Williams. Though known as a hothead, Jacobs had been painted as something of a saint by Bay Area writer Abe Kemp, who never missed a chance to tell his readers of Jacobs' heroics on the mound—heroics that showed the character of a man who toiled at his job while supporting a wife and five children. Kemp had a hard time glorifying Jacobs following this incident.

To make matters worse, the umpire Jacobs chose to attack—Henry Fanning—had but one arm. The week before the *Sacramento Bee* had hailed Fanning as one of the best umpires in the league; and when Portland's Larry French and Tony Rego had abused the umpire in a late September game, the *Bee* called the two cowards and bullies. So, even when Jacobs apologized to the umpire minutes later, he elicited no sympathy from the crowd, who had just witnessed a fallen, one-armed umpire carried off the field by a burly cop.

Williams ruled the next day that Jacobs would not be suspended, but that he would merely forfeit part of his playoff money. The ruling seemed contrary to Landis' 1927 edict arising from the Frank Brazill case, in which the commissioner declared automatic suspension when physical violence was used against an umpire. *Bee* sports editor Rudy Hickey wrote that "a lifetime ban would not be too severe." A *Bee* editorial the day after the incident called for the same punishment.

The game proceeded with only two umpires, rather than the playoff quota of three. A stiff wind through the Moreing Field outfield turned the tight ballgame into a slugfest. Shortly after order was restored in the fourth inning, Ray Rohwer hit a grand slam home run, accounting for the Senators' sixth run of the inning and staking the home team to a 6-1 lead. Rohwer then followed with a solo home run in the sixth to put his team ahead 7-1.

The Seals bunched four wind-aided hits in the seventh off starter Vinci to cut the Senators' lead to 7-5. In the eighth, Senators second baseman Johnny Monroe's fly ball also benefitted from the wind, falling for a double down the left field line to score Rohwer and increase the score to 8-5.

The Seals scored twice in the ninth and had the tying and winning runs on base with two outs. Out came old Doc Crandall to relieve Vinci; in stepped pitcher Dutch Ruether, a .316 hitter, to pinch-hit for Gordon Jones. With darkness beginning to settle, Crandall struck out Ruether. The series was tied at one game apiece.

The two teams returned to Moreing Field Saturday afternoon and 8,000 fans watched Sacramento carry a 3-2 lead into the eighth. They then watched pitcher Pudgy Gould once again lose his stuff to surrender six hits and five runs over the last two innings.

Pinelli led off the eighth for the Seals with a single. Averill lined out before Suhr lashed a double off the center field wall to score Pinelli. Jolley drew an intentional pass and Thurston was nicked by a pitch to load the bases. After Rhyne struck out, it looked as though the Senators might survive the inning since the light-hitting Joe Sprinz was up. However, the young catcher fisted one to center to drive in two runs, making the score 5-3. The Senators scored in the bottom of the eighth, but they lost a chance to tie the game when Osborne failed to slide on a play at the plate and was tagged out.

Consecutive hits by Johnson, Pinelli and Averill in the ninth provided the Seals with the final 7-4 margin. In something of a surprise for such a pivotal game, Nick Williams had started pitcher Sloppy Thurston, who had a record of 9-7 and a 4.59 ERA for the year and was considered a better first baseman than pitcher. The gamble paid off as Thurston, whose nickname belied the sartorial splendor for which he was known, threw an eight-hit, complete-game victory. Prior to the game the Senators learned that shortstop Ray French, who had not missed a game all year, would not be able to play for the rest of the series. French had been knocked unconscious by a bad-hop ground ball hit by Gus Suhr in game two. His replacement, Lennie Backer, a .266 hitter, would fill in admirably at short and in the leadoff position, hitting .450 and not committing an error in the series. However, French could cover as much ground as any shortstop in the league. Losing his defense and leadership severely dampened the Senators' chances against a team like the Seals.

Saturday at Recreation Park, the series resumed its high-scoring ways. Sacramento scored nine runs in the seventh and eighth innings to post a 12-11 win. The Seals chased Crandall after just 2⅓ innings in which they scored four runs. Max Rachac and Hollywood-aquisition Dick Bonnelly gave up six more runs as the Seals took a 10-3 lead into the seventh. Then Herb "Buckshot" May began to falter, managing to secure only one out in the seventh. Gordon Jones and Walter Mails came in, but neither could stem a five-hit, four-run rally by the Senators. In the eighth the Senators again bunched four hits to score five more runs and take a 12-10 lead. The big blows in the rallies were home runs by Sheely, Rohwer and Hoffman, as well as a two-run pinch single by Hank Severeid. When the nearly three-hour hit parade had ended, Sacramento had tallied 21 hits, San Francisco 20. With the 12-10 win, Sacramento evened the series at two games apiece.

For 6½ innings on Sunday it looked like the pitchers had finally regained control. San Francisco's Marvin Moudy surrendered only four hits and three runs, while Laurie Vinci gave up three runs on eight hits. In the home half of the seventh, however, this modicum of restraint broke. As the *Bee* put it:

"The game cracked up when the Seals came to bat [in the seventh]. Ten runs on nine hits were rung up by the San Franciscans. Vinci was bumped hard and Ray Keating was simply slaughtered. Roy Johnson started it all with a triple and before the inning was over was up again to hit a home run with two on. It was just a terrible hitting barrage."

The final score of game five was 15–3 and the series now stood 3-2 in favor of the Seals. Rather than impressing, the weekend slugfests seemed to put off at least one baseball purist, an unnamed writer for the *Bee*: "For teams that are battling for a pennant, much less first and second half champions, the contests are dragging and lacking the glitter and spirit of real combats. Apparently both clubs are pretty well shell-shocked and the strain is telling."

Indeed, the season had been long, even for the Pacific Coast League. With the split season, teams played only 190 or so regular season games—less than the standard 200 and more that characterized the decade—but the Seals and Senators had endured two pennant races, a pressure-packed three-game playoff for the second-half title and now a best-of-seven playoff series. Even in 1928 there were better ways to earn a cut of $9,000.

Tuesday, October 16, was a mild Indian summer day at Moreing Field, and a less-than-capacity crowd turned out. The Sacramento Chamber of Commerce decided to award each member of the Senators a "costly travelling bag" prior to game six, rather than banking on a post-series celebration to award the gift. The Senators would not have to wait long to begin packing their new bags.

Once again, the ballgame started as a pitcher's duel, this time between Dutch Ruether and Pudgy Gould. After six innings the two teams were deadlocked at four runs apiece. The Senators knocked around Ruether in the bottom of the fourth with a three-run rally. They led off the inning by putting runners on second and third, with Hoffman singling and Koehler doubling. McLaughlin hit a sacrifice fly ball to Jolley to score Sacramento's second run of the game. Sheehan then homered to give Sacramento a 4–3 lead.

The Seals tied the game in the fifth when Sheely booted Pinelli's bunt and then threw the ball wildly down the right field line. The two errors gave the Seals two runners in scoring position with Averill, Suhr and Jolley coming up. Gould battled the three sluggers. Averill popped out to short. Suhr popped out to second, but Johnson tied the game at 4–4 by beating Monroe's errant throw home. Jolley then flied out to end the inning; Gould had averted what could have been a disastrous inning.

In the home half of the fifth, the Senators chased Ruether from the game, but failed to score despite loading the bases with one out. Marvin Moudy came in to relieve and induced Koehler, the Senators' hottest hitter, to hit into an inning-ending doubleplay. Sacramento's best chance of the day came up empty. Though they added a run in the sixth, it was not enough.

Sloppy Thurston (Don Hazelwood)

Sacramento's undoing came in the seventh. Gould hit Moudy with a pitch to start the inning. Johnson, who had been having trouble with Gould all series, then hit a two-run homer. Following a walk to Pinelli, Crandall came in to relieve, whereupon he yielded singles to Averill, Suhr and Thurston, the last blow driving in two runs. Rachac came in to end the inning, but by then the Seals had scored five runs. The outburst ended the scoring as Moudy sailed along to shut down Sacramento the rest of the way to pick up his second win of the series. Final score: Seals 9, Senators 5.

The San Francisco Seals had beaten the Sacramento Senators, four games to two, winning the first-ever split-season pennant in PCL history. Sacramento's surprisingly strong team had come up short.

In the end, the Senators could not quell the San Francisco hitters. Sacramento starting pitchers threw a lot of pitches and innings during the stretch drive for the second-half pennant. During the regular and post seasons, Vinci pitched 354 innings, Keating 314, the first and fourth highest in the league. Gould threw fewer than 250 innings, but most of those came down the stretch. By the time the final playoff series had arrived, the Senators' three top pitchers were tired. Keating managed to throw only five innings in the six game-series; Vinci and Gould turned in 15 innings apiece in their two outings, but the latter especially lost his stuff past the midpoint in his two ballgames.

As the Senators' pitching struggled, the Seals' hitting prospered. For the six-game series, San Francisco hit .379. Though they hit only two home runs (both by Johnson), they averaged three doubles a game and hit well in the clutch. The entire starting lineup enjoyed a productive series: Jolley (.517), Averill (.483), Suhr (.458), Sprinz (.407), Pinelli (.357), Johnson (.333, 2 HR), Thurston (.333) and Rhyne (.296). The Senators also hit well, with a team batting average of .350 and good numbers throughout the lineup: Koehler (.480), Backer (.450), Rohwer (.412, 3 HR), Monroe (.409), Sheehan (.400, 1 HR), Osborne (.360), Sheely (.304, 1 HR) and Hoffman (.300, 1 HR).

The series proved a pitcher's nightmare and a less-than-artistic success. For Sacramento it had been a chance to play—and almost beat—the big boys. The 1928 season had been a fun ride.

Perhaps *Bee* writer Rudy Hickey's epitaph for the year said it best: "It would be mighty poor sportsmanship to say the best club did not win. It would have been a nice thing for the Senators to have won the flag, but the season has been a huge success. [The game] ended Sacramento's best year in baseball and no tears are due or justified."

In fact, overall league attendance rebounded from a lackluster 1927 to top the two million mark for only the second time. Hollywood, in the running for both the first- and second-half pennants, showed the most improvement, while Sacramento also enjoyed a big jump from the year before.

Following are the 1928 league attendance figures announced by the league:

San Francisco	414,000
Hollywood	363,000
Missions	250,000
Sacramento	237,000
Oakland	230,000 (88,000 less than '27)
Los Angeles	186,000
Portland	130,000 (43,000 less than '27)
Seattle	96,000 (46,000 less than '27)

Ray Keating (George E. Outland)

1928 Final Standings

First-half standings

	W	L	Pct.
San Francisco	58	34	.630
Hollywood	53	39	.576
Sacramento	50	42	.543
Missions	49	43	.533
Los Angeles	48	44	.522
Oakland	40	52	.435
Portland	37	55	.402
Seattle	33	59	.359

Second-half standings

	W	L	Pct.
Sacramento	62	37	.626
San Francisco	62	37	.626
Hollywood	59	40	.596
Oakland	51	48	.515
Missions	50	49	.505
Portland	42	57	.424
Los Angeles	39	60	.394
Seattle	31	68	.313

Team batting leaders

Average:	San Francisco — .308
Runs:	San Francisco — 1,129
HRs:	San Francisco — 182

Individual batting leaders

At-bats:	Ray French, Sacramento — 814
Average:	Smead Jolley, San Francisco — .404
Runs:	Earl Averill, San Francisco — 178
Hits:	Smead Jolley, San Francisco — 309
2B:	Gus Suhr, San Francisco — 64
3B:	Roy Johnson, San Francisco — 16
	Tony Governor, Oakland — 16
HR:	Smead Jolley, San Francisco — 45
RBI:	Smead Jolley, San Francisco — 188
Total bases:	Smead Jolley, San Francisco — 516
Stolen bases:	Evar Swanson, Missions — 49

Individual pitching leaders

Winning percentage:	Dutch Ruether, San Francisco — .806 (29-7)
Games won:	Dutch Ruether, San Francisco — 29
Games lost:	Earl Collard, Seattle — 23
Most games:	Pudgy Gould, Sacramento-Oakland — 55
Most shutouts:	Elmer Jacobs, San Francisco — 6
Most complete games:	Dutch Ruether, San Francisco — 28
	Jack Knight, Seattle-Portland — 28
Most innings:	Jack Knight, Seattle-Portland — 331
ERA:	Elmer Jacobs, San Francisco — 2.56

All-Stars

A vote of 21 baseball writers chose the following all-star team for 1928:

RF	Smead Jolley (Seals)		3B	Jimmy McLaughlin (Sacramento)
LF	Roy Johnson (Seals)		SS	Dudley Lee (Hollywood)
CF	Earl Averill (Seals)			Lyn Lary (Oakland)
C	Johnny Bassler (Hollywood)		P	Dutch Ruether (Seals)
1B	Earl Sheely (Sacramento)		Util	Sloppy Thurston (Seals)
2B	Johnny Kerr (Hollywood)			

Chapter 11

1929 — The "Other Team" Shares the Glory

When the Salt Lake City Bees moved to Hollywood in 1926, filling the void left by the Vernon Tigers' departure to San Francisco, it looked as though the league had settled on a blissful new alignment. The new league structure promised greater revenues and more harmony. The poor-drawing Salt Lake franchise now shared the West's largest city and best ballpark — Wrigley Field. That meant no more costly train rides to Utah for the other PCL clubs. The divisive feud between the Los Angeles and Vernon ownership groups vanished. San Francisco — the league's baseball hotbed — now had continuous baseball in Recreation Park, a circumstance certain to boost league attendance. Even Oakland, which stood to lose the most with continuous baseball across the bay in San Francisco, was placated when the league agreed to pay the Oaks $140,000 if they would go along with the new alignment.

At first, this new organization operated more smoothly than it had in years. But this was, after all, the Pacific Coast League, where intra-league squabbles were a way of life. Ironically, the major dispute came between friends Bill Lane and William Wrigley. Now that they shared the same ballpark, the Hollywood and Los Angeles owners became increasingly alienated from one another. And as they did, the other Pacific Coast League owners were only too eager to jump into the fray.

"The fight between the magnates is a hotter one than the games on the field," wrote *Los Angeles Times* sportswriter Matt Gallagher in May. What was the source of so much trouble? What could have caused such a fight? In a word, women.

More specifically, the brouhaha was over Ladies Day at Wrigley Field. William Wrigley wanted to have Ladies Day — when women could attend ballgames for free — every game at his ballpark. Moreover, he wanted his tenant — Lane's Hollywood Stars — to do the same. Lane resisted, claiming that admitting women free cost him money. The other league owners agreed, saying that the practice reduced their cut of the gate as well. They had no problem with the traditional Wednesday, Thursday and Friday Ladies Day that most teams offered, but such practices on Tuesdays (the day a series opened) and weekends were going too far.

Wrigley first installed a ladies free policy in 1926, and the other owners soon objected. Rather than discontinue the policy, Wrigley agreed to give the visiting ballclub its 40 percent share and the league its 5 percent of what the women would have paid. Maintaining this policy in 1928 cost the Angels 32 cents for every woman admitted to the ballpark, which added up to more than $30,000 on the year, according to a report in the *Sporting News*.

Wrigley saw this money as building the future for the game and chafed at the league's shortsightedness. "We must cultivate baseball fans here," he declared. "The game has been on the decline and our only salvation is to interest women, who once interested, will be the means of taking the men folks to the games on Saturdays and Sundays instead of to the beaches or for auto rides."

In truth some of the women attending Coast League games, regrettably, already displayed the tendencies of the most boorish male fans. The *Sporting News* reported several incidents, including one at a game between Portland and Hollywood wherein an enraged woman rushed onto the field and beat an umpire over the head with her parasol after a disputed call. In another reported incident, "An excited feminine fan at one of the San Francisco–Oakland games last week got so stirred up that she threw a pop bottle before she had done any drinking. Another spectator sitting in front of her was on the receiving end of the bottle and a policeman endeavored to take the woman out of the park, but she hung to her seat. There was considerable argument, but she won and stayed for the game."

These were exceptions, however, and women on the coast—as in the major league ballparks—mitigated the rowdiness that occurred in the grandstands. As women became more and more common at the ballparks, the level of civility rose. Hollywood owner Bill Lane did not care as much about civility as he did the bottom line. So when Wrigley insisted that he sign a lease for Wrigley Field that included a provision for admitting women free every day, Lane balked.

President Harry Williams affirmed Lane's position and had support from the other owners. Grudgingly Wrigley relented, but he clung to his promise to offer Ladies Day every day of the week, citing a league bylaw that allowed him to set his own admission prices. A league vote in March 1929 rescinded the bylaw, with Portland owner Tom Turner the most strident voice against Wrigley. Turner relied heavily on the revenues from his club's games in Wrigley Field to make ends meet and was adamantly opposed to the women-free policy. To underscore his opposition, Turner, in a show of political spite, began lobbying for a late March start to the PCL season. In previous years, Wrigley jammed his ballpark for March exhibition series between his Chicago

Cubs and other major and minor league opponents. Turner's action was clearly intended to limit this source of income from Wrigley.

Wrigley was enraged and threatened to "junk" the Angels and proceed with the major league exhibition games. "I will carry the matter to the highest courts of the land if necessary to get my constitutional rights," he said. "I bought the Los Angeles club to have a nice grounds for the Cubs in the spring. It hasn't paid a dime interest on the investment so far as the Coast League club is concerned. I'm just about tired of the petty policies. Unless there is a change of heart, the park will be closed for 1930."

Wrigley said he would re-open Vernon's 3,000-seat ballpark to spite the other owners. Not dependent upon income generated by the Angels, Wrigley's move would have hurt league revenues and taken his gem of a ballpark out of the circuit, symbolically lowering the status of the PCL.

Turner, Cal Ewing and Bill Lane joined forces to approve a March 26 opener, flatly denying Wrigley's appeal for an April 3 start. Stinging from the loss, Wrigley escalated his effort to conduct Ladies Day every day of the week. Eventually he took the issue to the National Board of Arbitration, recognizing his prospects were dimmed by the fact that Cal Ewing was one of the board's members. On July 8, 1929, the board decided against Wrigley. He could have his Ladies Day on Wednesday, Thursday and Friday like everybody else; the rest of the week the women paid.

"The decision is a joke, but we are part of a joke system and we will abide by the verdict," said Wrigley, who did not follow through on his threat to move the team to the Vernon ballpark or to sell the Angels outright.

Thereafter, the good relationship between Wrigley and Lane never fully recovered, and after repeated haggling over the lease and other issues, Lane decided to move his team in to the friendlier clime of San Diego, a city Lane began considering as a new home as early as 1929 when his ballclub took spring training there. It was not until after the 1935 season, however, that Lane finally made his move and established the San Diego Padres.

The squabbles also affected PCL President Harry Williams, who had been installed in 1926 mainly on the strength of Wrigley's influence. Though he had little power for establishing policy, Williams clearly opposed Wrigley on the Ladies Day issue. In December 1928 it appeared that Williams' stance might have cost him his job. After 24 votes, the league's owners were split 4–4 on a new president; moreover the tie was between former president William McCarthy and Judge McCredie. Williams was no longer in the running, his support in the southland had crumbled, Lane favored McCredie and Wrigley, ironically, favored his old nemesis, McCarthy.

The impasse was not broken and the meeting adjourned until January, when the directors agreed to reopen the vote. Almost sheepishly, Williams argued his case:

Five years ago I did not ask anybody to vote for me, nor have I since. After all, the real test of a league president is the record which that league has made under his administration.

During the last five years the circuit has been condensed, with a great saving in transportation, and continuous baseball provided in San Francisco. The past five years the prosperity of the league has far exceeded that of any corresponding period. The two greatest seasons in the history of the league in point of attendance were enjoyed during these five years, and in one of these years the minor league attendance record for all time was broken. In one of those years the Coast League drew approximately half as many paid admissions as one of the major leagues despite the fact that we had a circuit population of about 3,000,000 as against at least 15,000,000 embraced in that major league circuit.

These are just the high spots in the business record of the league the past five years.

In January 1929, after just two ballots Williams was re-elected for two more years at a salary of $10,000 annually. The deadlock was broken when Bill Lane decided to vote for the current president after receiving unspecified concessions. Once Lane went with Williams, the other directors voted unanimously for him as well.

In the shadow of a legend

The relationship between the two San Francisco ballclubs—the Seals and the Missions—was not as fractious as that between the Angels and the Stars. There was the usual dickering over the amount of rent the Missions would pay the Seals to use Recreation Park, but by and large the two teams coexisted peacefully. This relationship heated somewhat in 1929, when the Missions emerged from the Seals' shadow.

"The Missions have never had a following here, but Red Killefer is determined to get one this year," wrote the *San Francisco Chronicle*'s Ed Hughes.

Killefer, one of the league's best managers during the decade, also assumed the role of team president from McCarthy late in 1928 so that the latter could launch what proved to be an unsuccessful bid for the league presidency. Hired in 1928, Killefer signed a three-year deal, reportedly at a salary higher than any other PCL manager in history. In 1929 he made it a priority to improve the team's identity in San Francisco. He started by renaming the ballclub. "The Mission Bells are no more. From now on it is the Mission Reds and the team gets its moniker from the fiery thatch of its leader, Red Killefer," reported the *Sporting News*. "Killefer never did like the dingdong sound of Bells anyway."

This was the third name in four years for the Mission club. When the former Vernon Tigers moved to San Francisco, they dubbed themselves the Mission Bears and dressed in blue and gold. The out-of-towners failed to recognize that the Bay Area already had a blue and gold team called the Bears.

And the University of California at Berkeley did not appreciate someone try-ing to appropriate its mascot's name. The university filed suit, which it subse-quently dropped when the Missions scrapped the bear identity and became the Mission Bells.

Though occasionally known as the Monks, the Missions maintained the Reds nickname through the 1937 season—their last in San Francisco. By and large, however, the team was known simply as the Missions. When the team returned to Southern California in 1937, they became known as the Hollywood Stars, replacing Bill Lane's team of the same name.

The 12-year life of the Missions was an experiment that never fully suc-ceeded; San Francisco was first and foremost the Seals' town. The Missions began with William McCarthy, the former league president. McCarthy and shipping magnate Stanley Dollar teamed up to buy the Vernon club and establish residence in Recreation Park. McCarthy had enjoyed good relations with the Seals, who welcomed an opportunity to extract additional income by leasing out their ballpark when they were on the road.

This relationship was so good that the Seals had no compunction about selling their best pitcher, Dutch Ruether, to their intercity rivals. The Seals unloaded Ruether when he demanded a signing bonus from the Seals prior to the 1929 season, just like he had received the year before when the Seals lured him away from the New York Yankees. At $7,500, Ruether was no bargain, but he was a major addition to the Missions' staff and gave them one of the best rosters—top to bottom—in the league.

Beginning in December 1928, Killefer began to reshape his team, which had finished disappointingly out of the running during the previous season. Given a modest $25,000 bankroll for obtaining players, Killefer started by buying Eddie Mulligan's contract from the Pirates. He then purchased outfielders Pete Scott and Walter Christensen, from Cincinnati; catcher Fred "Bootnose" Hofmann came from the Boston Red Sox and pitcher Bert Cole, the "temperamental" lefty who had languished in Portland and Seattle, was obtained. With the additions of Ruether and Cole, the Missions had one of the more memorable pitching staffs of the era: Herman Pillette, Harry Krause, Bill Hubbell, Herb McQuaid, Ernie Nevers, Mert Nelson, Ruether and Cole. For the 40-year-old Krause, the season marked his last year in baseball. His PCL record of 249-220 was the third highest win total in league history.

Outfielders Irwin "Fuzzy" Hufft and Ike Boone had been obtained in mid–1928. Hufft came from Seattle, while Boone was delivered from Portland in a trade for outfielder Eddie Rose and catcher Rod Whitney. The two left-handed hitters were custom-made for Recreation Park's short right field fence. In 1928, Hufft finished with a .371 average, 46 doubles, 30 home runs, and 143 runs batted in. In 1929 he topped all those numbers: .379 average, 57 doubles, 39 home runs and 187 runs batted in. Great as these numbers were,

Fuzzy Hufft (Bob Brady)

they could not compare to Boone's 1929 season, one of the truly great offensive performances in the history of organized baseball.

The 32-year-old Boone was widely known throughout baseball as one of the game's premier sluggers. He was one of three baseball-playing brothers. Collectively, Danny, Ike and Bill Boone amassed 4,345 hits and 436 home runs, while hitting .361. The latter two numbers are the best by brothers in the history of minor league baseball. Danny's career spanned 15 years in which in collected 1,648 hits, 214 home runs and a .356 batting average, but it was Ike who was the best of the three brothers.

Isaac Morgan Boone was born in Samantha, Alabama, on February 17, 1897. He began his career in professional baseball when he left the University of Alabama in 1920 to play for Cedartown in the Georgia State League. In 290 at-bats that first season, he hit .403. He earned a trip to New Orleans of the

Ike Boone (Tony Pirak)

Southern League the following year, where he led the circuit with a .389 average, 46 doubles and 27 triples. The performance bought the 6-foot, 200-pounder a cup of coffee with the New York Giants in 1922. But after only two at-bats, Giant Manager John McGraw sent Boone back down to the minors. Before he was through, Boone would make seven more trips to the majors, but his longest stint was only two-plus years with the Boston Red Sox from 1923 through 1925. Though his major league career consisted of only 355 games and 1,154 at-bats, Boone did manage a highly credible .319 career average with the Giants, Red Sox, White Sox and Dodgers. Boone, like many of the PCL's slugging outfielders, was clumsy in the field. Even a *Sporting News* article that sung Boone's praises had to admit that "Isaac Morgan Boone may not resemble a gazelle as he roams the outfield pastures."

It was in the minors, however, where Boone clearly distinguished himself. Playing 13 years in the top five circuits—Pacific Coast, International and Texas Leagues, and the American and Southern Associations—Boone compiled a lifetime batting average of .370. That is the best mark in the history of organized baseball. Boone finally called it quits in 1936, when he served as player-manager for Toronto, finishing a minor league career in which he amassed 2,521 hits, 215 home runs and 1,334 runs batted in.

His best season came in 1929. All Boone did for Red Killefer's Missions was to set the all-time record for total bases with 553 in 198 games. He did that by hitting a league-leading .407, and also leading the league in home runs (55), runs batted in (218), runs (195) and hits (323). He was just two hits shy of the organized baseball record for most hits in a season — Paul Strand's 325, set in the high altitude of Salt Lake City. Boone actually did not take the league lead in batting until September when he hit in 20 straight games, raising his average 15 points to .405.

When Boone continued on his tear in 1930 by hitting .448 in the first 83 games, he earned his first trip to the Brooklyn Dodgers, ending his association with the Missions and the Pacific Coast League.

In 1929, Boone and the Seals' Smead Jolley delighted San Francisco baseball fans with their brute power. Though he took a back seat to Boone, Jolley enjoyed another sensational year at the plate, hitting .387 and 35 home runs while driving in 159 runs with his 314 hits.

Jolley's power was one of the few ingredients left over from the 1928 pennant-winning ballclub. Outfielders Earl Averill and Roy Johnson, along with shortstop Hal Rhyne, were lost to the major leagues. Catcher Joe Sprinz and pitchers Oliver Mitchell and Buckshot May could not come to terms and were sold to other minor league ballclubs. The Seals did field another excellent team, filling Rhyne's spot with young Frankie Crosetti and installing Gus Suhr at his natural first base position. During the season, Suhr earned the attention of major league scouts, many of whom called Suhr the PCL's best prospect. The Seals also found room on the roster for a young pitcher named Vernon "Lefty" Gomez. At six-foot-two and 165 pounds, Gomez looked so skinny to Strub that he had milk delivered to the pitcher's home every morning to help fatten him up. On the year Gomez went 18-11 with a 3.43 ERA. Elmer Jacobs (21-11, 3.47 ERA), Curtis Davis (17-13, 3.97 ERA) and Sloppy Thurston (22-11, 4.40 ERA) helped the Seals exceed the expectations of most of the league's sportswriters.

The ballclub finished the first half of the season with a 59-39 record, good enough for second place in both the league and the city.

Killefer's Mission Reds won the first-half pennant despite losing nine straight games in April. The turning point for the Missions came against the Angels at Recreation Park on April 25. The San Francisco club had already dropped the first two games to Los Angeles and appeared well on the way to their tenth straight loss, trailing 6–0 in the bottom of the ninth inning. But the Missions rallied, with doubles by Fuzzy Hufft and Mickey Finn helping them tie the score. Two innings later they pushed across the winning run to end the losing streak. From that point on there was no looking back.

The Missions' performance made the league owners reconsider a preseason vote to discontinue the split-season format. With the Missions threatening to run away with the pennant—thereby hurting late season attendance—the owners declared the ballclub the first-half champions just prior to the Fourth of July.

For San Francisco's "other" team, the first-half title was a satisfying triumph in a town dominated by the Seals. But the season was only half over and there was a team in Southern California with hopes for a flag of its own.

A crowded field

The hasty decision to split the season gave new hope to several teams for the second half. Whereas only four teams played better than .500 baseball in the first half, six teams did so in the second half. Two teams that played poorly all year long—Seattle and Sacramento—would not have been helped if the season had been split every week.

Bill Klepper, the former Portland owner whose 1922 ban from baseball had been lifted, returned to the Pacific Coast League as the owner of the Seattle franchise. Actually, this was Klepper's second stint with the Indians; he had served as their president prior to his departure for Portland. Seattle, despite the bat of Ox Eckhardt (.354, 7 HR, 70 RBI) and the experience of veteran manager Ernie Johnson, finished dead last in the overall standings with a .332 winning percentage. They could not hit (last in the league), field (again, dead last), or pitch. And all year long, Klepper struggled to draw enough fans to the ballpark to make his payroll.

Lew Moreing of Sacramento had much the same problem. Just a year after his team's high-water season, the Senators slipped badly and fan support waned. With his club en route to a 39-64 second-half record, Lew Moreing began jettisoning players in July in a series of cost-cutting moves. Then he threatened to move the franchise to his hometown of Stockton, where his club already played its Sunday morning game. Moreing began playing one week-day game in Stockton as well in 1929. Later he began negotiating the sale of the franchise to a group in San Diego, but that deal quickly fell apart.

Art Koehler and Johnny Monroe again shone for the Senators, and Emil "Irish" Meusel even played for the team for a time, but the club never climbed out of the second division and finished in seventh place overall. Probably of greatest significance to Sacramento fans was that 1929 marked the debut of Tony Freitas, who went on to a three-decade career in the majors and minors. In so doing he became the minor league's winningest left-handed pitcher, and in 1942 he pitched Sacramento to its only Coast League pennant.

Portland started the 1929 season worse than both Sacramento and Seattle, but battled back in the season's second half to finish a respectable fourth with a 57-46 record. The club's 33-66 first-half performance could be blamed on owner Tom Turner, who completely revamped his roster prior to the season and then juggled it almost weekly to find the right combination of players.

While the team's poor play might have warranted such a shuttling of players, the ballclub's roster seldom looked the same from one year to the next. Turner was noted for taking frequent cross-country trips in search of new talent. Adding to the team's identity crisis was Turner's decision prior to the 1929 season to drop the team's Beaver nickname. From now on the franchise would be called the Ducks, Turner declared. But halfway through the season, bowing to chamber of commerce pressure, Turner renamed the team again, dubbing them the Rosebuds. The name Ducks, it was alleged, reflected badly on Portland, suggesting it might receive too much rainfall.

Even if he could not settle on a name, Turner finally did hit on a satisfactory playing combination during the second half and in late August his team vaulted from sixth place to first by winning 16 consecutive games. First baseman Jim Keesey paced the weak-hitting Beavers-Ducks-Rosebuds by hitting .349 with 12 home runs and 124 RBI. Pitchers Roy Mahaffey (21-25, 4.01 ERA) and Curt Fullerton (19-18, 4.50 ERA) were the club's top pitchers on the year, but lack of pitching scotched Portland's hopes for a second-half title.

The Oakland Oaks also made a second-half run for the pennant. All year long they played above average ball, finishing fourth overall with a .549 winning percentage. The most memorable event for the 1929 Oaks came on Thursday, July 11, when Roy Carlyle hit what was unofficially the longest home run in baseball history — 618 feet. The blast came off Missions pitcher Ernie Nevers, the ex–Stanford All-American fullback. The ball landed on the roof of a house at 1212 Park Avenue, outside the Oaks' Emeryville ballpark and was not found until several days later. Carlyle, an outfielder, had an outstanding year, belting 22 home runs and driving in 108 runs on his way to a .348 average. Buzz Arlett once again led Oakland hitters with his typical numbers — .374 average, 39 home runs, 189 runs batted in — but he was challenged by 21-year-old catcher Ernie Lombardi, who batted .366 with 24 home runs and 109 runs batted in. Two years later, Lombardi started his 17-year Hall of Fame career. He played with the Brooklyn Dodgers, Cincinnati Reds, Boston Braves and New York Giants. Also on his way to the majors was second baseman Jimmy Reese who in 1930 would finally rejoin teammate Lyn Lary with the Yankees on the strength of a .337 batting average.

As a team, the Oaks hit .302 and scored 1,034 runs — impressive numbers, but only fifth best in the league. Indeed, the 1929 baseball seemed to have more juice than ever, and the league batting average increased to .302 — the highest in league history.

The Angels set their team batting record that year, hitting .303 and for the first time since 1926 winning more than they lost. They also hit 180 home runs, led by outfielders Wally Berger (40) and Earl Webb (37), first baseman Chick Tolson (28), and second baseman Ray Jacobs (20). In addition to power, the Angels showed speed; Fred Haney stole 56 bases and the recently returned Jigger Statz swiped 37. Angels pitching proved to be the weak point in 1929,

Ernie Nevers (John E. Spalding)

as evidenced by their 4.78 team earned run average. However, Clyde Barfoot somehow managed an 18-12 record on his way to a 314-243 record in the minor leagues. Manager Marty Krug took the heat for his team's 47-52 first-half record and was fired after six and a half years at the helm. He was replaced by Jack Lelivelt, who guided the Angels to a 57-46 second-half record. He managed through the 1936 season, piloting some of the best ballclubs in minor league history.

But in 1929 the Angels had to take a back seat in their own city.

Hooray for Hollywood

Just as the Missions were the "other" team in San Francisco, so were the Stars in Los Angeles. The team bore the name of the nearby movie-star city, but actually played all their home games in Los Angeles. Born in 1926 when Bill Lane moved his Salt Lake franchise out west, the Hollywood ballclub suffered an identity crisis from its inception. Following a warm reception in February 1926 by the Hollywood Chamber of Commerce and the Business Men's Club, Lane almost immediately disagreed with the town's movers and shakers over the name of his team. They wanted the team to be called the Stars, a name that would promote Hollywood's movie and entertainment image. Lane preferred to hang on to the old team name, Bees, and his club opened spring training that first year sporting Bee emblems on their jerseys. Soon, however, Lane relented and agreed to call his club the Stars, but as often as not the club was called by its unofficial moniker—the Sheiks. By any name, the newcomers eventually earned a following, creating a rivalry between the two local teams that grew almost as hot as the relationship between Lane and Wrigley.

Oscar Vitt—"Old Os"—managed the 1929 club, which joined in with the heavy-hitting action that year by hitting a club record .311 and leading the league with 1,233 runs scored. Despite this hitting, the Stars finished in fourth place in the first half.

But the team had been building and was ready for an improved second half. Bill Rumler finally earned reinstatement after his role in the 1919 betting scandal, and at the age of 37 the former PCL batting champion rejoined his former ballclub. Surprising everyone, Rumler picked up where he had left off, compiling the third best batting average in the league, .386. Elias Funk, acquired in May from the Yankees as part of an earlier deal, hit .384, further improving what had been a weak outfield. Also in May, Howard Burkett came from the Angels to take over second base from Mike Maloney who had failed to meet expectations. But the biggest boost to the Stars' hopes came in July when veteran catcher Hank Severeid arrived following his release by Sacramento in a cost-cutting move. Most PCL teams regularly worked two catchers, and the Stars were weak behind Johnny Bassler. When Bassler went down with an injury in August, the move to obtain Severeid became brilliant. The 38-year-old catcher had 15 years of major league experience under his belt, including two World Series, and had helped Sacramento with its 1928 pennant drive; he was able to handle the pressure of another race for the championship. During August and September, Severeid lit up PCL pitchers by hitting .415 and driving in 72 runs in the 79-game stretch run.

Valuable as Severeid turned out to be, the season belonged to Frank Shellenback. As the league's best pitcher, he put together a 26-12, 3.97 ERA season. As always, he was just as masterful at the plate (.322 average, 12 HR, 37 RBI). Paced by this performance and a solidified lineup, the Stars battled throughout the summer and early fall for the second-half crown. It was a particularly heated race; six teams still had a chance as the season wound down. But two teams emerged from the pack. As the season entered its final week, Hollywood clung to a two-game lead over the Missions.

Though they trailed, the Missions may have been in the more enviable position. Their opponent for the seven-game final series was last-place Seattle. Hollywood, on the other hand, had to face a much-improved Portland team. But neither the Stars nor the Missions looked like a team that wanted to win the championship; over the last two weeks of the season, both played only .500 ball. On the last Saturday of the season, the Missions regained some of their earlier momentum when Herman Pillette threw a no-hitter. Pillette walked a man in the first and was perfect the rest of the way in the 4–0 win. San Francisco then won the second game of the doubleheader to close the gap to one game entering the final Sunday doubleheader. The Stars were still in good shape, however, needing only one win to clinch a tie for the pennant. A sweep meant the second-half honors were theirs.

A sweep did, in fact, take place, but it was Portland that did the sweeping, easily defeating the Stars 4–1 and 9–2. As *Los Angeles Times* writer Bob Ray put it: "Unable to win the second-half race for themselves, the Stars were shoved into the playoffs by the Seattle Indians, who conveniently handed the Missions a couple of surprising drubbings."

Hollywood, indeed, backed into the second-half title, but they now had a chance to show the rest of the league that they were a better team than the Missions. The 1929 PCL championship series would begin Tuesday, October 8, in San Francisco.

1929 championship series

With slightly better pitching and fielding, the Missions, on paper, were better balanced and appeared the better team. Yet hitting would be the key to the series, as each team presented a fearsome lineup of batsmen. The Missions led the league with a .319 average and featured two of the game's best hitters in Boone and Hufft. Hollywood could point to its own prowess at the plate, including a .311 team batting average and the league's highest run production. The lineups the two teams fielded promised a close, explosive series:

Mission Reds

Eddie Mulligan, 3b (.279, 3 HR, 56 RBI)

Mickey Finn, 2b (.347, 5 HR, 64 RBI)

Ike Boone, rf (.407, 55 HR, 218 RBI)

Pete Scott, cf (.335, 12 HR, 55 RBI) or

Walter Christensen, cf (.319, 0 HR, 47 RBI)

Jack Sherlock, 1b (.336, 14 HR, 156 RBI)

Fuzzy Hufft, lf (.379, 39 HR, 187 RBI)

Gordon Slade, ss (.302, 16 HR, 115 RBI)

Fred Hofmann, c (.300, 11 HR, 72 RBI)

Herman Pillette (Tony Pirak)

Pitchers

Bert Cole (24-12, 3.45 ERA)
Herman Pillette (23-13, 3.59 ERA)
Bill Hubbell (11-7, 3.79 ERA)
Herb McQuaid (12-4, 4.29 ERA)
Ernie Nevers (7-8, 4.56 ERA)
Dutch Ruether (14-9, 4.71 ERA)
Merton Nelson (17-10, 4.80 ERA)
Harry Krause (7-9, 5.33 ERA)

Hollywood Stars

Dudley Lee, ss (.262, 4 HR, 71 RBI)
Russ Rollings, 3b (.324, 6 HR, 86 RBI)
Elias Funk, cf/lf (.384, 13 HR, 125 RBI)
Hank Severeid, c (.359, 24 HR, 124 RBI)
Johnny Bassler, c (.251, 0 HR, 37 RBI)
Bill Rumler, rf/lf (.386, 26 HR, 120 RBI)
Harry Green, rf/lf (.279, 4 HR, 45 RBI)
Mickey Heath, 1b (.349, 38 HR, 156 RBI)
Cleo Carlyle, cf (.347, 20 HR, 136 RBI)
Howard Burkett, 2b (.242, 5 HR, 53 RBI)

Pitchers

Augie Johns (17-10, 3.89 ERA)
Frank Shellenback (26-12, 3.97 ERA)
Buzz Wetzel (17-15, 4.04 ERA)
George Hollerson (13-13, 4.40 ERA)
Joe Marticorena (9-9, 5.77 ERA)
Walt Kinney (12-12, 4.25 ERA)
Hank Hulvey (14-11, 6.07 ERA)

The Missions put their "on paper" advantages to work in the opening game of the series, posting a 7–2 win as they collected 15 hits and received a strong performance from Dutch Ruether. Gordon Slade's two-run homer in the second off Augie Johns staked the Missions to a 1–0 lead, which they followed with three more in both the third and seventh innings. Finn, Boone, Scott, Hufft, Slade and Hofmann all had two or more hits for the Missions. Ruether gave up nine hits and went the distance. The only blight on the day for San Francisco came off the field; only 2,000 fans turned out at Recreation Park to watch the West Coast's Fall Classic. Disappointingly, none of the three weekday games in San Francisco drew more than 2,000 fans.

In game two, Red Killefer again turned to a left-hander. This time Bert Cole went the entire way to beat the Stars. Cole was not nearly as effective as Ruether, allowing 12 hits and needing a two-run eighth inning rally by his teammates to secure the 8–6 win. A fight between the Missions' Red Baldwin and the Stars' Lester Cook, a fan uprising over a call by umpire Cady and a surprise firecracker outburst added excitement to the proceedings.

On Thursday Herman Pillette returned to the mound for his first appearance since his no-hit performance against Seattle. After holding Hollywood hitless for two innings—extending his streak to 15 innings—

Pillette fell apart. The right-hander surrendered six runs and ten hits in the next three innings, finally departing in the seventh, his team trailing 6–4. Hollywood eventually won 11–5. The hitting hero for the Stars was Cleo Carlyle, whose four for five included two home runs, a triple and four runs batted in. Elias Funk and Johnny Bassler added three hits each, as did pitcher Frank Shellenback who hit a home run and drove in three runs to help his cause.

With the series heading to Los Angeles, the Stars' hopes were looking up. And Shellenback once again turned in a hero's performance in the opener at Wrigley Field. Entering the ninth, the Stars trailed 3–2 with nobody on and two outs. Vitt went to the bench and put Shellenback up to bat as a pinch-hitter. Merton Nelson was on the mound in relief, ready to shut down the Stars and put the Missions in an enviable three games to one series lead. Shellenback, however, refused to play his part in the scenario.

"Frank tied the score with a home run—a tremendous clout far over the left center wall and into the row of little cottages on the other side of the street," is how *San Francisco Chronicle* writer Prescott Sullivan described Shellenback's heroics.

Carlyle followed in the tenth inning with a two-out double that scored Funk to give Hollywood a 4–3 win. In keeping with local custom, jubilant fans showered Funk and the Stars with thousands of seat cushions. The series stood even at two games apiece.

The dramatic victory was tempered by the beaning of Bill Rumler in the eighth inning by a Herb McQuaid fastball. Rumler fell unconscious and was rushed to the hospital for x-rays, but he recovered in time to play in the series finale. The beaning appeared to unnerve McQuaid, who could not find the plate after the incident and left the game in favor of Nelson.

Buzz Wetzel pitched eight strong innings for Hollywood, allowing just eight hits to the Missions, who played without Ike Boone, out with a stomach ache. Hank Hulvey threw two innings of hitless relief to earn the victory.

The Missions' skid continued on Saturday. Though the team garnered 10 hits, it could produce only three runs, falling to the Stars 6–3. Dutch Ruether took the loss, while Augie Johns earned the win. Ruether was bunted out of the box in the sixth inning, when the Stars recognized the pitcher suffered from an injured knee. Harry Green led off with a bunt single and Mickey Heath followed with another. Johnny Bassler then bunted the two runners over, allowing Maloney to hit the sacrifice fly that resulted in the eventual winning run. Hofmann and Slade homered for the Missions, but once again Boone sat out and his bat was sorely missed.

Boone finally returned for the sixth game of the series—a Sunday affair before 10,000 fans. Two of the league's more legendary pitchers squared off: for the Missions, Bert Cole; for the Stars, Frank Shellenback. Spitballer Shellenback had already stemmed the Missions' momentum, pitching and hitting his team to victory in the getaway game in San Francisco and then deflating their hopes with his dramatic homer in game four. Now he had the opportunity to end the Missions' season and earn his team the Pacific Coast League championship.

For seven innings it looked as though Shellenback had met his match in Cole. The two pitchers locked horns for a 3–3 tie entering the bottom of the eighth. Then the Missions fell apart.

Howard Burkett led off the inning with a single to center. Funk then bunted and appeared to run into the ball, but the umpire ruled otherwise. Catcher Red Baldwin alertly picked Burkett off second; however, in the ensuing rundown, Eddie Mulligan threw the ball away and Burkett returned safely to second. Two hitters later, Bill Rumler returned from his beaning by stroking a single to left to drive in a run. Heath then doubled to score two more. Singles by Bassler, Maloney and Lee closed out the hitting, but by now Hollywood led 8–3.

Shellenback cruised through the ninth inning for his second win of the series. Boone's bat had been silenced, 0 for 4. For the series the slugger hit a quiet .333 (6 for 18, 1 double, 2 RBI).

It was a disappointing ending for Boone and the Missions, who for the season played the coast's best baseball. In the championship series they hit .312 (versus Hollywood's .324), but came up short in the clutch—a fact as much attributable to Frank Shellenback as any shortcoming on the part of the Missions. After the game more than 2,000 Hollywood fans milled about outside the clubhouse. As each Star player emerged, he was greeted by a rousing cheer. For the players and fans the win was sweet. For 69-year-old Bill Lane it was even sweeter. After his bitter feud with Wrigley and 14 years without a PCL pennant, redemption was finally his. "Boss Bill Lane had a big smile on his weather-beaten face tonight," wrote Sullivan in the *Chronicle*.

For Hollywood the 1929 championship signalled a bright start for the 1930s. Lane's club went on to win another pennant in 1930, the first-half title in 1931, and then, as the San Diego Padres, the 1937 championship. The Missions, on the other hand, never came close again, finishing above .500 only once more. Their 101 wins in 1934 were good enough for second place, but the club finished an amazing 35½ games behind the Los Angeles Angels, one of the greatest minor league ballclubs of all time. Even though the future for both clubs was markedly different, the 1929 season gave each respect in their cities that they had never before enjoyed.

As a league the PCL had overcome scandal, internecine politics and isolation from the East Coast power structure to grow in stature as the 1920s progressed, becoming the preeminent minor league in the land. Soon the nation suffered the Great Depression, and a decade later world war. The Pacific Coast League would survive the arrival of the farm system and the all-but-mortal blow of major league relocation to its two largest cities in the 1950s.

But these events were yet to come. As darkness fell on the Pacific Coast League's final day of 1929, the future had never been brighter.

1929 Final Standings

First-half standings

	W	L	Pct.
Missions	63	35	.643
San Francisco	59	39	.602
Oakland	56	43	.566
Hollywood	52	47	.525
Los Angeles	47	52	.475
Sacramento	46	53	.465
Seattle	39	60	.394
Portland	33	66	.333

Second-half standings

	W	L	Pct.
Hollywood	61	42	.592
Missions	60	43	.583
Los Angeles	57	46	.553
Portland	57	46	.553
San Francisco	55	48	.534
Oakland	55	48	.534
Sacramento	39	64	.379
Seattle	28	75	.272

Team batting leaders

Average:	Missions—.319
Runs:	Hollywood—1,233
HRs:	San Francisco—193

Individual batting leaders

At-bats:	Dudley Lee, Hollywood—848
Average:	Ike Boone, Missions—.407

Runs: Gus Suhr, San Francisco—196
Hits: Ike Boone, Missions—323
2B: Buzz Arlett, Oakland—70
3B: Ox Eckhardt, Seattle—17
HR: Ike Boone, Missions—55
RBI: Ike Boone, Missions—218
Total bases: Ike Boone, Missions—553
Stolen bases: Fred Haney, Los Angeles—56

Individual pitching leaders

Winning percentage: Frank Shellenback, Hollywood .684 (26-12)
Games won: Frank Shellenback, Hollywood—26
Games lost: Roy Mahaffey, Portland—25
Most games: Fred Pipgras, Seattle—58
Most shutouts: Elmer Jacobs, San Francisco—4
                         Roy Mahaffey, Portland—4
Most complete games: Roy Mahaffey, Portland—32
Most innings: Roy Mahaffey, Portland—370
ERA: Lefty Gomez, San Francisco—3.43

Chapter 12

In Their Own Words

More than a thousand players graced Coast League ballparks during the 1920s. Here, in their own words, is how six of these players described their experiences during interviews conducted in 1992.

Tony Freitas
Born: May 5, 1908
Pitcher
Sacramento Senators, 1929–1932; Portland Beavers, 1933; Sacramento Solons, 1937–1942, 1946–1950

(Freitas is the winningest left-handed pitcher in minor league history, compiling a 342-238 lifetime record.)

There was a fella down around Mill Valley, a cab driver who was an old semipro ballplayer. He used to come up and do a lot of duck hunting in the Sacramento area where Buddy Ryan was. Of course Buddy Ryan was manager of the Sacramento Solons. So he got to talking to Buddy Ryan and says there's a young fella over in Mill Valley I'd like to have you look at. This was in 1928 when I first reported to spring training. I tried out and then they sent me to Phoenix in the Arizona State League. The next year I came up to the Solons.

My first year in 1928 I made $200 a month. I do not know if that was typical for a young player then or not. I'm out of the sticks of Mill Valley, just a country boy. I was just glad to put on the uniform and get paid for the game I'd play for nothing. I loved the game, I loved to pitch and I loved to get out there and compete.

I never did throw what you'd call a good fastball. A curveball with good control and a changeup. I'd throw my fastball not even fifty percent of the time. A changeup off the fastball, then maybe a breaking ball. The changeup was my best pitch in fooling a hitter and getting him off stride. The secret to hitting is timing. So the secret of pitching is getting them off of time. And that's by changing speeds.

Tony Freitas (John E. Spalding)

You also have to throw strikes so you're ahead of the hitter. When they get ahead of you they can look for a certain pitch and then it is not good for the pitcher. But if you throw the first ball over for a strike you can work the corners and move the ball around.

The PCL was a pretty good league. In fact they called it a third major league at one time. A real hitter's league.

I had a chance in the American League and a chance in the National League and I never felt good back there. The heat and humidity were terrible. Could not get any sleep. In 1942 Branch Rickey said how do you feel about going back to the big leagues? And I said Mr. Rickey I like it here, this is my backyard, I like the climate here, the people and everything about it. I'm not interested in going back to the big leagues. He said "I'm glad you told me because I came out here to purchase you and take you back to St. Louis."

You gotta be lucky to have a career as long as I did. I was a very lucky boy. I did not have the ability some of the other pitchers had but I was lucky.

Carl Dittmar
Born: March 21, 1901
Shortstop
San Francisco Seals, 1927; Los Angeles Angels, 1928–1938

I'd been playing in Augusta, Georgia, and I was recognized by Ty Cobb—he used to live down there—and he recommended me to the Seals. I was about 25. Nick Williams was my first manager for the Seals. He was all right, but I could hardly get used to him because I was only there one year. He and I roomed together some of the time, but he hardly ever stayed in his room. They used to move us players around, we never had a regular roommate. I suppose they had a reason for that.

Recreation Park was a big wooden structure. The first time I played there I thought the outfield fences were awfully close. I remember the Booze Cage. We had to walk past it to get our bats. It was just a screen, chickenwire, you know, in front of the fans and they used to throw dirt at us and call us everything. It was mostly all men as I recall, drinking, hollering and carrying on. They gave everybody a bad time, not just the visiting team, but they were not too hard on me when I played for the Seals.

I was tickled to death to get to the Pacific Coast. The chance to jump that high, not many people do it. My first year I was just getting acclimated. I did not think much of anything, just playing. I was sold by the Seals to the Angels. I do not have the slightest idea how much they sold me for. Not very much, not in those days.

In Los Angeles I roomed with Jigger Statz for about five years. He was a great outfielder, one of the best. A very, very nice fellow. He hoped to play in the majors, but as the years went by and he was not as active it got harder. It did not frustrate him though. He was easy going and took it in stride. Jigger really stands out above everybody I played with. I think he was the best player back then. O'Doul was quite a player, too. He was a very good hitter. I could never understand why he was not in the big leagues at that time.

Truck Hannah was another player. He was a quiet, easy going guy, but he would get mad. He was a big man, you know, about six-foot-two or six-foot-three and about 200 pounds. He had a big, real heavy catcher's mitt. I never saw anything like it in all of baseball. He could never catch a ball one-handed—not with that glove. Had a big bat, too. I used a 33-ounce bat, about 32 inches. I used a Doak fielding glove. Made by Bill Doak. We did not have gloves of different sizes in those days. They were all small.

We had a very big, very hot rivalry with Hollywood. Not like in San

Francisco. There was not much of a rivalry between the Seals and the Missions. San Francisco was mainly a Seals town. But the Angels always filled up the ballpark when we played Hollywood.

One park I did not like to play in was Oakland. Emeryville ballpark. It was strange, but I never played well there. I do not know why. I wish I could have found out why, then maybe I would have done better there.

I think we could have beaten over half the clubs in the big leagues in 1933 and 1934. We had great ballclubs. Before that we were good, too. A lot of our fellas went up to the majors.

I thought I'd get a chance to play in the majors, but the opportunity never presented itself. I had a couple of good years and thought I might go to the Cubs—we belonged to the Cubs. But they had two shortstops so I never had a chance. I played nine years in the league and was treated very nice. I was with the right club.

Dallas Locker
Born: July 21, 1898
First base
Vernon Tigers, 1921–1923

Hell, we used to play a 196 game schedule. We shared Washington Park with Los Angeles. One week we'd be the home team, then the next week they would be. Then the team would go up to Sacramento and play seven games, then spend a week in San Francisco. Always we played seven games. Travel on Monday and doubleheaders on Sundays. After San Francisco we'd go up to Portland and Seattle and then Salt Lake.

Salt Lake had this crackerbox ballpark by today's standards. One game Pete Schneider hit all these home runs. Five of them. I remember the game because I hit a home run and do not think I ever hit another home run in the Coast League.

They say [Vernon owner] Eddie Maier and his old lady were worth $4 million and $8 million dollars—chicken feed nowadays. Anyway, I remember he used to sit over our dugout. About the fourth or fifth inning we'd look over there and he'd be asleep. But he was a good guy, good to the players. We all just called him Ed.

Our manager Bill Essick was one of the smartest guys I ever ran across in baseball. And I played in the Texas League, the Southern League and the Coast. The greatest manager I ever played for. He never did instruct me too much, though I remember he gave me a compliment once on my hitting— after he chewed my ass all the way to first base.

We were a hustling team. Vernon used to outdraw Los Angeles because we were more entertaining. Especially our second baseman Carl Sawyer. He

Gus Suhr (John E. Spalding)

was quite a clown. If we were up six or eight runs in a game, he'd catch the ball behind his back. Never missed one that I saw. The fans loved it and they never knew what he was going to do.

Another player I remember was Ping Bodie. He came down from the Yankees in 1922 and was my roommate. He and I would break curfew together. Looking back, I'd probably have been a better baseball player if I had any sense.

Gus Suhr
Born: January 3, 1906
Infield
San Francisco Seals, 1926–1929

My father and mother came from the old country. They did not go for my playing baseball too much. Neither of my parents knew a ball from a strikeout. Sometimes I had to sneak playing ball. Of course my father died before I got to be a professional baseball player.

When I could find time I played, but I had a paper route every day. I'd deliver the *Bulletin* in the afternoon, then on Sunday mornings I had the *Examiner* route. I would like to have played a little more, but those routes mixed me up.

Sometimes I played on Sundays. That was when they had a lot of Sunday baseball there in San Francisco. They had some good teams. Very good. I never played in the big games, I was just a small kid. I played with the Sunset Federals and the Midgets—a fellow named Anson Orr had the club.

A fellow, a special policeman, I cannot remember his name, he saw me playing in the Sunday leagues and signed me up with the Seals.

Charlie Graham was the fella that signed me up. He seemed to be a nice fella. A fella by the name of Putnam—he was part owner of the Seals also. He was one of these jolly guys, he was a big shot, you know, trying to help somebody. Doc Strub was the other owner. I did not know much about him. Graham knew more about baseball than the other two put together. He had the most say about signing players.

At that time in the Pacific Coast League, when I was playing, most of the big league players came down to play out here. So there was a lot of good ballplayers, believe me.

I started in 1925, you know, and I was shipped out to Quincy in the Three-I League as a first baseman. And that year I never played anything else but first base. Then in 1926 they were kind of weak at shortstop on the Seals. They had two fellas who were a little older than me. Johnny Saypo and Nobby Paynter I believe were their names. Gee whiz, I could not play first base because Bert Ellison was the manager and that was his position. At that point it was about all he could play. So I just hung around the bench for two weeks.

Then we went to Oakland. We had a seven-game series, we played all week, you know. On Sunday, Bert says to me "Suhr, we're short at shortstop. Would you play there?" So I went out and played a helluva game, two games in fact. Sunday morning I had one putout and six assists, I remember that. And in the afternoon game I had seven assists. No errors.

We had an off-day Monday, then we played L.A. Tuesday in Recreation Park. Jigger Statz, I'll never forget this, he hit the first ball down to me. I got it and then I threw that son of a gun over Bert Ellison's head plenty wild. Then I was off! Then I went to third base. Then to second base. I could never get to first base, though. Not with the manager playing the position.

I played in every game one year—201 games. And the year before that I played in 191. I think that was about all they played. Gosh, they played an awful lot of games.

I remember one game in the 1928 playoffs against Sacramento. It was the last game I think. We had them three games to one and we needed one more game to win it. We were playing up in Sacramento. Doc Crandall was pitching against us. This game went a long time, a tie ball game. It was 3 to 3 going into the ninth. I remember Earl Averill getting a base hit that put us ahead 4 to 3. And then I got a base hit that made it 5 to 3. They did not score in the bottom of the ninth and we were the champions of the league that year.

Earl Averill had to be one of the best players I ever played with. Yeah, I'd say that was right. Roy Johnson, another outfielder, he was real good, too.

Some of the better players I played against? Gee, let me see, Sacramento, they had a catcher Koehler and a pitcher Keating. Oakland had Jimmy Reese and Lyn Lary. Hollywood had Johnny Kerr and Dudley Lee, I remember them. Very good. In L.A., when Dittmar left our club—he was a shortstop— he was very good. Jigger Statz was good. There was Fuzzy Hufft in Seattle, he could hit like the devil, but he could not field and he had a poor throwing arm. The Missions had Swanson in center field—he was quite a ballplayer.

I guess Shellenback was one of the toughest pitchers. He was a spitball pitcher. Then there was Krause. Lefty Vinci, a Sacramento boy, was pretty good, too.

I loved the game, really. It was not for the money. I liked making money, but that was not the reason I played. Some of those boys in the majors made $700, $800 a month. You know, that was good money in those days. I was going for a big $175 when I first broke in the Coast League.

It was a lot of fun. I had a tough time not playing first base for a couple of years. That was kinda rough. But I'd have to say I'm glad I played then compared to nowadays.

Lou Almada
Born: 1908
Outfielder
Seattle, 1929–31

(Lou Almada's brother, Mel, was the first Mexican-born player to play in the major leagues.)

I had been up with the New York Giants a season or two before as a pitcher. I signed a contract with Sam Crawford when I was still in high school. He saw me pitch during the winter league. I graduated in February 1927 and was playing in the winter league in November, December before that in Brea. I won two championships at L.A. High. I mean our team did, of course, but I did all the pitching. Anyway, he saw me pitch three games in the winter league. I pitched a one-hitter, a two-hitter and a one-hitter and all were

Lou Almada (Don Hazelwood)

shutouts. It so happens that two of the pitchers I beat were young big league prospects—a fella named Foster and another named Archie Campbell.

Crawford thought after watching me pitch three games that I could go up there to the big leagues and pitch. So he called me and said that he had talked to McGraw and he offered me a contract. Crawford was to get $2500 and I was to get $2500 if I was retained by the club. And then I'd get $750 a month, which seemed like a million dollars to me then.

When this contract came in both my mother and my older sister told me I should take it, not go to college because my father was in debt. He worked for the Mexican consulate. He was up there in San Francisco, straightening the place out up there. But instead of two or three months, they kept him there for three to four years. He used to come down on the Lark twice a month to see the family. He just accrued some debt staying there in the hotel. My dad told me not to listen and to go to college. I was going to go to USC, where I was a waterboy three years as a kid. We lived just a block and a half from the school.

But I decided to sign the deal with the Giants and did extremely well during the week at Sarasota, Florida. But I got caught in a sleet storm and I almost caught pneumonia and had to stay there in the hotel for two days while the club went on. I did not tell anybody what happened but I got soaking wet and could not find a car back into town, so I had to walk two hours into town. The doctor took care of me for 40 hours.

I took a train and then a ferry to New Jersey to join the club for an exhibition game. When I joined the ballclub about May 19 or 20 up there in New Haven, the president of the club and the manager McGraw met me at the train and told me you're pitching today. I pitched and had an easy game. I won 7 to 2. The next day Lindbergh flew the Atlantic. We were in about the third or fourth inning when they announced that Lindbergh was flying to Paris.

How I got into the Coast League? I was playing the outfield there for the San Clemente Cubs or whatever they called them in 1928.

I was working for the engineers setting up new tracts of land in San Clemente. Walking over those hills in the back of San Clemente put me in terrific shape. Ernie Johnson, who was the manager of Seattle and who lived in Laguna, must have gone over and seen a couple of those games. I did not really know that at the time. But I was hitting well and he offered me a contract.

I joined the club as one of twelve outfielders for spring training. Three of them were sure to stay there—Dave Barbee, a fella named Wade and I forget what the other one's name was, but I know they were regulars. And among the rest of us there was one position open. One position for eight of us.

I'd go out to practice an hour early and stay an hour late, shagging balls or just trying to learn something about baseball from the coaches. Anyway, I made the team. I did not get to play much the first three weeks or so. I started playing after someone was hurt and I remember standing in about three inches of water. This was in the old Rainier Ballpark. A fella named Dugdale ran that ballpark. It sloped off into low spots. And it rained for an inch and a half or two during the evening and morning, but that first game I played they had nine thousand people there.

I met Mr. Dugdale. To me he was a fat old man. I was 20, 21 years old and he was a man in his sixties and very heavy. I remember vividly a ball being foul tipped and went through the back screen and hit Mr. Dugdale right on the nose. They had to carry him out. He was knocked out. The backstop was all rusted because they were not repairing anything up there because they did not have any money. He always used to sit behind home plate, but I remember him not coming back after that for a couple of weeks.

The first year I had a place up there at the Vance Hotel where everybody stayed. Six rooms were adjoining and anybody could walk into your room. I began to notice my toothbrush would be wet and I had not used it. And I was missing a handkerchief or two. So I decided to move out. Mr. Gildersleeve, who owned the Benjamin Franklin Hotel, told me he had a room I'd like on the second floor there and that he'd give me a real good deal. So I moved over there. Charlie Falk from Santa Clara came up in the summer to join the ballclub, moved in and helped me pay for half the room.

They gave me the name of "Ladies Day Louie" there. A fella named Blake had a radio sports program for half an hour [and he] was staying at the Benjamin Franklin — he and his wife. During the summer I was beginning to play and I was hitting the ball well. I did not do much early in the week, but Ladies Day was Thursday and Friday. It was just young people, people from the university who did not have anything else to do. There were not that many jobs around then, especially after the crash. We'd get five or six thousand people out there because all it would cost them was ten cents. I'd hit real good during those Ladies Days, just by coincidence. I remember hitting a double to win one game, a home run another time, and a single one other time — all in the clutch. Seemed like I always got three or four hits. So this fella Blake told me, "Whenever it's Ladies Day you do so well. You must be a ladies man. I got a name for you — Ladies Day Louie."

That name stuck with me even after I left Seattle. I'd come back to visit sometimes and they'd say "Ladies Day Louie's in town."

My first year I was in 98 or 100 games and I hit pretty well for a rookie. Then the next year I was a regular playing center field. Oscar Eckhardt was a fella who hit .400 a couple of times I was there. Could not field worth a darn. In fact, some of the cartoons in the paper would draw a basket on his head and say something like "Oscar, this is what you should have out there."

Bill Klepper owned the ballclub when I was there. Klepper was a short, little fat man. Very short and quite fat and bald. Nice person, but nervous. He just could not pay his players. My father was not working then, so I sent money home. On paydays, I'd tell a cab driver to be ready and after the games I would not even shower. I'd take my uniform off, put on my clothes and get in the cab and head for the Horton Bank. The first six or seven checks could be cashed, but after that there wasn't enough money.

If they could not cash your check, we'd usually get an advance from the hotel until Klepper earned or borrowed enough money to pay us. That's the way it went on even when my brother Mel was up there. My brother wired Landis telling him that he had not been paid in several months. Landis wired him back and said that "if you're not paid in 24 hours consider yourself a free agent."

Boston was about to buy him and he could have made himself some money. Well, somebody called Klepper and told him that my brother was going to be a free agent. So Klepper brought cash over and paid Mel all he owed him. About four days later, he sold him to Boston for $25,000. Klepper was able to catch up on his debts and pay off the rest of the players with that.

Klepper did work hard to keep the club going. He was a dedicated man who put everything he had into the club and he was not taking much for himself. We got paid every fifteen days. When we had good weekend crowds we'd be all right. If not then we were in trouble. There were times there that if we did not have Ladies Day, we'd have only seven or eight hundred people. Then the weekends if we were playing one of the better clubs — like the Los Angeles club or the San Francisco club — we'd get a better turnout. If we played a club that was down like Sacramento or the Missions or Oakland we would not draw. It was an interesting time.

Dolph Camilli
Born: April 23, 1907
First Baseman
San Francisco Seals, 1926–27; Sacramento Solons, 1929–1933

There was not much you could do in those days for fun after the games. You had to play ball and you had to take care of yourself. We'd go swimming and when I was playing in Sacramento we'd go rent a boat and use the motor out on the river. And all season we used to follow the movies and the picture world. You had a lot of good movies, you know the old timers. Great movie actors, some which we'd meet when we were down in L.A.

Ballplayers were not really thought of as celebrities, but we were well thought of. We had a good following, but it was not like it is today. I used to walk right down Market Street and no one knew me. In New York, though, I could walk out of the subway and would not walk fifty feet and they'd know who I was. So there's the difference in the minor and majors. There was quite a bit of difference between the two. Major league ballplayers, geez, when I was a kid I thought they were invincible.

I thought the Pacific Coast League was a very good league and it was tough to break into that class of ball. In those days there were a lot of players who were in that league that never got out — they should have made the majors, but they did not have enough room in the majors then. They just picked the cream of the crop and left the rest there that could have played in the majors.

We had six spitball pitchers in the league. In those days they were allowed. Shellenback, he was a major league pitcher in the minors, I'll tell you. He could pitch. All those spitball pitchers were tough, they had good ones and it was legal. They loaded 'em up so much you could see the stuff flying off the ball when they delivered it. Not like your modern day spitball pitcher—they put enough on there so they do not get caught. Shellenback was a great athlete, too, a good hitter. He could pitch, he could do everything. He belonged in the big leagues, no doubt about it.

The Coast League had a lot of major league players but I do not think it was a third major league. Some of the players were on the way down. They were good, but. . .

Naturally, everybody wanted to go to the big leagues. That was where the money was. In the big leagues you got maybe twice as much as you'd get in the minors, and even that was not a heck of a lot. In those days they did not pay that kind of money. If you got to the big leagues and made five and six thousand dollars a year that would be a great starting salary. In the minors you were lucky if you made $500 a month. Some of them got more if they came down from the big leagues, they'd get a better salary because of their experience. Some of them would get a thousand or so, but very few did.

Yeah, I remember how I got signed to the big leagues. A guy named Doyle, he was the Coast League scout for the Cubs, he'd seen me. Then they sent Pants Rowland out to double check on me. He followed me and decided he liked what he saw and they made a deal for me late in the year in 1933 for 1934 delivery. They were gonna pay Sacramento $25,000 for me. They agreed to give the ballclub $12,500 when I reported, and then $12,500 if they kept me through the month of May, the way I understood it.

Well, it turned out that a month before the 1933 season was over they wanted to know if I'd report right then and there. I was glad to go, so I went up in '33 for three weeks. The Cubs turned around and mailed Sacramento a check for the full amount.

I was only with the Cubs a short time. I liked the Cubs, the organization. I liked the fans, they were great, but I did not stay there long. Mr. Veeck—not Bill Veeck, Jr., his father—he was the general manager of the Cubs, but he died the winter after my first season. I liked him and I know I would have stayed with the Cubs if he stayed alive. Anyway, he was not there the following year, 1934, and I was going good, I thought. Charlie Grimm was still playing first base. I'd play a short time, then he'd play—back and forth. Finally, they decided they wanted the experienced ballplayer and they had a chance to get the first baseman from the Phillies for me and they traded me. So that was that.

I started playing when I was eight, nine years old, and that's about all I'd do was baseball. It is a sport that demands a long-term education so to speak. My mother encouraged me to play as a kid, but my father did not get too excited over it. He thought we kids should go to work. My mother liked for us to go out and play, you know, she knew we enjoyed it.

When I was a kid I suppose I hoped to be a ballplayer, but I thought it was too far out of reach. I could not imagine. I mean pro ballplayers were men.

Even the guys I started playing with were men and there were very few kids among 'em.

I do not know if he discovered me, but Nick Williams signed me for the Seals. Williams started talking to me about playing pro ball. Naturally, I wanted to play and so we put together a good contract. They gave me exactly what I asked for. It was a good contract. I got a little money to sign and what they called an iron-clad contract in those days. They had to give me the money they signed me for the whole year. In those days that was kind of rare; today it seems to be the norm.

Williams became the manager later on. As a matter of fact I played for him up in the Utah-Idaho League. I was up there in Logan, Utah, the Seals had a farm team there. I was up there part of both years. Later on he was manager of the Seals when I came back. He was not a good manager in my opinion. The guy was, I do not know how to explain it, he was not considered a good manager, not by me.

He did not even have signs. To give signs he'd holler out and clap his hands and stuff like that, instead of having regular signs like the other teams. Smart players playing against us picked up the signs pretty easy.

I remember the Seals' owners very well. I hate to say what I think of Doc Strub. I did not think much of him. He was a shrewd businessman and he treated the ballplayers — at least he treated me — badly. He was all for himself and for the money. I had a case of tonsillitis up at spring training and Nick Williams told me to go back to the city to have it taken care of. He said the Seals would take care of it, but they never did. Every time they would get the doctor's bill they would refuse it. The next thing I know they had an agency out after me to collect the money. That was Strub that did that. I do not have much regard for him. That was a helluva way to treat a ballplayer.

Putnam was one of the three. When you went in to speak contract, the three of them would be in there and they'd pick you to pieces. But Putty later on, came over and spoke to me when I was in Sacramento. He shook my hand and said I was going great and looked good and he was very nice.

Of course, Charlie Graham was a real quiet man, a real nice man. He was the baseball person, he played ball. A real fatherly type man. Charley was a good person.

The Seals? Some of the greatest characters! We had Walter Mails for one thing. Walter was quite a fella. A real good guy and he had a lot of energy. I liked Walter. He was cocky and he could be very insulting in a lot of ways to people. Oh, you know, just talking. He thought nothing about telling you what he thought of you, whether he did not like you or if you dressed funny or something. Mails mainly relied on his fastball. He did not have much of a curve, and very seldom threw a change of pace. He was a guy who could really fire the ball and there were very few who threw any harder than Walter.

They stuck that nickname on him, Duster, because he supposedly threw at a lot of hitters. But when I was in Sacramento later on I do not remember him throwing at any hitters. He might have moved them back a little, dusted them off, not really throwing at them. A pitcher has to do that if he wants to get control of the ballgame, unless you've got outstanding stuff like Walter Johnson. He never said a word they said, and he never threw at anybody. Did not have to. He just threw it by everybody. Most pitchers are not that great so you gotta move the hitter back every once in a while, or knock 'em down.

There was not too much of that really in the Coast League. We had more of that when I was at Brooklyn, we had beefs with every club in the league.

Bert Ellison was the manager when I joined the club in 1926. Bert was a good guy, a good ballplayer and a pretty good manager. He got disgusted with the team—I do not know what happened—and he quit right then and there right in the middle of the season. That's when they called me back from Logan, Utah, to join the team. And I started right away.

Then we had O'Doul, who was a very colorful player, a great ballplayer. Lefty was a great guy and very well liked by everybody.

We had a great hitting outfield. We had big Smead Jolley, who just passed away recently. Smead was a big, easy going guy. I do not think I saw Smead ever get mad at anybody. He sure hit the ball hard and had a lot of power. Jolley was one of the hardest hitters I saw. And he was a bad-ball hitter. He could hit 'em off his shoetops or up around his head. A big strong guy who could swing the bat, not a good outfielder, but he could swing the bat. He was only up in the majors for a very short time. A lot of good hitters in those days did not stay up there. Ike Boone was another one with the Missions. Same type of hitter, a big strong guy who could not hit in the majors and there's two or three others like that. Fuzzy Hufft, he was good in that small park, but you put him in a big park and he could not hit good. There were quite a few of those kind of guys.

The Seals also had outfielders Roy Johnson and Earl Averill, a young fella who came from the Northwest—he's in the Hall of Fame. He was a real good outfielder, good hitter, great fielder. Earl was a good guy. He was kind of quiet, but he was a determined person. He just went about doing his business, doing the things he had to do. He was very good with the bat. Good fielder, too.

Recreation Park had a short right field that favored the left-handed hitters. I played in a couple of big league parks later that were very similar: in Philadelphia, the Baker Bowl, and at Brooklyn, Ebbets Field, the very short right field and the high screen. But they had their own characteristics, of course. People loved it because you had all these balls hit against the fence and all that. Here's these balls popping for doubles. Even the Polo Grounds was a park altogether different than any other park I've ever seen.

The clubhouse at Rec Park was just an old two-story building out in center field. The second story was the home club's clubhouse. It was all under a roof, no fancy paint job or anything. I've seen barns that were just as good. And then the visiting clubhouse was downstairs. We had about three showers.

I liked Sacramento after I went up there, but as a visiting player it was a tough park to play in. They had a stiff wind coming in over the right field fence. There were not too many balls hit over that fence. Of course left field at that time was a little easier, and later on as the ball got livelier it became a home run park for right-handed hitters. I do not recall seeing 20 balls hit over the right field fence all year—and I used to hit about half of them—that included our club and the visiting club.

Lew Moreing owned the Sacramento team. Lew was a great person, a real nice man. Wonderful guy. Treated his players terrifically. He was for the ballplayers. I can truthfully say that Lew Moreing was the finest owner I ever met. He had the players' interest at heart. He could not pay much money because they did not draw that many people. He was putting what money he did make from the ballclub into wheat. He had a farm down in Stockton and he lost it all. The poor man, as old as he was, had a silver mine up in the Sierra and went up and tried to work that but he died broke. It was a darn shame. A wonderful man.

I enjoyed playing in the Coast League very much. I met my wife up in Sacramento and the Coast League brought you as close to the big leagues as you can get. The difference between the big leagues and the Coast League was not that great. The only difference was that in the big leagues you saw a good pitcher mostly every day, where in the Coast League you did not. It was a good class of ball.

Chapter 13

The All-1920s Team

Imagine an all-star team for which Hall of Famers Earl Averill, Ernie Lombardi or Tony Lazzeri were eligible but not selected. The fact that these players did not make the All-1920s Pacific Coast League team shows how good the league really was — and how difficult it was to select the team. There were simply too many good players to choose from.

As is the case when selecting any all-star team, worthy players are left off. Players like Jigger Statz, called by many the greatest minor league outfielder ever, could not make either the first or second team. Statz's stature grew during the 1930s as he maintained a level of performance and skill that few could ever match.

Choosing an outfield from among the PCL's greatest hitters was not easy. In fact, virtually every position presented difficult choices for the four committee members. For example, shortstop Tony Lazzeri, whose 1925 season (.355, 60 HR, 222 RBI, 202 Runs) is now legend, and who enjoyed a great career in the majors, was not chosen; Hal Rhyne and Ray French outperformed Lazzeri in the Coast League during the 1920s. Still other worthy players did not meet the minimum selection criterion of playing at least three years in the PCL during the decade.

Difficult as the decisions were, the task was still enjoyable for the selection committee, which was comprised of four men with expertise and interest in Pacific Coast League history:

Dick Beverage — president, Pacific Coast League Historical Society and author Dick Beverage attended his first PCL game in 1946. He became an Oaks fan during the years of Casey Stengel and still finds it difficult to understand why the Athletics did not change their nickname when they moved to Oakland in 1968. In 1987, he founded the Pacific Coast League Historical Society, which has grown to more than 500 members. He is the author of book-length team histories of the Los Angeles Angels and Hollywood Stars and is currently researching a history of the San Francisco Missions.

Dick Dobbins — historian and author Dobbins saw his first PCL game in 1945, and has attended hundreds of games up and down the coast. Dick has an outstanding collection of memorabilia, papers and documents chronicling the history of the Pacific Coast League. Dick has written many articles on the history of the league and recently published a book on San Francisco Bay Area baseball history.

Scott Mackey — author As the author of this book, Mackey has been researching minor league baseball for several years and has also written several articles on California minor league teams and players. He is a member of the Society for American Baseball Research, the Pacific Coast League Historical Society and the National Association of Baseball Writers and Broadcasters.

Bill Weiss — statistician and author As the preeminent minor league statistician, Bill has been compiling baseball statistics since 1948. He was the official statistician for the Pacific Coast League from 1950 through 1988. He merged his statistician business with the old Howe News Bureau to form Howe Sportsdata International in 1989. Since 1989, he has been the Pacific Coast League Historian. He has also been associated with the California League since 1949, the Pioneer League since 1952, and the Northwest League since 1955.

Each committee member was asked to use the following criteria in selecting the All-1920s team:

1. The player must have competed in at least three seasons in the PCL during the 1920s. Subsequent or previous performance in the PCL or other league (including majors) should not be considered.

2. The player must have demonstrated consistent, high-quality play.

3. The player must have been very valuable to the success of his ballclubs.

Beyond these basic criteria, each committee member used his own perspective, judgment and standards.

A major criterion Dick Beverage employed was how the player contributed to winning. He cited Kilduff and Rhyne as good examples. "They excelled during three Seals pennants. The same applies for pitchers Wieser Dell with Vernon, McWeeny with the Seals, and Elmer Jacobs, who was consistent and the ace of the 1926 Angels."

Of some of his other choices, Beverage wrote, "No one really stands out at first base. Strand's numbers are inflated at Salt Lake City. I like Eldred's career numbers."

"Tough choices!" is how Bill Weiss described selecting his All-1920s team. "I tried to take defensive ability and performance into consideration, especially with infielders. At third base, for example, Eddie Mulligan didn't hit as well as Brazill or others, but he was the best fielder over a period of years, an excellent base runner and a leader on the field."

In selecting Slade and Rhyne over Lazzeri at shortstop, Weiss noted that the future Hall of Famer was next to last in fielding among regular shortstops in 1925. "Also, 39 of his 60 homers were in Salt Lake—enough said! I tend to downgrade all of Salt Lake hitting performances to a degree.

"Very hard to leave off players like Reese, Kamm, French, Statz, Kremer, Gregg, Krause and Pillette."

Dick Dobbins echoed Weiss's sentiment. "This was a more difficult task than I had presumed. How can one leave the likes of Ernie Lombardi and Earl Averill off the list? It wasn't easy, but there were more deserving. It was difficult limiting performance to just the decade. Vean Gregg, Chester Chadbourne and others were great players, but not in the 1920s. I was surprised at how many solid pitchers the Solons had, though none qualified for my top eight. Too bad they didn't play for the Tigers or the Seals."

Selecting players

Each committee member selected the following number of players: six outfielders, eight pitchers, and two players for each of the remaining positions including utility. Selected players were ranked within their position (e.g. first, second, etc.) by each member.

The number one player at a position named by a committee member received 10 points, the number two player nine points, etc. The point totals of all four committee members were then added together and the player receiving the most points at a position (top three outfielders and top four pitchers) was named to the first team. Runners-up were named to the second team and anyone receiving points earned Honorable Mention.

When the ballots were tabulated and the team selected, the only unanimous selection was at catcher, where Sacramento's Art Koehler was the choice. The toughest competition came at second base, where Johnny Kerr and Pete Kilduff each earned 20 points, while Jimmy Reese was only two points behind. Johnny Monroe and Paddy Siglin also received votes.

Most notable about the first team is that 10 of the 15 spots are filled by players who played for the San Francisco Seals. "I'm a bit distressed at the 'weight' of the Seals," wrote Dobbins about his choices. "But of course they did win four pennants." Simply put, the Seals consistently fielded the best players, dominating the all-star teams in the 1920s. It should not be a surprise, then, that they dominate a team chosen some seven decades later.

Following are the players selected as the Pacific Coast's best of the 1920s. Their point total is in parentheses, with a maximum possible score of 40.

The First Team (points received—maximum 40)

First base:	Bert Ellison (39)
Second base: (tie)	Johnny Kerr (20)
	Pete Kilduff (20)

Third base: Eddie Mulligan (38)
Shortstop: Hal Rhyne (39)
Outfield: Buzz Arlett (34)
                         Paul Waner (31)
                         Smead Jolley (28)
Catcher: Art Koehler (40)
Utility: (tie) Ray Jacobs (28)
                         Gus Suhr (28)
Pitchers: Elmer Jacobs (36)
                         Doc Crandall (35)
                         Frank Shellenback (35)
                         Wieser Dell (26)

The Second Team

First base: James Poole (18)
Second base: Jimmy Reese (18)
Third base: Frank Brazill (28)
Shortstop: Ray French (19)
Outfield: Ike Boone (27)
                         Lefty O'Doul (24)
                         Brick Eldred (11)
Catcher: (tie) Truck Hannah (18)
                         Sam Agnew (18)
Utility: Jimmy Caveney (20)
Pitchers: Doug McWeeny (25)
                         Oliver Mitchell (22)
                         Bob Geary (11)
                         Harry Krause (9)

Honorable Mention (other players receiving votes)

Gordon Slade, ss (18); Willie Kamm, 3b (10); Jigger Statz, of (10); Mickey Heath, 1b (9); Johnny Monroe, 2b (9); Paddy Siglin, 2b (9); Earl Averill, of (8); Paul Strand, of (8); George Boehler, p (7); Ray Keating, p (3).

Appendix:
The Players

The following list was compiled using the *Reach Guides* (1920 through 1929) and the *Official Rosters and Club Records* published by the Pacific Coast League. *The Baseball Encyclopedia* (Macmillan) and *Total Baseball* (Harper-Collins) were used as references for nicknames and spellings for those players who appeared in the major leagues. Don McPherson's carefully compiled list of Pacific Coast League players featured in the Zeenut baseball card series was used to check player names for non–major leaguers. For some players, however, no secondary reference source could be found and they are therefore listed as their name appears in the *Reach Guides* or the *Official Rosters*. In some cases, the listing is by the last name only.

Because of so much movement on rosters, particularly early and late in the seasons, it is impossible to list every player who ever filled a roster spot; however, those who played in 10 or more games from 1920 through 1922 and 15 or more games from 1923 through 1929, as well as pitchers with 45 or more innings pitched during a season, have been included in this appendix.

In some cases, players were traded during the season from one Pacific Coast League club to another. A player who played on two or more teams is indicated by a slash (for example, *1921 P/O* means the player was on the Portland and Oakland teams during the 1921 season). To avoid too much confusion, the player's name is listed under one team (the team for whom the player began the season). In like manner, many players logged innings at two or more positions. For consistency's sake, position descriptions have been simplified to pitcher (p), catcher (c), infielder (if) or outfielder (of), and only that description used in the official rosters is used.

The dates listed in parentheses are the inclusive dates during the 1920s only. No attempt was made to chronicle the years before or after the decade. The following abbreviations are used to designate teams:

LA   Los Angeles
H   Hollywood (prior to 1926 this was the team from Salt Lake City)
O   Oakland
P   Portland
M   Missions (prior to 1926 this was the team from Vernon, California)
Sac Sacramento
SF   San Francisco Seals
SL   Salt Lake
Sea Seattle
V   Vernon

Los Angeles Angels

Aldridge, Victor E. (Vic); p
  (1920–1921)
Andrews, R.J.; of (1920)
Baldwin, Earl P. (Red); c (1921–1923)
Barfoot, Clyde R. (Foots); p (1928–1929)
Bassler, John L.; c (1920)
Beck, Clyde E.; if (1922, 1924–1925)
Berger, Walter A. (Wally); of
  (1928–1929)
Bigbee, Lyle R. (Al); p (1924)
Billings, John A. (Josh); c (1924)
Brazill, Frank L.; if (1926–1927)
Brown, Charles R. (Curley); p (1920)
Burkett, Howard L.; if (1928, 1929
  LA/H)
Butler, John S. (Trolley Line); (1929)
Byler, C.A. (Butch); c (1924)
Carroll, Dorsie L. (Dixie); of
  (1921–1923)
Casey, Thomas; c (1921)
Chelsey, Harry (Childs); p (1928–1929)
Cox, Elmer J. (Dick); of (1927)
Crandall, James Otis (Doc); p (1920,
  1921 LA/O, 1922–1926)
Crandall, Karl; if (1920)
Crawford, Samuel E. (Sam, Wahoo
  Sam); of (1920–1921)
Cruise, Walton Edwin (Walt); of
  (1924)
Cunningham, Bruce L.; p (1927–1928)
Daly, Thomas D. (Tom); c (1922,
  1923 LA/P)
Day, Clyde H.; p (1926)
Deal, Charles A. (Charlie); p (1922,
  1923 LA/V)
Dittmar, Carl H.; if (1928–1929)

Douglas, Kenneth A.; p (1922)
Dumovich, Nicholas (Nick); p
  (1920–1922, 1924)
Durst, Cedric M.; of (1924)
Dwyer, Raymond; if (1926)
Ellis, George W. (Rube); of (1920–1921)
Ennis, Russell Elwood (Hack); c (1925)
Gabler, Glen J.; p (1928)
Gardner, Hal W.; p (1927)
Glazner, Charles F. (Whitey); p
  (1925–1926)
Golvin, Walter G.; p (1923–1924)
Griggs, Art Carle; if (1920–1923)
Grimes, Oscar Ray (Ray); if (1924–1925)
Gunther, Fred; if (1924–1925)
Hamilton, Earl A.; p (1926–1927)
Haney, Fred G. (Pudge); if (1920, 1929)
Hanna, Roy; p (1923)
Hannah, James Harrison (Harry,
  Truck); c (1926–1929)
Hemingway, Edson M. (Ed); if
  (1926–1927)
Holling, Carl; p (1929)
Holmes, Lester A.; p (1926)
Hood, Wallace J. (Wally); of
  (1923–1928)
Horan, Joseph P. (Shags); of (1925
  LA/V)
Horne, Berlyn D. (Berly, Trader); p
  (1929)
Hughes, Thomas J. (Long Tom); p
  (1920–1925)
Jacobs, Raymond F. (Ray); if
  (1923–1929)
Jacobs, William Elmer (Elmer); p
  (1925–1926)

Jahn, Arthur C. (Art); of (1926–1927)

Jenkins, Joseph D. (Joe); c (1924 SL/LA)

Jensen, Forrest D. (Woody); of
(1927–1928)

Jones, Percy L.; p (1923)

Jones, Robert W. (Bob, Ducky); if
(1928–1929)

Kahn, Owen E. (Jack); if (1927)

Keating, Raymond H. (Ray); p (1920)

Kerrigan, George; if (1927)

Killefer, Wade H. (Red); of
(1920–1922)

Krug, Martin J. (Marty); if
(1923–1927)

Lapan, Peter N. (Pete); c (1920)

Lindimore, Howard S.; if (1921–1923)

Lyons, George T. (Smooth); p
(1921–1923)

McAuley, James E. (Jim); if
(1920–1925)

McCabe, William F. (Bill); of
(1922–1923)

McDonald, Charles C. (Tex); if (1920)

Milstead, George E. (Cowboy); p
(1925)

Mitchell, John F. (Johnny); if
(1926–1927)

Mosolf, James F. (Jim); of (1928)

Moss, Raymond E. (Ray); p (1927)

Murray, Robert H.; if (1929)

Myers, Elmer G.; p (1924)

Niehoff, John A. (Bert); if (1920–1921)

Norton, O.K.; c (1928)

Osborn, John Bode (Bob); p (1928)

Parker, Arthur G.; if (1929)

Payne, George W.; p (1924–1925)

Pertica, William A. (Bill); p (1920)

Peters, Wilbert A.; (1928–1929)

Phillips, Elmer; p (1925, 1926 LA/H)

Piercy, William B. (Bill, Wild Bill); p
(1927)

Plitt, Norman W.; p (1928–1929)

Ponder, Charles Elmer (Elmer); p
(1922–1923)

Ramsey, C.A. (Buck); p (1924)

Read, Bert; c (1926)

Rego, Antone (Tony); c (1920,
1922–1923)

Reinhart, Arthur C.; (1921)

Roberts, Vaughn L.; p (1929)

Robertson, Lawrence; p (1923)

Root, Charles H. (Charlie); p
(1924–1925)

Sandberg, Gustave E. (Gus); c
(1925–1929)

Sanders, Herbert A. (Harry); p (1927)

Scherf, Charles; if (1927)

Schulmerich, Edward Wesley (Wes);
of (1927–1929)

Smith, Alfred K. (Al); p (1927)

Soria, D.J.; p (1921)

Spencer, Edward R. (Tubby); c
(1924–1925)

Spencer, Vernon M. (Vern); of (1922)

Staley, George Gaylord (Gale); if
(1926–1928)

Stanage, Oscar H.; c (1921)

Statz, Arnold J. (Jigger); of
(1920–1921, 1925–1926, 1929)

Sullivan, John L.; of (1922)

Tait, Douglas J. (Doug, Poco); of
(1925–1926)

Thomas, Claude A. (Lefty); p
(1920–1923)

Tierney, Martin; if (1928)

Tolson, Charles J. (Chick); if
(1928–1929)

Twombly, Clarence E. (Babe); of
(1922–1925)

Wallace, Robert M.; p (1922–1923)

Walsh, August S. (Augie); p (1929)

Walters; if (1923)

Warren, Dallas; c (1928–1929)

Weathersby, Earl E. (Tex); p
(1927–1928)

Webb, William Earl (Earl); of (1929)

Weinert, Phillip W. (Phil, Lefty); p
(1924)

Weis, Arthur J. (Butch); of
(1926–1927)

Whaley, William C.; of (1924–1925)

Wright, Wayne B. (Rasty, Doc); p
(1925–1928)

Yarrison, Byron W. (Rube); p (1926)

Zeider, Rollie H. (Bunions); if (1920,
1921 LA/V)

Oakland Oaks (Acorns)

Adams, Spencer D.; if (1924)

Alten, Ernest M. (Ernie, Lefty); p
(1920–1921)

Anton, Leroy F.; if (1928)

Arlett, Alex (Pop); if (1920)

Arlett, Russell L. (Buzz); p, of (1920–1929)

Baker, Delmer D.; c (1923–1925, 1927)

Boehler, George H.; p (1924–1925, 1927–1928, 1929 O/LA)

Boehling, John Joseph (Joe); p (1920)

Bool, Albert J. (Al); c (1926–1928)

Bratcher, Joseph W. (Joe, Goobers); of (1924–1928)

Brenton, Lynn D. (Herb, Buck); p (1922)

Brooks, Jonathon J. (Mandy); of (1928–1929)

Brown, Don M.; of (1922)

Brubaker, Ray K.; if (1920–1929)

Byler, C.A. (Butch); c (1925)

Caffey; of (1922)

Carlyle, Roy E. (Dizzy); of (1929)

Cather, Theodore P. (Ted); of (1921–1924, 1925 O/Sac)

Caveney, James C. (Ike); if (1927, 1928 O/SF)

Chavez, Harold P.; if (1922–1923)

Colwell, Ira J.; p (1923)

Cooper, Arley Wilbur; p (1927–1928)

Cooper, Claude W.; of (1920–1925)

Craghead, Howard O. (Judge); p (1926–1929)

Daglia, Peter G. (Pete); p (1926, 1928–1929)

Dean, Monroe H.; if (1928–1929)

Delaney, Arthur D. (Swede); p (1925–1927)

Dickerman, Leo L.; p (1926–1927)

Dorman, Charles W. (Charlie); c (1920)

Dumovich, Martin; p (1928–1929)

Eley, Orville; p (1922–1923)

Eller, Horace O. (Hod); p (1922)

Fenton, John J.; if (1925–1929)

Fitzsimmons, Thomas W. (Tom); if (1920)

Flowers, D'Arcy R. (Jake); if (1924–1925)

Foster, George C.; p (1924)

Frazier, Foy; of (1928–1929)

Freeman, Alexander V. (Buck); p (1926)

Gingliardi, Henry; if (1920)

Goebel, Edwin (Ed); of (1924)

Gould, Albert F. (Al, Pudgy); p (1926–1927, 1928 O/Sac)

Governor, Antone (Tony); of (1926–1929)

Guisto, Louis J. (Lou); if (1920–1921, 1923–1927)

Hamilton; if (1920)

Harris, Grant G.; p (1924)

Hasty, Robert K. (Bob); p (1927–1928)

Holling, Carl; p (1920)

Howard, Ivon C.; if (1922)

Hurst, Robert C.; p (1929)

Jeffcoat, Charles; p (1929)

Johnson, Osborne R.; of (1923)

Jones, Gordon L.; p (1922)

Kaiser, Julius; p (1925)

Kasich, Charles P.; p (1929)

Kerns, Bernard; if (1921, 1922 O/SL)

Knight, John W. (Schoolboy); if (1920–1923)

Koehler, Arthur R. (Art); c (1921–1922)

Kopf; if (1922)

Krause, Harry W. (Hal); p (1920–1928)

Kremer, Remy P. (Ray); p (1920–1923)

Kunz, Earl D. (Pinches); p (1924–1925, 1926 O/SF)

Lafayette, George R. (Frenchy); if (1922–1924, 1925 O/P)

Lane, William (Bill); of (1920)

Lary, Lynford H. (Lyn); if (1925–1928)

Lombardi, Ernest N. (Ernie, Schnozz); c (1927–1929)

McCarren, William J. (Bill); if (1924)

McDonald, Romie; c (1925 O/SL)

McEvoy, Louis A. (Lou); p (1928–1929)

McGaffigan, Mark A. (Patsy); if (1923)

McIsaac, Gus; if (1929)

McKenry, Frank Gordon (Pete); p (1925–1926)

McNally, Glen E.; if (1926)

Maderas, A. J.; if (1922–1924)

Mails, John Walter (Duster, The Great); p (1923–1924)

Makin, George T.; if (1925–1926)

Marriott, William E. (Bill); if (1922)

Massey; of (1923)

Meusel, Emil F. (Irish); of (1928)

Miller, Lawrence H. (Hack); of
(1920–1921, 1925–1926)
Mitze, Honus; c (1920–1922)
Murchio, George; p (1923–1924)
Murphy, Arthur; if (1927)
Paul, William; if (1920)
Pickering, Urbane H. (Pick); of
(1925–1926)
Pinelli, Ralph A. (Babe); if (1921)
Pruett, Hubert S. (Hub); p
(1925–1926)
Raftery, Don C.P. (Pat); p (1920)
Read, Addison J.; c (1921–1929)
Reese, James H. (Jimmy); if
(1925–1929)
Ruegg, Joseph A.; if (1921)
Schino, Stanley; of (1929 O/SF)
Seibold, Harry (Socks); p (1921)
Shinners, Ralph P.; of (1926–1927)
Smith, Marvin H. (Red); if (1923)
Sparks, Herman W.; p (1927–1928)
Spellman; c (1920)
Steward, George C.; if (1924)
Stewart, John; p (1926)
Thomas, Chester D. (Pinch); c (1923)
Uhalt, Bernard B. (Frenchy); of (1929)
Valla, Eugene (Gene); of (1927)
Vergez, John L. (Johnny); if
(1928–1929)
Volkman, Ray; c (1929 O/P)
Weaver, Harry A.; p (1920)
Wells, Lyle A.; p (1923)
Wetzel, Charles E. (Buzz); p (1928
O/P/H)
Wetzel, Frank B. (Dutch); of (1923)
White, Albert J.; if (1921)
Whiteman; of (1923)
Wilie, Dennis E. (Denney); of
(1920–1923)
Winn, George B. (Breezy); p
(1920–1922)

Portland Beavers (Lucky Beavers, Ducks, Rosebuds)

Ainsmith, Edward W. (Eddie); c (1928
P/Sea)
Baecht, Edward J.; p (1929)
Bagwell, William M. (Bill, Big Bill);
of (1926–1927)
Baker, Delmer D. (Del); c (1920–1921)

Barbee, David M. (Dave); of (1928
P/Sea)
Barnabe, Charles E.; of (1920)
Bates, Charles W.; of (1928–1929)
Baumgartner, Stanwood F. (Stan); p
(1926)
Beck, John; p (1929)
Bedient, Hugh C.; p (1924)
Benton, Stanley W. (Rabbit); if
(1924–1925)
Berry, Charles F.; c (1926)
Biemiller, Harry L.; p (1922)
Bigbee, Carson L. (Skeeter); of (1928
P/LA)
Blue, Luzerne A. (Lu); if (1920)
Boone, Isaac M. (Ike); of (1928 P/M)
Borrelli, Nick C.; of (1929)
Bourg, Arthur S. (Art); of (1920–1921)
Bowman, Joseph E.; p (1929)
Branom, Dudley E.; if (1927)
Brazill, Frank L.; if (1922–1924)
Brooks, Vernon; p (1920)
Burns, Dennis; p (1925–1926)
Bush, Leslie A. (Bullet Joe); p (1929)
Butler, Willis E. (Kid); if (1921)
Byler, C.A. (Butch); c (1923 P/LA)
Cascarella, Joseph T.; p (1929)
Chatham, Charles L. (Buster); if
(1929)
Cissell, Chalmer William (Bill); if
(1926–1927)
Cochrane, Gordon S. (Mickey); c
(1924)
Cole, Albert G. (Bert); p (1928)
Coleman, Ralph O.; p (1921–1922)
Cooper, Guy (Johnny); if (1929)
Couch, John D. (Johnny); p (1927,
1928 P/H)
Cox, Elmer J. (Dick); of (1920–1924)
Cronin, James J. (Jim); if (1929)
Crosby, William Lee; c (1925)
Crumpler, Roy M.; p (1922, 1923
P/SL/P)
Daly, Thomas D. (Tom); c (1924)
Davis, Isaac M. (Ike); if (1928)
Deal, Charles D.; if (1925)
Distel, George A. (Dutch); if (1924)
Eckert, Charles W. (Ox); p
(1923–1925)
Elliott, Harold B. (Rowdy); c (1922)
Ellison, George R.; p (1921)

Elsh, Eugene Reybold (Roy); of (1926)
Fischer, William C. (Bill); c (1927)
Fisher, August H. (Gus); c (1921)
Freeman, Harvey B. (Poke); p (1922)
French, Lawrence H. (Larry); p
    (1927–1928)
Frey, Carl; of (1929)
Fuhrman, Alfred G. (Ollie); c (1922)
Fullerton, Curtis H. (Curt); p (1929)
Galewood; of (1920)
Gardner, Harry R.; p (1924)
Genin, Walter; of (1921)
Glazier, John B.; p (1920)
Grantham, George F. (Boots); if
    (1921)
Gressett, Leo (Tex); of (1922–1924)
Hale, Samuel D. (Sam, Sammy); if
    (1921–1922)
Harris, David S. (Sheriff); of (1929)
Haserot, Lee; if (1928)
Hassler, Joseph F. (Joe); if (1929)
Hasty, Robert K. (Bob); p (1925
    P/Sea)
High, Charles E. (Charlie); of
    (1922–1925)
Hillis, Malcolm D. (Mack); if (1929)
Hollingsworth, John B. (Bonnie); p
    (1925)
Hughes, William N. (Bill); p (1927)
Hunnefield, William F. (Wild Bill); if
    (1925)
Jahn, Arthur C. (Art); of (1929 P/SF)
Johnson, Ernest R. (Ernie); if
    (1926–1928)
Johnson, Robert L. (Indian Bob); of
    (1929)
Johnson, Sylvester W. (Syl); p
    (1920–1921)
Jones, John W. (Skins); if (1923–1925)
Juney, Frank L.; p (1920)
Kallio, Rudolph (Rudy); p (1920, 1921
    P/SL)
Keefe, David E. (Dave); p (1924, 1926
    P/Sac)
Keesey, James W. (Jim); if
    (1928–1929)
Kenworthy, William J. (Bill, Duke); if
    (1924)
Kilhullen, Joseph I. (Pat); c (1922)
King, A.V. (Rip); c (1921–1922)
King, Edward Lee (Lee); of (1923)

Kingdon, Westcott W. (Wes); if
    (1920)
Kinney, Walter W. (Walt); p (1927)
Knight, Elma R. (Jack); p (1929)
Knothe, Wilfred E. (Fritz); if (1928)
Koehler, Arthur R. (Art); c (1920)
Krug, Martin J. (Marty); if (1921)
Lafayette, George R. (Frenchy); if (1926)
Lamb, Lyman R.; of (1925)
LeBourveaux, DeWitt W. (Devo); of
    (1928)
Leverenz, Walter F. (Tiny); p
    (1922–1925)
Leverette, Gorham V.; p (1926)
Lewis, George E. (Duffy); of (1925)
Lingrel, Ray; p (1926)
McCann, Robert Emmett (Emmett); if
    (1922–1925)
McCurdy, Alfred L.; if (1926–1927)
Mahaffey, Lee Roy (Roy, Popeye); p
    (1929)
Maisel, George J.; of (1920)
Mangum, Leo A. (Blackie); p (1926)
Martin, Patrick F. (Pat); p (1925)
Mee, Thomas W. (Tommy, Judge); if
    (1921)
Meeker, Charles Roy (Roy); p
    (1925–1926)
Metz, Leonard R. (Lenny); if (1926,
    1927 P/O)
Middleton, James B. (Rifle Jim); p
    (1922–1923)
Miller, Jacob G. (Jake); of (1924)
Nixon, Albert R. (Al); of (1928)
O'Brien, Parry; of (1927)
O'Dell, Ray; if (1929)
Onslow, John J. (Jack); c (1923)
Ortman, Fred W.; p (1925–1929)
Ostenberg, Leo C.; if (1929 P/H)
Paten, Hazen; if (1921–1922)
Payne, George W.; p (1926)
Pillette, Edward G. (Ted); p (1923
    P/SL/P)
Pillette, Herman P. (Old Folks); p
    (1921, 1924–1925)
Plummer, William L.; p (1921)
Polson, Harry G.; p (1920, 1921 P/SL)
Ponder, Charles Elmer (Elmer); p
    (1927–1928)
Poole, James R. (Jim, Easy); if
    (1921–1924)

Powers, John Lloyd (Ike); p (1929)
Prothro, James T. (Doc); if
 (1926–1927)
Query, Ray; c (1924)
Quesinberry; p (1921)
Rachac, Max J.; p (1924–1925, 1926
 P/Sac)
Rego, Antone (Tony); c (1928–1929)
Richards, R.L.; if (1929)
Riconda, Henry P. (Harry); if (1925)
Rohwer, Ray; of (1925, 1926 P/Sac)
Ross, George Sidney (Sid); p (1921)
Ross, Samuel I. (Sam); p (1920–1922)
Rowland, Charles L. (Chuck); c (1925)
Sargent, Joseph A. (Joe, Horse Belly);
 if (1922)
Saunders, John; c (1928)
Schaller, Walter (Biff); of (1920)
Schandeling, Nathan; c (1927)
Schroeder, Clyde M.; p (1920,
 1923–1924)
Scott, Kenneth; p (1921)
Sigafoos, Francis L. (Frank); if
 (1927–1929)
Siglin, Wesley P. (Paddy); if (1920)
Smith, Elmer J.; of (1926–1928)
Smith, Marvin H. (Red); if (1926)
Spranger, Carl W. (Kibby); if (1920)
Staley, George Gaylord (Gale); if
 (1929)
Stokes, Albert J. (Al); p (1925)
Storti, Lindo I. (Lin); if (1927)
Strand, Paul E.; of (1926–1927)
Stumpf, William F. (Bill); if (1923)
Sullivan, James R. (Jim); p
 (1922–1923)
Sutherland, Harvey S. (Suds); p (1920,
 1922–1923)
Thomas, Charles G. (Babe); if (1924)
Thorpe, James F. (Jim); of (1922)
Tobin, Frank E.; c (1926)
Tomlin, Edwin C. (Ed); p (1927–1929)
Walberg, George E. (Rube); p (1922)
Washburn, Royce; if (1926)
Wendell, Lewis C. (Lew); c
 (1926–1927)
Winters, Jesse F. (Buck); p (1924–1925)
Wisterzil, George C. (Tex); if (1920)
Wolfer, Merle J. (Ike); of (1921–1924)
Woodall, Charles Lawrence (Larry); c
 (1929)

Wuestling, George (Yats); if
 (1928–1929)
Yarrison, Byron W. (Rube); p
 (1922–1925)
Yelle, Archie J.; c (1927)
Yerkes, Charles Carroll (Carroll); p
 (1927–1928)
Young, Clyde; if (1921)
Zeider, Rollie H. (Bunions); if (1923)

Sacramento Senators (Solons)

Alley, Daniel; c (1926)
Backer, Leonard H. (Lennie); if
 (1926–1929)
Becker, David Beals (Beals); of (1924
 Sac/Sea)
Brown, Harry; of (1923–1924)
Brown, Henry E.; if (1925)
Brown, Roy; (1927)
Bryan, Edward C. (Eddie); p (1929)
Burke, William E.; of (1928–1929)
Cady, Forrest L. (Chick); c (1920)
Camilli, Adolph L. (Dolph); if (1929)
Canfield, Carroll M.; p (1922–1923,
 1925–1926)
Canfield, Wallace; p (1925–1926)
Cano, John R.; p (1929)
Cochran, Charles B.; of (1923–1925)
Colwell, Ira J.; p (1922 Sac/O)
Compton, Ann Sebastian (Pete,
 Bash); of (1920–1921, 1922 Sac/SF)
Cook, Lester S. (Doc); c (1920–1923)
Cooper, Claude W.; of (1927)
Crandall, James Otis (Doc); p (1928,
 1929 Sac/LA)
Crowley, Dan; (1929)
Cunningham, William A. (Bill); of
 (1925–1926)
Davis, John Wilbur (Bud, Country,
 Wilbur); if (1924–1926)
Elliott, Harold B. (Rowdy); c (1921)
Faeth, Anthony J. (Tony); p (1920,
 1921 Sac/V)
Fittery, Paul C.; p (1920–1923)
Flynn, Thomas B.; p (1928–1929)
Freitas, Antonio (Tony); p (1929)
French, Raymond E. (Ray); if
 (1925–1929)
Gardner, Melvin; if (1927)
Gillick, Lawrence; p (1929)

Gorman, Edward M.; of (1924)
Gould, Albert F. (Al, Pudgy); p (1929)
Grover, Roy A.; if (1920)
Hall, Charles L. (Charley, Sea Lion); p
(1924)
Hammock, Sterling; (1929)
Hampton; p (1922–1923)
Harris, B.; c (1929)
Harris, Joseph (Moon); of (1929)
Hemingway, Edson M. (Ed); if
(1923–1924)
Hoag, Myril O.; of (1929)
Hoffman, Clarence C. (Dutch); of
(1925–1928)
Hollander; if (1920)
Hughes, William N. (Bill); p
(1923–1925, 1926 S/P)
James, William L. (Seattle Bill); p
(1924)
Jones, Carroll E. (Deacon); p (1920)
Jones, Gordon L.; p (1921 Sac/Oak)
Kallio, Rudolph (Rudy); p
(1926–1928)
Keating, Raymond H. (Ray); p
(1925–1929)
Keefe, David E. (Dave); p
(1927–1928)
Knight, John W. (Jack, Schoolboy); if
(1926–1927)
Koehler, Arthur R. (Art); c (1923–1929)
Kopp, Merlin H. (Manny); of
(1920–1928)
Krasovich, Anthony; if (1929)
Kunz, Earl D. (Pinches); p
(1920–1922, 1928, 1929 Sac/Sea)
McGaffigan, Mark A. (Paddy, Marty);
if (1920–1922)
McGee, Francis D. (Frank, Tubby); if
(1927)
McGinnis, George; if (1923–1924)
McLaughlin, James R. (Jim); if
(1925–1929)
McNeeley, George Earl (Earl); of
(1922–1924)
Mails, John Walter (Duster, The
Great); p (1920)
Manger; (1922)
Martin, Elwood G. (Speed); p
(1925–1926)
Mathews, Wid C.; of (1924)
Matteoni; (1922)

Meusel, Emil F. (Irish); of (1929)
Mollwitz, Frederick A. (Fritz); if
(1920–1924)
Monroe, John A. (Johnny); if
(1926–1929)
Niehaus, Richard J. (Dick); p
(1920–1921)
O'Brien, Parry; of (1929)
Orr, William J. (Billy); if (1920–1921,
1922 Sac/Sea)
Osborne, Frank R.; of (1926–1929)
Pearce, Walter; if (1922)
Penner, W. Kenneth (Ken); p
(1920–1923)
Peters, Henry L.; p (1922–1924)
Pfahler, Fred; if (1926)
Pick, Charles T. (Charlie); if
(1921–1924)
Prough, Herschel Clinton (Clint, Bill);
p (1920–1924)
Rachac, Max J.; p (1927–1929)
Rohwer, Claude; if (1923)
Rohwer, Ray; of (1927–1929)
Rose, Peter; of (1921)
Ryan, John Bud (Buddy); of
(1920–1924)
Schang, Robert (Bobby); c
(1920–1924)
Schinkel, A.H.; of (1922)
Schneider, Peter J. (Pete); of (1925
Sac/V)
Severeid, Henry L. (Hank); c
(1927–1928, 1929 Sac/H)
Shea, Elmer F. (Specs); p (1921–1924,
1926–1927, 1928 Sac/O)
Shea, Mervyn D.J. (Merv); c
(1922–1926)
Sheehan, Leslie (Les); if (1920–1922, '28)
Sheely, Earl H. (Whitey); if (1928)
Shellenback, Frank V. (Shelly); p
(1925)
Siglin, Wesley P. (Paddy); if
(1923–1926)
Singleton, John E. (Sheriff); p
(1927–1928)
Smith; of (1924)
Stanage, Oscar H.; c (1922)
Stoeven, Harold; if (1929)
Sweeney, James; of (1926)
Thompson, Harold (Harry); p
(1923–1924)

Vinci, Laurie A.; p (1924–1929)
Wachenfeldt, Eugene B.; c (1925)
Watson, M.W.; of (1925)
Yellowhorse, Moses J. (Chief); p (1923–1924)

Salt Lake Bees (1920–1925) — Hollywood Stars (1926–1929) (Sheiks)

Agnew, Samuel L. (Sam); c (1928)
Albert, William M.; of (1929)
Anfinson, Edward A.; c (1922–1923)
Barry; if (1921)
Bassler, John L. (Johnny); c (1928–1929)
Baum, Charles A. (Charley, Spider); p (1920)
Betts, Hugh; p (1922)
Blaeholder, H.A.; p (1921–1922)
Bonnelly, Richard C. (Dick); p (1928 H/Sac)
Bonowitz, Joe; of (1929)
Boroja, Anthony; of (1928)
Borton, William Baker (Babe); if (1920)
Bouton, Carl H.; if (1927)
Brinley; p (1921)
Bromley, John R.; p (1920–1922)
Brown, Don; if (1921)
Byler, C.A. (Butch); c (1920–1922)
Carlyle, Hiram Cleo (Cleo); of (1928–1929)
Cartwright, Joseph; if (1922)
Cavet, Tiller H. (Pug); p (1928)
Chesterfield, Roy; p (1929 H/P)
Connolly, Joseph G. (Coaster Joe); of (1925)
Cook, Lester S.; c (1924–1927, 1929)
Coumbe, Fred N. (Fritz); p (1923–1925)
Cravath, Clifford C. (Gavvy); of (1921)
Cullop, Henry Nicholas (Nick); p (1920)
Davis; if (1923)
Duchalsky, Jim; p (1923)
Edwards, Leo E.; c (1921)
Frederick, John H. (Johnny); of (1923–1927)
Fullerton, Curtis H. (Curt); p (1926–1927, 1928 H/P)
Funk, Elias C. (Liz); of (1929)

Gay, Frank M.; if (1921)
Ginglardi, Henry; of (1921 SL/P)
Gleichmann, Gustave; if (1922)
Gooch, Charles F. (Charlie); if (1925–1927)
Gould, Albert F. (Al, Pudgy); p (1920–1923)
Green, Harry R.; if (1929)
Griffith; of (1920)
Hanger; of (1921)
Heath, Minor W. (Mickey); if (1927–1929)
Henkle, H.; p (1922 SL/Sea)
Hillis, Malcolm D. (Mack); if (1926)
Hodges; of (1920)
Hollerson, George; p (1926, 1929)
Holley, Thomas G.; if (1927–1928)
Hood, Wallace J. (Wally); of (1920)
Hosp, Frank; of (1920)
Hulvey, James Hensel (Hank); p (1924–1929)
Jacobs, Arthur E. (Art); p (1927)
Jenkins, Joseph D. (Joe); c (1920–1924)
Johns, August F. (Augie, Gus); p (1929)
Johnson, Ernest R. (Ernie); if (1920)
Jourdan, Theodore C. (Ted); if (1921)
Kallio, Rudolph (Rudy); p (1922–1925)
Kerns, Bernard; if (1923)
Kerr, John F. (Johnny); if (1925–1928)
Kinney, Walter W. (Walt); p (1928–1929)
Krug, Martin J. (Marty); if (1920)
Lazzeri, Anthony M. (Tony); if (1922–1925)
Lee, Dudley E.; if (1926–1929)
Leslie, Roy R.; if (1923–1926)
Leverenz, Walter F. (Tiny); p (1920–1921)
Lewis, George E. (Duffy); of (1921–1924)
Lewis, Samuel I.; p (1922)
Light; of (1922)
Lindimore, Howard S.; if (1924–1926)
Lowell, Edwin; if (1927)
Lynn, Byrd; c (1921)
McCabe, Richard J. (Dick); p (1922–1929)
McDowell, James; if (1927)

McNulty, Patrick H. (Pat); of
(1927–1928)
Maloney, Michael (Mike); if (1929)
Marticorena, Joseph (Joe); p (1929)
Mathews, Wid C.; of (1922)
Mulcahy, John P. (Phil); p (1924–1928)
Mulligan, Edward J. (Eddie); if (1920)
Murphy, Dennis J.; c (1927)
Murphy, William A. (Bill); p
(1926–1928)
Myers, Elmer G.; p (1922–1923)
O'Doul, Francis J. (Lefty); of
(1924–1926)
O'Neil, Joseph Henry (Harry); p
(1924–1926)
Ostenberg, Leo C.; if (1928)
Pearce, Walter; if (1923–1924)
Peters, John W. (Shotgun); c
(1923–1926)
Piercy, William B. (Wild Bill); p (1925)
Pierotti, Leonard; if (1926)
Pittinger, Clarke A. (Pinky); if (1924)
Ponder, Charles Elmer (Elmer); p
(1924–1925)
Redman, Gus; c (1926 H/Sea)
Rehg, Walter P. (Wally); of (1928–1929)
Reiger, Elmer J.; p (1920–1922)
Reilly; (1920)
Rhodes, John Gordon (Gordon,
Dusty); p (1928)
Riley, James N. (Jim); if (1922)
Rollings, William Russell (Russ, Red);
if (1929)
Roth, Robert F. (Braggo); of (1928)
Rumler, William J. (Bill); of (1920,
1929)
Sand, John Henry (Heinie); if
(1920–1922)
Schick, Maurice F. (Morrie); of (1922)
Segrist, John W.; of (1927)
Shea, Patrick H. (Red); p (1927 H/P)
Sheehan, Leslie (Les); of (1923–1927)
Sheely, Earl H. (Whitey); if (1920)
Shellenback, Frank V. (Shelly); p
(1926–1929)
Siglin, Wesley P. (Paddy); if
(1921–1922)
Singleton, John E. (Sheriff); p
(1923–1926)
Strand, Paul E.; of (1921–1923)
Stroud, Ralph V. (Sailor); p (1920,

1925, 1926 H/LA)
Swartz, Monroe; p (1921 SL/Sea)
Sweeney, James; of (1927)
Sypher, Clarence (Rowdy); c (1929)
Teachout, Arthur J. (Bud); p (1927)
Thomas, Claude A. (Lefty); p (1924)
Thurston, Hollis J. (Sloppy); p
(1920–1922)
Tierney, James A. (Cotton); if (1927)
Twombley, Clarence E. (Babe); of
(1927–1928)
Vitt, Oscar J. (Ossie, Old Os); if
(1922–1927)
Welch, Frank T. (Bugger); of (1928
H/SF)
Wera, Julian V. (Julie); if (1928)
Wetzel, Charles E. (Buzz); p (1929)
Wilhoit, Joseph W. (Joe); of
(1922–1923)
Worth; (1920)
Zoeller, Frank H.; of (1926)

San Francisco Seals

Agnew, Samuel L. (Sam); c (1920–
1926, 1927 SF/H)
Alten, Ernest M. (Ernie, Lefty); p
(1922, 1923 SF/V)
Anfinson, Edward A.; c (1920–1921)
Averill, Howard Earl (Earl); of
(1926–1928)
Baker, Loris R.; if (1926–1927, 1929)
Baloff, Steven N. (Nino); p (1920)
Bodie, Frank S. (Ping); of (1927, 1928
SF/M)
Brower, Frank W. (Turkeyfoot); of
(1925–1926)
Buckley, Timothy; p (1923)
Burger, George; p (1924)
Camilli, Adolph L. (Dolph); if
(1926–1927)
Caveney, James C. (Ike); if
(1920–1921, 1929)
Cole, Albert G. (Bert); p (1920)
Coleman, Parke Edward (Ed); of (1929)
Compton, Anna Sebastian (Pete,
Bash); of (1923)
Connolly, Joseph G. (Coaster Joe); of
(1920, 1926)
Corhan, Roy G. (Irish); if (1920)
Couch, John D. (Johnny); p
(1920–1921, '29)

Coumbe, Fred N. (Fritz); p (1922)
Courtney, Henry S. (Harry); p (1922–1923)
Crockett, James W. (Davey); p (1924–1925)
Crosetti, Frank P.J. (Frankie); if (1928–1929)
Crumpler, Roy M.; p (1921)
Davis, Curtis B. (Curt, Coonskin); p (1929)
Davis, D.K. (Daka); p (1922)
DeVitalis; p (1920)
Dittmar, Carl H.; if (1927)
Donovan, Gerald T.; if (1928–1929)
Ellison, Herbert S. (Bert, Babe); if (1921–1926)
Fitzgerald, Justin H. (Mike); of (1920–1921, 1922 SF/Sac)
Flashkamper, Raymond H. (Ray, Flash); if (1923, 1925)
Geary, Robert N. (Bob, Speed); p (1922–1927)
Gillenwater, Claude; p (1922)
Glynn, Vallery G. (Val); p (1929)
Gomez, Vernon L. (Lefty); p (1929)
Griffin, Martin J. (Marty); p (1924–1926)
Hanson, Sydney; p (1926)
Hasbrook, Robert L. (Ziggy); if (1920)
Haworth, Homer Howard (Cully, Howie); c (1929)
Hendryx, Timothy G. (Tim); of (1923–1926)
Hodge, Clarence Clement (Shovel); p (1923–1924)
Jacobs, William Elmer (Elmer); p (1928–1929)
Johnson, Roy C.; of (1926–1928)
Jolly, Smead P.; of (1925–1929)
Jones, Gordon L.; p (1928, 1929 SF/H/Sac)
Jordon, Roy; p (1920)
Kamm, William E. (Willie); if (1920–1922)
Keefe, Robert F.; p (1921)
Kelly, Joseph H. (Joe); of (1922–1925)
Kennedy, E.H.; of (1920)
Kerr, Richard H. (Dickie); p (1926)
Kilduff, Peter J. (Pete); if (1922–1926)
Koerner, Philip A.; if (1920)
Kunz, Earl D. (Pinches); p (1927)

Lang, B.M.; p (1926)
Langford, Elton J. (Sam); p (1929)
Lewis, Samuel I.; p (1920–1921)
Love, Edward H. (Slim); p (1920)
McCrea, Francis W. (Frank); c (1927)
McIsaacs, Gerald; c (1929)
McQuaid, Herbert G. (Herb); p (1920–1921, 1922 SF/LA)
McWeeny, Douglas L. (Doug, Buzz); p (1922–1923, 1925)
Mails, John Walter (Duster, The Great); p (1926–1929)
Martin, Sidney W.; p (1927)
May, William Herbert (Herb, Buckshot); p (1927–1928)
Miller, J.; (1922)
Miller, Ralph J.; if (1922)
Mishkin, Solly; if (1927–1928)
Mitchell, Oliver C.; p (1922–1928)
Moudy, Marvin J. (Dick); p (1925–1928)
Mulligan, Edward J. (Eddie); if (1923–1927)
O'Connell, James J. (Jimmy); of (1920–1922)
O'Doul, Francis J. (Lefty); p, of (1920, 1927)
Paynter, Norbert (Nobby); if (1924–1926)
Penebsky, Adolph; c (1929)
Pfeffer, Edward J. (Jeff); p (1925)
Pinelli, Ralph A. (Babe); if (1927–1929)
Rath, Morris C. (Morrie); if (1921)
Reed, Robert; c (1929)
Rego, Antone (Tony); c (1927)
Rhyne, Harold J. (Hal); if (1922–1925, 1928)
Ritchie, Peter (Pete); c (1924–1925)
Ruether, Walter H. (Dutch); p (1928)
Schick, Maurice F. (Morrie); of (1920–1921)
Schmidt, Walter J.; c (1929)
Schorr, Ernest; p (1924)
Scott, James (Death Valley Jim); p (1920–1924)
Seaton, Thomas G. (Tom); p (1920)
See, Charles H. (Charlie, Chad); of (1922)
Shea, Patrick H. (Red); p (1922–1924)
Sheehan, John T. (Jack); if (1927)

Smith, Casey; p (1920)
Sprinz, Joseph C. (Joe, Mule); c (1928)
Stokes, Albert J. (Al); c (1927)
Suhr, August R. (Gus); if (1926–1929)
Taylor, Leo T. (Chink); if (1926)
Thurston, Hollis J. (Sloppy); p
  (1928–1929)
Turpin, Harold; p (1927)
Valla, Eugene (Gene); of (1922–1926)
Vargas, Andrew J.; c (1924,
  1926–1928)
Walsh, James T.; if (1920)
Walsh, Lee T. (Dee); if (1921–1924)
Walters, John; p (1929 SF/P)
Waner, Lloyd J. (Little Poison); of
  (1925)
Waner, Paul G. (Big Poison); of
  (1923–1925)
Williams, Guy; p (1924–1927)
Wingo, Absalom H. (Al, Red); of
  (1929)
Wolter, Harry M.; of (1920)
Yelle, Archie J.; c (1920–1926)

Seattle Indians (Siwashes, Suds)

Adams, John Bertram (Bert, Jack); c
  (1920–1922)
Adams, Spencer D.; if (1922)
Allington, William B.; of (1929)
Almada, Louis (Lou, Ladies Day
  Louie); of (1929)
Anderson, Andrew; of (1929)
Bagby, James C.J. (Sarge, Jim); p (1924)
Baldwin, Earl P. (Red); c (1920,
  1924–1926)
Baldwin, Henry C. (Ted); if
  (1924–1926)
Ballenger, Pelham A.; if (1927)
Barbee, David M. (Dave); of (1929)
Barker, Dixie; c (1928)
Barney, Edmund J. (Ed); of
  (1922–1923)
Bates, Raymond; if (1921)
Best, Clifford; p (1926)
Bigbee, Carson L. (Skeeter); of (1927
  Sea/P)
Blake, John Frederick (Sheriff, Fred);
  p (1923)
Blevins, Bruce; p (1929)
Bohne, Samuel A. (Sam, Sammy); if
  (1920)

Borreani, Charles; c (1927–1929)
Bowman, Elmari W. (Big Bow); if
  (1924)
Brady, Clifford F. (Cliff); if
  (1924–1927)
Brandt, Edward A. (Ed); p (1927)
Brazill, Frank L.; if (1925)
Brenton, Lynn D. (Herb, Buck); p
  (1920–1921)
Brett, Herbert J. (Duke); p
  (1926–1927)
Burger, George; p (1922–1923)
Callaghan, Martin F. (Marty); of
  (1926–1927)
Caveney, James C. (Ike); if (1926
  Sea/O)
Chamberlain, Joseph J. (Joe); if (1928)
Chekelak, Stephen; p (1925)
Collard, Earl C. (Hap); p (1928–1929)
Connolly, Thomas F. (Blackie); if
  (1922)
Cox, Frank; c (1928–1929)
Crane, Samuel B. (Sam, Red); if
  (1922–1924)
Cueto, Manuel (Potato); if (1922)
Cunningham, William A. (Bill); of
  (1920–1921, 1928)
Cutshaw, George W. (Clancy); if
  (1924–1925)
Dailey, Joseph; p (1920–1922)
Daly, Thomas D. (Tom); c (1925)
Dell, William G. (Wieser); p (1924)
Demaree, Albert W. (Al); if
  (1920–1921)
Dumovich, Nicholas (Nick); p, of
  (1925)
Easterling, Paul; of (1926–1927)
Eckhardt, Oscar G. (Ox); of (1929)
Edwards, James C. (Jim Joe, Little
  Joe); p (1927–1929)
Eldred, Ross C. (Brick); of
  (1920–1927)
Elliott, Carter W.; if (1920–1921)
Elliott, James T. (Jumbo Jim); p
  (1925–1926)
Ellsworth, Floyd W. (Chuck); if
  (1926–1929)
Emmer, Frank W.; if (1924–1925)
Evans, Oscar; (1928)
Falk, Charles (Charlie); if (1929)
Finneran, Joseph I. (Happy); p (1922)

Fisch, Elbert; p (1929)
Francis, Ray J.; p (1921)
Fussell, Frederick M. (Red, Fred,
  Moonlight Ace); p (1924–1925)
Gardner, Harry R.; p (1920–1923)
Geary, Robert N. (Bob, Speed); p
  (1920–1921)
Gibeke; (1925)
Graham, Kyle (Skinny); p (1927–1929)
Gregg, Sylveanus A. (Vean); p
  (1922–1924)
Griggs, Arthur (Sandow); if (1926)
Hartford, Bruce D. (Harry); if (1920)
Hasty, Robert K. (Bob); p (1926)
Herman, Floyd C. (Babe); if (1925)
Hetherly, Clarence W.; if (1929)
Hood, Wallace J. (Wally); of (1922,
  1929)
House, Andrew; p (1927–1929)
Hudgins, James P. (Jimmy); if
  (1926–1928)
Hufft, Irwin V. (Fuzzy); of
  (1926–1927, 1928 Sea/M)
Jacobs, John; of (1928)
Jacobs, William Elmer (Elmer); p
  (1921–1923)
Janvrin, Harold C. (Hal); if (1923)
Jenkins, Joseph D. (Joe); c
  (1926–1927)
Jessee, Daniel E.; if (1926)
Johnson, Ernest R. (Ernie); if (1929)
Johnson, Wheeler R. (Doc); if (1923)
Jones, Percy L.; p (1924)
Kallio, Rudolph (Rudy); p (1929)
Kenworthy, William J. (Bill, Duke); if
  (1920–1921)
Kimmick, Walter L. (Wally); if (1927)
Knight, Elma R. (Jack); p (1927–1928)
Knothe, Wilfred E. (Fritz); if (1929
  Sea/P)
Labetich, John J.; (1929)
Lafayette, George (Frenchy); of (1921)
Lamanske, Frank J. (Lefty); p (1929)
Lane, William (Bill); of (1921–1926)
Lawrence, William H. (Bill); of (1929)
Lee, Harry; p (1926)
Lucas, Fred; p (1925)
McCabe, William; of (1925)
McDaniels, Osborne C.; if (1929)
Mack, Frank G. (Stubby); p
  (1921–1922)

Martin, Elwood G. (Speed); p (1928
  Sea/M)
Martin, Sidney W.; p (1926–1927)
Mearkle, Clyde; if (1923)
Middleton, R.H.; of (1920–1921)
Miljus, John K. (Johnny, Jovo); of
  (1925–1927)
Mitchell, John F. (Johnny); if (1928)
Muller, Frederick W. (Freddie); if
  (1928–1929)
Murphy, Rod; if (1920–1921, 1922
  Sea/Sac)
Nance, Clyde L.; p (1927–1928)
Neis, Bernard E. (Bernie); of (1928)
Nixon, Albert R. (Al); of (1920)
Oldring, Rueben H. (Rube); of (1921)
Olney, Walter W.; if (1928–1929)
Orr, William J. (Billy); if (1923)
Osborne, Frank R.; of (1924)
Patterson, William; if (1921)
Peters, Wilbur; p (1926, 1927 Sea/LA)
Pigg, Victor; p (1923)
Pipgras, Fred J.; p (1929)
Plummer, William L. (Bill); p
  (1924–1925)
Purdy, Everett V. (Pid); of (1927)
Ramage, C.; if (1923)
Ramsey, C.A. (Buck); p (1925
  Sea/LA, 1926)
Ritchie, Peter (Pete); c (1923 Sea/SF)
Rohrer, W.W. (Dad); c (1920)
Rohwer, Ray (Home Run Ray); of
  (1923–1924)
Ruble, William Arthur (Art); of (1928)
Schmidt, Walter J.; c (1927–1928)
Schorr, Ernest; p (1920–1922)
Schulte, Frank A. (Wildfire); of (1922
  Sea/O)
Schwab, Harry A.; if (1926)
See, Charles H. (Charlie, Chad); of
  (1921)
Seibold, Harry (Socks); p (1920)
Sherlock, John C. (Monk); if
  (1926–1928)
Smith, George S.; p (1929)
Spencer, Edward R. (Tubby); c
  (1921–1922)
Steinecke, William R. (Bill); c (1929)
Strand, Paul E.; of (1920)
Stryker, Sterling A. (Dutch); p (1925)
Stueland, George A.; p (1924)

Stumpf, William F. (Bill); if
(1920–1922)
Sullivan, Charles E. (Charlie); p (1928)
Sullivan, Tom B.; of (1928)
Sutherland, Harvey S. (Suds); p
(1924–1925, 1927)
Taylor, Harry W. (Handsome Harry);
if (1929)
Teachout, Arthur J. (Bud); p (1928)
Tesar, John; p (1923)
Tobin, Frank E.; c (1920–1924, 1925
Sea/P)
Twombley, Clarence E. (Babe); of
(1926)
Wade, Charles W.; of (1929)
Wares, Clyde E. (Buzzy); if (1920)
Welsh, James C. (Jimmy); if
(1923–1924)
Williams, Carl; p (1923–1924)
Wilson, Gomer R. (Tex); p (1928)
Wisterzil, George J. (Tex); if (1921)
Wolfer, Merle J. (Ike); of (1928)
Yaryan, Clarence Everett (Yam); c
(1923)
Young, George; if (1928)
Zamlock, Carl E.; if (1920)

Vernon Tigers (1920–1925) San Francisco Mission Reds (Missions, Mission Bells, Mission Reds, Bells, Bears) (1926–1929)

Alcock, John F. (Scotty); of
(1920–1921)
Baldwin, Earl P. (Red); c (1927–1929)
Barfoot, Clyde R. (Foots); p
(1925–1927)
Becker, David Beals (Beals); of (1925)
Berger, Fred E.; of (1928–1929)
Blakesley, James L. (Jim); of (1924–1925)
Bodie, Frank S. (Ping); of (1922–1923)
Boone, Isaac M. (Ike); of (1926, 1929)
Bott; if (1923)
Brazill, Frank L.; if (1928 M/P)
Brenzel, William R. (Bill); c
(1928–1929)
Bryan, Edward C. (Eddie); p
(1924–1928)
Cadore, Leon J.; p (1924)
Camp, H.; c (1920)

Carson, Al; p (1923)
Caster, George J. (Ug); p (1929)
Chadbourne, Chester J. (Chet, Pop);
of (1920–1924)
Christensen, Walter N. (Cuckoo); of
(1929)
Christian, C.V. (Jim); p (1924–1927)
Cole, Albert G. (Bert); p (1926, 1929)
Cross, D.; p (1921)
Cruz, Cecil; p (1923)
Davenport, Claude E. (Big Dave); p
(1928)
Deal, Charles D. (Charlie); if (1924)
Dell, William G. (Wieser); p
(1920–1922, '23 V/Sea)
DeVormer, Albert E. (Al); c (1920)
Doyle, Jesse H. (Jess); p (1922)
Dumovich, Nicholas (Nick); p (1927)
Eckert, Charles W. (Buzz); p
(1926–1927)
Edington, Jacob Frank (Frank,
Stump); of (1920–1921)
Faeth, Anthony J. (Tony); p (1922)
Finn, Cornelius F. (Neal, Mickey); if
(1925–1929)
Fisher, Robert Taylor (Bobby, Tom);
if (1920)
Foster, George (Rube); p (1923)
French, Raymond E. (Ray); if
(1921–1923)
Fromme, Arthur H. (Art); p (1920–1921)
Gilder, Raymond; p (1922–1923)
Gillespie, Robert F.; of (1923–1927)
Gorman, Charles; c, if (1921, 1923)
Green, Harry R.; if (1928)
Griffin, Westel H. (Wes); if
(1924–1928)
Hannah, James Harrison (Harry,
Truck); c (1921–1924, 1925 V/P)
Hawks, Nelson L. (Chicken); of (1922)
Hemingway, Edson M. (Ed); if (1925)
High, Hugh J. (Bunny); of
(1920–1923)
Hofmann, Fred (Bootnose); c (1929)
Holling, Carl; p (1928)
Hooper, Harry B.; of (1927)
Houck, Byron S. (Duke); p (1920,
1922 V/P)
Hubbell, Wilbert W. (Bill); p (1929)
Hufft, Irwin V. (Fuzzy); of; (1929)
Hughes, William N. (Bill); p (1928)

Hyatt, Robert Hamilton (Ham); if (1920–1923)
James, William H. (Big Bill); p (1922–1923)
Johnson, George; p (1925)
Jolley, James; p (1922–1923)
Jones, Robert W. (Bob, Ducky); if (1926–1927)
Kimmick, Walter L. (Wally); if (1924)
Krause, Harry W. (Hal); p (1929)
Locker, Dallas; if (1921–1923)
Long, Thomas A. (Tommy, Tripling Tommy); of (1920–1921)
Love, Edward H. (Slim); p (1921)
Ludolph, William F. (Wee Willie); p (1924–1928)
McDaniel, Osbourne C.; if (1927–1928)
McDowell, James (Jim); if (1924–1926)
McGraw, Robert E. (Bob); p (1921)
McQuaid, Herbert G. (Herb); p (1929)
May, Frank S. (Jakey, Joker Jake); p (1922–1923)
Menosky, Michael W. (Leaping Mike); of (1924)
Mitchell, John F. (Johnny); if (1920)
Mitchell, William (Willie); p (1920–1921)
Moore, Albert J. (Al); of (1925)
Morse, Newell O. (Bud); (1929)
Morse, Peter Raymond (Hap); if (1920–1921)
Mueller, Arthur; if (1920)
Mulligan, Edward J. (Eddie); if (1929)
Murphy, Daniel (Dan); c (1920–1926)
Nelson, Merton A. (Mert); p (1928–1929)
Nevers, Ernest A. (Ernie); p (1928–1929)
O'Brien, Parry; of (1921)
Oeschger, C. Joseph (Joe); p (1926 M/O)
Oldham, John C. (Red); p (1925)
Oliver, Thomas N. (Rebel); of (1924–1927)
O'Shea; (1925)
Parker, S.R.; if (1927)
Penner, Kenneth W. (Ken); p (1924–1925)

Piercy, William B. (Bill, Wild Bill); p (1920)
Pillette, Herman P. (Old Folks); p (1926–1929)
Rader, Donald R. (Don); if (1923)
Redfern, George H. (Buck); if (1925)
Rieger, Elmer J.; p (1923)
Rodda, William T.; if (1926–1929)
Rose, Edward (Ed, Eddie); of (1926–1927, 1928 M/P)
Rosenberg, Phil; of (1928)
Ruether, Walter H. (Dutch); p (1929)
Sawyer, Carl F. (Huck); if (1921–1923)
Schang, Robert M (Bobby); c (1925)
Schmidt, Walter J.; c (1926)
Schneider, Peter J. (Pete); p, of (1920–1924)
Scott, Floyd J. (Pete); of (1929)
Sellers; p (1924)
Shellenback, Frank V. (Shelly); p (1920–1921, 1923–1924)
Sherlock, John C. (Jack, Monk); if (1929)
Shore, Ernest (Ernie); p (1921 V/SF)
Slade, Gordon L. (Oskie); if (1923–1929)
Smallwood, Walter C. (Walt); p (1920–1921)
Smith, James Carlisle (Red, Carlisle); if (1920–1922, 23 V/LA)
Swanson, Ernest Evar (Evar, Swanny); of (1925–1928)
Sypher, Clarence (Rowdy); c (1928)
Thomas, Claude A. (Lefty); p (1924)
Thompson, Lafayette F. (Fresco, Tommy); if (1925)
Vache, Ernest L. (Tex); of (1926)
Wade, Richard F. (Rip, Dick); of (1927)
Walters, Albert J. (Roxy); c (1926–1927)
Warner, John R. (Jack); if (1923–1925)
Weinert, Phillip W. (Phil, Lefty); p (1927)
Weis, Arthur J. (Butch); of (1928)
Whitney, Rodney E. (Rod); c (1923–1927, 1928 M/P)
Wolfer, Merle J. (Ike); of (1925)
Zanic, John; c (1923)
Zeider, Rollie H. (Bunions); if (1922)

Bibliography

Books

Alexander, Charles C. *John McGraw*. New York: Penguin Books, 1988.

Benson, Michael. *Ballparks of North America*. Jefferson, North Carolina: McFarland & Company, Inc., 1989.

Beverage, Richard E. *The Angels, Los Angeles in the Pacific Coast League, 1919–1957*. Placentia, California: The Deacon Press, 1981.

_____. *The Hollywood Stars, Baseball in Movieland, 1926–1957*. Placentia, California: The Deacon Press, 1984.

Blake, Mike. *The Minor Leagues: A Celebration of the Little Show*. New York: Wynwood Press, 1991.

Cox, James A. *The Lively Ball: Baseball in the Roaring Twenties*. Alexandria, Virginia: Redefinition, Inc., 1989.

Creamer, Robert W. *Babe: The Legend Comes to Life*. New York: Simon and Schuster, 1974.

DiMaggio, Dominic, and Bill Gilbert. *Real Grass, Real Heroes*. New York: Kennsington Publishing Corporation, 1990.

Graham, Frank, and Bill Hyman. *Baseball Wit and Wisdom: Folklore of a National Pastime*. New York: David McKay Co., Inc., 1962.

Grobani, Anton. *Guide to Baseball Literature*. Detroit, Michigan: Gale Research Company, 1975.

Gunther, Marc. *Basepaths: From the Minor Leagues to the Majors and Beyond*. New York: Charles Scribner's Sons, 1984.

Halberstam, David. *Summer of '49*. New York: Avon Books, 1990.

Hodges, Russ, and Al Hirshberg. *My Giants*. New York: Doubleday & Company, Inc., 1963.

James, Bill. *The Bill James Historical Abstract*. New York: Villard Books, 1986.

Kahn, Roger. *Good Enough to Dream*. New York: Doubleday & Company, Inc., 1985.

Lamb, David. *Stolen Season*. New York: Random House, 1991.

Lange, Fred W. *History of Baseball in California and Pacific Coast Leagues, 1847–1938*. Oakland: self-published, 1938.

Lord, Myrtle Shaw. *A Sacramento Saga*. Sacramento, California: Sacramento Chamber of Commerce, 1946.

Maranville, Walter. *Run, Rabbit, Run*. Cleveland: Society for American Baseball Research, 1991.

Obojski, Robert. *Bush League*. New York: MacMillan Publishing Company, Inc., 1975.

O'Neil, Bill. *The Pacific Coast League: 1903–1988.* Austin, Texas: Eakin Press, 1990.

Porter, David L. *Biographical Dictionary of American Sports.* New York: Greenwood Press, 1987.

Reach Official American League Guide. Philadelphia: A.J. Reach, 1920–1927; A.J. Reach, Wright & Ditson, 1928–1929.

Reichler, Joseph L., ed. *The Baseball Encyclopedia.* New York: Macmillan Publishing Co., Inc., 1990.

Reidenbaugh, Lowell. *Take Me Out to the Ball Park.* St. Louis: The Sporting News Publishing Company, 1983.

Rice, Grantland. *The Tumult and the Shouting.* New York: A.S. Barnes & Company, 1954.

Rickart, Paul A., ed. *The Sporting News Record Book for 1926.* St. Louis, Missouri: Charles C. Spink & Son (reprinted by Horton Publishing Company, 1988).

Ritter, Lawrence S. *The Glory of Their Times.* New York: William Morrow, 1984.

Rowe, David G., ed. *Pacific Coast League Official Record Book, 1903–1954.* San Francisco: Pacific Coast League of Professional Baseball Clubs, 1955.

Sann, Paul. *The Lawless Decade.* Greenwich, Connecticut: Fawcett Publication, Inc., 1971.

Schroeder, W.R. *Helms Athletic Foundation Pacific Coast League Baseball Record.* Los Angeles, California: Helms Athletic Foundation, 1940.

Society for American Baseball Research. *Minor League Baseball Stars*, Volume I. Manhattan, Kansas: Ag Press, Inc., 1984.

_____. *Minor League Baseball Stars*, Volume II. Manhattan, Kansas: Ag Press, Inc., 1985.

_____. *Minor League Baseball Stars*, Volume III. Birmingham, Alabama: EBSCO Media, 1992.

Spalding, John E. *Always on Sunday: The California Baseball League, 1886 to 1915.* Manhattan, Kansas: Ag Press, Inc., 1992.

Spink, J.G. Taylor. *Judge Landis and Twenty-Five Years of Baseball.* New York: Thomas Y. Crowell Company, 1947.

_____, ed. *The Sporting News Record Book for 1921.* St. Louis, Missouri: Charles C. Spink & Son (reprinted by Horton Publishing Company, 1988).

Sullivan, Neil J. *The Minors: The Struggles and the Triumph of Baseball's Poor Relation from 1876 to the Present.* New York: St. Martin's Press, 1990.

Thorn, John, and Pete Palmer, eds. *Total Baseball.* New York: HarperPerennial, 1993.

Tomlinson, Gerald. *The Baseball Research Handbook.* Kansas City: Society for American Baseball Research, 1988.

Tormont. *20th Century Baseball Chronicle.* Montreal, Canada: Tormont Publications, Inc., 1992.

Weiss, William J., ed. *1991 Pacific Coast League Record Book.* Tempe, Arizona: Pacific Coast Baseball League, 1991.

Werstein, Irving. *Shattered Decade, 1919–1929.* New York: Charles Scribner's Sons, 1970.

Woodford Associates. *A History of Baseball in the San Francisco Bay Area: San Francisco Giants Official 1985 Yearbook, Special Historical Edition.* San Francisco: Woodford Associates, 1985.

Yallopp, David A. *The Day the Laughter Stopped.* New York: St Martin's Press, Inc., 1976.

Pacific Coast League Record Books

The Pacific Coast League published several annual record books for the leagues and individual teams. The following were consulted for statistical and roster information:

Hollywood Baseball Club, Vernon Club, Mission Club (to 1946 inclusive). Pacific Coast League Baseball, 1947.
Los Angeles Baseball Club (to 1946 inclusive). Pacific Coast League Baseball, 1947.
Oakland Baseball Club (to 1946 inclusive). Pacific Coast League Baseball, 1947.
Pacific Coast League Baseball League, 1903 to 1946, Club Records and Other Features, Volume I. Pacific Coast League Baseball, 1947.
Portland Baseball Club (to 1946 inclusive). Pacific Coast League Baseball, 1947.
Sacramento Baseball Club, Tacoma Club, Fresno Club (to 1946 inclusive). Pacific Coast League Baseball League, 1947.
San Diego Baseball Club, Salt Lake Club, Hollywood Club (to 1946 inclusive). Pacific Coast League Baseball, 1947.
San Francisco Baseball Club (to 1946 inclusive). Pacific Coast League Baseball, 1947.
Seattle Baseball Club. Pacific Coast League Baseball, 1947.

Periodicals

Baseball America, 1991–1992.
Baseball News, official publication of the National Association of Professional Baseball Leagues, Inc., 1991–1992.
California League Newsletter, 1990–1992.
The Los Angeles Times, 1919–1930.
Oldytime Baseball News, 1991–1992.
Pacific Coast League Potpourri, newsletter of the Pacific Coast League Historical Society, 1990–1992.
The SABR Bulletin, newsletter of the Society for American Baseball Research, 1991–1992.
The Sacramento Bee, 1919–1930.
The San Francisco Chronicle, 1919–1930.
Seattle Post-Intelligencer, 1924.
The Sporting News, St. Louis, Missouri, 1919–1930.

Articles

Cusick, Dennis. "Gedeon Treated Just Like Those Banned Players." *Sacramento Bee*, September 17, 1991.
_____. "Sacramento's Pitcher of Success: Tony Freitas." *Sacramento Bee*, August 9, 1987.
Daniels, Stephen M. "The Hollywood Stars." *Baseball Research Journal*, 1975.
Davids, L. Robert. "Nick Cullop, Minor League Great." *Baseball Research Journal*, 1975.
Franks, Joel. "Of Heroes and Boors: Early Bay Area Baseball." *Baseball Research Journal*, 1987.
Goldstein, Ed. "The Yankee-California Connection." *Baseball Research Journal*, 1990.
Gutman, Dan. "Bring Back the Spitter? No!" *Baseball Research Journal*, 1991.

Hibner, John. "Last Hurrah for the Seals." *Baseball Research Journal*, 1989.

Hilton, George W. "The 1919 White Sox Depicted." *Baseball Research Journal*, 1975.

Katz, Lawrence S. "When Immortals Returned to the Minors." *Baseball Research Journal*, 1990.

Lovitt, Dan. "Seattle Wins the Pennant! Seattle Wins the Pennant!" Unpublished, 1992.

Luse, Vern. "Research of Minors Yields Major Finds." *Baseball Research Journal*, 1984.

McCormack, Frank. "Bring Back the Spitter? Yes!" *Baseball Research Journal*, 1991.

Pietrusza, David. "Critters, Flora and Occupations: Minor League Team Nicknames." *Baseball Research Journal*, 1989.

Rothe, Emil H. "Was the Federal League a Major League?" *Baseball Research Journal*, 1975.

Spalding, John E. "Unknown and Phenomenal: Minor League Batting Champions." *Baseball Research Journal*, 1987.

Swesey, Ben. "Ex-Dodger Kampouris Was Ahead of His Time." *Sacramento Bee*, November 5, 1989.

Tomlinson, Gerald. "A Minor League Legend: Buzz Arlett, The Mightiest Oak." *Baseball Research Journal*, 1988.

"Wm. Wrigley Jr. Co." *Fortune*. Time Inc. Magazine Company, New York, August 13, 1990.

Index

Acorns *see* Oakland Oaks
Agnew, Samuel L. (Sam) 50, 68, 73, 92, 98, 104, 196
Alcock, John F. (Scotty) 21
Aldridge, Victor E. (Vic) 41, 42
Almada, Louis (Lou, Ladies Day Louie) 184–188
Almada, Mel 184, 187–188
Alten, Ernest M. (Ernie, Lefty) 50
American Association 16, 44, 45, 61, 88, 101, 112, 131, 165
Angels *see* Los Angeles Angels
Arbuckle, Roscoe (Fatty) 15–16
Arlett, Russell L. (Buzz) 28, 53, 54, 56, 60, 75, 85, 89, 117, 119, 121, 122, 123, 132–135, 139, 168, 177, 196
Averill, Howard Earl (Earl) 1, 50, 123, 148–149, 150, 152, 153, 154, 155, 157, 158, 166, 184, 191, 193, 195, 196

Backer, Leonard H. (Lenny) 152, 155
Bagby, James C.J. (Sarge, Jim) 75
Bagwell, William M. (Bill, Big Bill) 121
Baker, Delmar D. (Del) 12, 31, 32, 132
Baker Bowl 191
Baldwin, Earl P. (Red) 75, 173, 175
Baldwin, Henry C. (Ted) 75
Ballenger, Pelham A. 127
Baltimore Orioles 101, 104
Barbee, David M. (Dave) 186
Barfoot, Clyde R. (Foots) 107, 140, 169
Bassler, John L. (Johnny) 158, 170, 173, 174, 175

Baum, Allan 11, 30, 69
Baum, Charles (Charley, Spider) 9–10
Bears *see* San Francisco Missions
Beavers *see* Portland Beavers
Beck, Clyde E. 111
Bees *see* Salt Lake Bees
Bells *see* San Francisco Missions
Benuvento, Rocky 31
Berger, Walter A. (Wally) 168
Beverage, Dick 193, 194
Black Sox scandal 1, 6, 11, 25
Blakesley, James L. (Jim) 76
Blue, Luzerne A. (Lu) 31, 38
Bodie, Frank S. (Ping) 76, 125, 137, 182
Boehler, George H. 75, 89, 107, 123, 129, 130, 132, 139, 140, 196
Bohne, Samuel A. (Sam, Sammy) 23
Boldt, James (Jim) 39, 67, 84
Bonnelly, Richard C. (Dick) 152
Bonneville Park: attendance at 1925 San Francisco Seals' game 96; effects on pitching and hitting 62, 114; history and description of 59, 127; Locker on 181; Seals' memories of 99; visiting teams' receipts at 80
Bool, Albert J. (Al) 132
Boone, Bill 164
Boone, Danny 164
Boone, Isaac M. (Ike) 114, 122, 128, 163–166, 171, 173, 174, 175, 176, 177, 191, 196
Borton, Babe 8–13, 19
Boston Braves 10, 48, 60, 92, 168
Boston Red Sox 25, 49, 62, 82, 99, 125, 126, 135, 165, 188
Bourg, Arthur S. (Art) 32, 33

Bowman, Elmari W. (Big Bow) 73, 86
Brady, Clifford F. (Cliff) 74, 75
Brandt, Edward A. (Ed) 127
Bratcher, Joseph W. (Goobers, Joe) 85, 119, 132
Brazill, Frank L. 77, 104–106, 112, 114, 117, 118, 119, 129–131, 151, 194, 196
Brewster, James 38–39
Brief, Bunny 61
Brooklyn Dodgers 125, 165, 166, 168, 191
Brooklyn Robins 117, 123, 129
Brooklyn Superbas 29
Broughm, Royal 75
Brower, Frank W. (Turkeyfoot) 91, 92, 99
Brown, Bob 64, 80
Brown, Don 31
Brubaker, Ray K. 75, 85, 119, 137
Bryan, Edward C. (Eddie) 76, 87
Buffalo Park 144
Burkett, Howard L. 170, 173, 175
Butler, Willis E. (Kid) 32
Byron, Bill 68–69, 79

Cady (umpire) 173
California Angels 137
California League 29, 98, 125
California State League 126, 131, 132, 143
California Winter League 44
Callaghan, Martin F. (Marty) 127
Camilli, Adolph L. (Dolph) 123, 188–192
Campbell, Archie 185
Cardinal Field 144
Carlyle, Hiram Cleo (Cleo) 173, 174
Carlyle, Roy E. (Dizzy) 168
Carroll, Dorsey L. (Dixie) 42
Carroll, Jack 97–98
Carson, Al 59
Cather, Theodore P. (Ted) 85
Caveney, James C. (Ike) 40, 122, 132, 135, 196
Cedartown (Georgia State League franchise) 164
Chadbourne, Chester J. (Chet, Pop) 18, 19, 22, 56, 195

Chase, Hal 9
Chicago Cubs 31, 32, 53, 102, 108, 110, 111–112, 114, 115, 160–161, 181, 189
Chicago White Sox 24, 40, 43, 73, 101, 125, 128, 129, 145, 147, 165
Christensen, Walter N. (Cuckoo) 163, 171
Christian, C.V. (Jim) 76, 89
Cincinnati Reds 39, 127, 168
Cissell, William (Bill) 128, 135
Clarke, Fred 69
Cleveland Indians 32, 82, 92, 149
Coates, Les 62
Cobb, Ty 50, 180
Cochrane, Gordon S. (Mickey) 1
Cole, Albert G. (Bert) 113, 122, 128, 163, 172, 173, 174
Coleman, Ralph O. 34–35
Collard, Earl C. (Hap) 157
Comiskey, Charles 24
Comiskey Park 109
Compton, Anna (Pete, Bash) 50
Conlin, Bill 142
Connolly, Joseph G. (Coaster Joe) 97
Cook, Jack 10–11, 14
Cook, Lester S. 173
Cooper, Arley Wilbur 132
Cotter, Harvey 102
Couch, John D. (Johnny) 21, 128
Coumbe, Fred N. (Fritz) 50, 62, 98
Courtney, Henry S. (Harry) 53–54, 72, 73
Cox, Elmer J. (Dick) 12, 31, 32, 33, 34, 35, 77, 129
Craghead, Howard O. (Judge) 117–118
Crandall, James Otis (Doc) 41, 52, 77, 89, 110, 117–118, 119–120, 122, 129, 146, 150, 151, 152, 154, 183, 196
Crane, Samuel B. (Sam, Red) 74, 75
Crawford, Samuel E. (Sam, Wahoo Sam) 1, 27, 41, 52, 184–185
Crockett, James W. (Davey) 95, 103
Crooke (umpire) 129–130
Crosetti, Frank P.J. (Frankie) 50, 146, 148, 149, 166
Cruise, Walton Edwin (Walt) 78–79
Cruz, Cecil 59
Cryer, George 109

Cullop, Henry Nicholas (Nick) 21, 102, 103
Cunningham, William A. (Bill) 39
Cutshaw, George W. (Clancey) 86

Dale, Jean 12–13
Dandalos, Nick (The Greek) 81
Davis, Curtis B. (Curt, Coonskin) 166
Davis, D.K. (Daka) 50
Davis, John Wilbur (Bud, Country, Wilbur) 115
Davis, Zachary T. 109
Dawson, Rex 17
Deal, Charles A. (Charlie) 52
Delaney, Arthur D. (Swede) 117, 132
Dell, William G. (Wieser) 5, 20, 21, 23, 26, 27, 28, 42, 52, 75, 194, 196
Demaree, Albert W. (Al) 40
Des Moines (Western League franchise) 124, 146
Detroit Tigers 25, 32, 38, 148
Devine, Joe 104
DeVormer, Albert E. (Al) 17, 19
Dickerman, Leo L. 117
Dittmar, Carl H. 180–181, 184
Doak, Bill 180
Dobbins, Dick 193–194, 195
Dollar, Stanley 163
Doran, William 12
Doubleday Park 144
Doyle, Jesse H. (Jess) 52, 56
Duchalsky, Jim 62
Ducks *see* Portland Beavers
Dugdale, D.E. 83, 122, 186–187
Dugdale Park *see* Rainier Valley Park
Dumovich, Nicholas (Nick) 52, 77
Dunn, Jack 101
Durocher, Leo 25
Durst, Cedric M. 77

Eason, Mal 129–131
Ebbets Field 191
Eckhardt, Oscar G. (Ox) 167, 177, 187
Edington, Jacob Frank (Frank, Stump) 19, 22, 26
Edmonds, Dick 144
Edmonds Field 144
Edwards, James C. (Jim, Joe, Little Joe) 127, 140

Eldred, Ross C. (Brick) 24, 74–75, 76, 86, 87, 122, 127, 194, 196
Elliott, James T. (Jumbo Jim) 122
Ellis, George W. (Rube) 5
Ellison, Herbert S. (Bert, Babe) 50, 56, 73, 83, 89, 90, 92, 93, 97, 99, 103, 104, 115, 183, 191, 195
Emeryville Park *see* Oaks Park
Essick, Bill 12–13, 16–18, 22, 52, 53, 181
Evans, Billy 149
Ewing, Cal 11–12, 14, 44, 54–55, 65–71, 80, 117, 119, 123, 128, 131, 135, 161

Falk, Charles (Charlie) 187
Fanning, Henry 150–151
Farmer, Frank 12
Farrell, John 71
Fawcett, Roscoe 9
Federal League 48, 81
Fenton, John J. 132, 135
Finn, Cornelius F. (Neal, Mickey) 126, 166, 171, 173
Finneran, Joseph I. (Happy) 17
Fisher, August H. (Gus) 33
Fisher, Robert Taylor (Bobby, Tom) 12, 19, 22, 26
Fittery, Paul C. 41, 42, 56, 58
Flashkamper, Raymond H. (Ray, Flash) 98–99
Fogalsong, Judge Frank 141
Foster, George (Rube) 75, 106
Frederick, John H. (Johnny) 62, 77, 94, 127
Freitas, Antonio (Tony) 46, 167, 178–180
French, Lawrence H. (Larry) 151
French, Raymond E. (Ray) 146, 149, 152, 157, 193, 194, 196
Fresno 64–65
Fromme, Arthur H. (Art) 20
Fullerton, Curtis H. (Curt) 168
Funk, Elias C. (Liz) 170, 173, 174, 175
Fussell, Frederick M. (Red, Fred, Moonlight Ace) 84

Gallagher, Matt 47, 53, 65, 135, 159
Gardner, Harry R. 75

Geary, Robert N. (Bob, Speed) 39, 50, 57, 58, 92, 95, 96, 97, 101, 102, 103, 104, 196
Genin, Walter 33
Georgia State League 164
Gillenwater, Claude 50
Glazier, John B. 12, 31
Glynn, Vallery G. (Val) 150
Golvin, Walter G. 77
Gomez, Vernon L. (Lefty) 1, 166, 177
Gould, Albert F. (Al, Pudgy) 59, 62, 63, 72, 119, 132, 139, 146, 150, 152, 153, 154–155, 158
Governor, Antone (Tony) 132, 157
Graham, Charles (Charlie) 7, 12, 43, 46, 49, 50, 54, 68, 92, 102, 126, 128, 132, 142, 146, 149, 183, 190
Graham, Kyle (Skinny) 127
Grantham, George F. (Boots) 33
Green, Harry R. 173, 174
Gregg, Sylveanus Augustus (Vean) 75, 82–83, 87, 195
Griffin, Martin J. (Marty) 87, 92, 95, 97, 102, 103
Griffin, Westel H. (Wes) 76
Griggs, Art Carle 52
Grimes, Oscar Ray (Ray) 78–79
Grimm, Charlie 189
Guyon, Joe 102

Hale, Samuel D. (Sam, Sammy) 33
Hamilton, Earl A. 112, 119, 122, 129
Haney, Fred G. (Pudge) 167, 177
Hannah, James Harrison (Harry, Truck) 111, 113, 114, 119, 122, 180, 196
Harkness, Harvey (Specs) 35
Hasty, Robert K. (Bob) 132
Hawks, Nelson L. (Chicken) 56
Heath, Minor W. (Mickey) 173, 174, 175, 196
Hemingway, Edson M. (Ed) 112, 114, 122, 129
Hendryx, Timothy G. (Tim) 73, 94, 99
Henry, Bill 109
Hickey, Rudy 151, 155
High, Charles E. (Charlie) 86
High, Hugh J. (Bunny) 12, 18, 19, 22, 26, 76

Hodge, Clarence Clement (Shovel) 53–54
Hoffman, Clarence C. (Dutch) 145, 149, 150, 152, 153, 155
Hofmann, Fred (Bootnose) 163, 171, 173, 174
Hollerson, George 173
Holley, Ed 102
Hollywood Stars 25, 38, 113–114, 127, 141, 147, 155, 159, 162, 163, 169–175, 180–181, 184
Hood, Wallace J. (Wally) 77, 94, 111, 112, 114, 118, 119
Hooper, Harry B. 1, 126
Houck, Byron S. (Duke) 17, 21
Howard, George E. (Del) 66
Howard, Ivon C. 61, 130
Hubbell, Wilbert W. (Bill) 163, 172
Hufft, Irwin V. (Fuzzy) 163, 164, 166, 171, 173, 191
Huggins, Miller 57
Hughes, Ed 81, 91, 97, 125, 137, 146, 162
Hughes, Thomas J. (Long Tom) 52, 98
Hughes, William N. (Bill) 58, 77
Hulvey, James Hensel (Hank) 61, 96, 127, 173, 174
Hunnefield, William F. (Wild Bill) 107
Hurlburt, Roy 8
Hyatt, Robert Hamilton (Ham) 19

Idaho Falls Spuds 138
Idaho League 21
Idora Park 131
Indiana-Illinois-Iowa League (Three-I League) 44, 60, 183
Indians see Seattle Indians, or see Cleveland Indians
International League 44, 45, 165

Jacobs, Raymond F. (Ray) 77, 112, 114, 122, 167, 196
Jacobs, William Elmer (Elmer) 75, 112, 119, 122, 129, 147, 149, 150–151, 158, 166, 177, 194, 196
Jahn, Arthur C. (Art) 111, 114, 122, 129

James, William H. (Big Bill) 52
Jenkins, Joseph D. (Joe) 78
Johns, August F. (Augie, Gus) 173, 174
Johnson, Ban 80–81
Johnson, Ernest R. (Ernie) 10, 21, 22, 137, 167, 186
Johnson, Roy C. 50, 123, 148–149, 150, 153, 155, 157, 158, 166, 184, 191
Johnson, Sylvester W. (Syl) 31, 38
Johnson, Walter (Big Train) 80, 191
Jolley, Smead P. 50, 60, 100–101, 123, 124, 125, 139, 148–149, 150, 152, 153, 154, 155, 157, 158, 166, 191, 196
Jones, Gordon L. 151, 152
Jones, Percy L. 73, 75, 84, 86
Junior World Series: of 1919 16; of 1924 88; of 1925 101–103

Kallio, Rudolph (Rudy) 35, 62, 97, 115, 122, 146
Kamm, William E. (Willie) 40, 43, 50, 53, 57, 195, 196
Keating, Raymond H. (Ray) 115, 140, 146, 150, 153, 155, 156, 184, 196
Keesey, James W. (Jim) 168
Kelly, Joseph H. (Joe) 50, 73
Kemp, Abe 18, 151
Kenworthy, William J. (Bill, Duke) 39–40, 65, 77
Kerr, John F. (Johnny) 127, 139, 158, 184, 195
Kilduff, Peter J. (Pete) 50, 73, 92, 95, 98–99, 104, 117, 194, 195
Killefer, Wade H. (Red) 10, 26, 41, 52, 67–68, 71, 73–74, 84, 87, 112, 126, 127, 162, 163, 173
Killefer, William (Bill) 52
Kingdon, Westcott W. (Wes) 32, 33, 35
Kinney, Walter W. (Walt) 173
Klepper, Walter 38
Klepper, William (Bill) 11, 14, 23, 38–40, 65, 66–67, 79, 84, 167, 187–188
Knight, John W. (Jack, Schoolboy) 145, 158
Koehler, Arthur R. (Art) 12, 58, 76, 92, 115, 122, 149, 150, 152, 155, 167, 184, 195, 196
Kopp, Merlin H. (Manny) 41, 72
Krause, Harry W. (Hal) 55, 61, 75, 117, 132, 163, 173, 184, 195, 196
Kremer, Remy P. (Ray) 54, 72, 195
Krug, Martin J. (Marty) 31, 32, 77, 84, 111, 114, 119, 120, 129–131, 169
Kunz, Earl D. (Pinches) 75, 140

Lafayette, George R. (Frenchy) 75, 85
Landis, Kenesaw Mountain 39–40, 45–46, 55, 65, 66, 81, 109, 115, 129, 130–131, 151, 187
Lane, Bill (owner of Salt Lake Bees) 10–11, 14, 61, 62–65, 66–69, 71, 77, 80, 81, 96, 123, 127, 159–161, 170, 175
Lane, William (Bill) 56, 74–75, 78, 82, 87, 89
Lary, Lynford H. (Lyn) 117, 119, 122, 132, 135, 137, 139, 158, 168, 184
Lazzeri, Anthony M. (Tony) 1, 62, 63, 94, 95–96, 98, 107, 114, 193, 195
Leard, Bill (Wild Bill) 113, 126
Lee, Dudley E. 127, 158, 173, 175, 176, 184
Lelivelt, Jack 169
Leslie, Roy R. 62, 77, 89
Lewis, George E. (Duffy) 59, 62, 64, 77, 89, 126
Lewis, Samuel I. 28, 42
Lindimore, Howard S. 77, 89, 94
Lingrel, Ray 128
Locker, Dallas 59, 181–182
Lockhardt, Charles 67, 68, 70–71, 73, 83, 84, 85, 112, 127
Logan Collegians 138, 190, 191
Lombardi, Ernest N. (Ernie, Schnozz) 1, 132, 168, 193, 195
Long, Thomas A. (Tommy, Tripling Tommy) 12, 22, 35
Los Angeles Angels 5, 8, 9–10, 15, 18, 20, 21, 23, 25, 26, 29–32, 40, 41, 48, 52–55, 77–79, 82–87, 93, 94–95, 98–99, 104, 108–121, 129, 138, 142, 155, 159–161, 162, 166, 168–169, 175, 180, 181, 183, 184, 188

Los Angeles Daily Times, covering the
  subject of: Wrigley Field 109
Los Angeles Times, covering the sub-
  ject of: "Battle of Avalon" 69–70;
  1922 Seals 53; 1924 pennant race
  85, 86; 1927 Oaks infield 135; 1929
  second-half championship won by
  Stars 171; feuding PCL owners 159;
  Grand Jury inquiry of bribes 12;
  PCL as major league 47
Louisville Colonels 101–103
Lucky Beavers see Portland Beavers
Ludolph, William F. (Wee Willie) 139
Lyons, George T. (Smooth) 52

McAuley, James E. (Jim) 41, 77
McCabe, Richard J. (Dick) 94
McCarthy, Joe 102, 114
McCarthy, William H. (Bill) 5–14, 39,
  54–55, 65–71, 80, 126, 161, 162, 163
McCredie, Judge William W. 11–12,
  29, 30, 31, 32, 35, 38, 69, 161
McCredie, Walter 12, 29, 30, 31, 34,
  35, 39, 112, 126
McDowell, James (Jim) 76, 122
McGaffigan, Mark A. (Paddy, Marty)
  41, 42
McGee, Francis D. (Frank, Tubby) 145
McGraw, John 57, 120, 165, 186
Mack, Connie 61
McLaughlin, James R. (Jim) 146, 149,
  150, 153, 158
McNeely, Earl 144
McNulty, Patrick H. (Pat) 127
McPherson, Don 197
McQuaid, Herbert G. (Herb) 50, 163,
  172, 174
McWeeny, Douglas L. (Doug, Buzz)
  53–54, 57, 73, 91, 92, 93, 97, 98,
  103–104, 107, 114, 194, 196
Magee, Lee 9
Magerkurth, George 131
Maggert, Harl 9–13, 22
Mahaffey, Lee Roy (Roy, Popeye) 168,
  177
Maier, Ed 14, 15–16, 26, 54, 67, 68,
  75, 80, 181
Mails, John Walter (Duster, The
  Great) 72, 75, 89, 130, 150, 152,
  190–191

Maisel, George J. 31
Maloney, Michael (Mike) 170, 174, 175
Marticorena, Joseph (Joe) 173
Martin, Elwood G. (Speed) 115
May, Frank S. (Jakey, Joker Jake) 52–
  53, 56, 59, 72, 75
May, William Herbert (Herb, Buck-
  shot) 125, 139, 152, 166
Mearkle, Clyde 73
Mee, Thomas W. (Tommy, Judge) 33
Menosky, Michael W. (Leaping Mike)
  76
Meusel, Bob 16
Meusel, Emil F. (Irish) 167
Middleton, James B. (Rifle Jim) 40,
  77
Miljus, John K. (Johnny, Jovo) 127,
  140, 149
Miller, Jack (Dots) 49, 50, 57, 115
Miller, Lawrence H. (Hack) 27, 42
Milwaukee Brewers 131
Minneapolis Millers 112
Mission Bells see San Francisco
  Missions
Mission Reds see San Francisco
  Missions
Missions see San Francisco Missions
Mitchell, John F. (Johnny) 18, 22,
  112, 114, 117, 119, 122, 129
Mitchell, Oliver C. 50, 51, 85, 89, 92,
  95, 103, 125, 150, 166, 196
Mitchell, William (Willie) 12, 21, 27
Mollwitz, Frederick A. (Fritz) 41
Monks see San Francisco Missions
Monroe, John A. (Johnny) 115, 122,
  149, 150, 151, 153, 155, 167, 195,
  196
Moreing, Charles 143–144
Moreing, Cy 143
Moreing, Lewis (Lew) 14, 66, 67–68,
  77, 115, 142, 143–144, 145, 167, 192
Moreing, William 143
Moreing Field: 1928 account 141;
  Camilli on 192; collection boxes at
  142; description and history of
  144–145; 1928 playoff and cham-
  pionship series at 149, 150–154
Morse, Peter Raymond (Hap) 22
Moudy, Marvin J. (Dick) 87, 92, 122,
  125, 152, 153, 154
Mueller, Arthur 19

Mulcahey, John P. (Phil) 89
Mulligan, Edward J. (Eddie) 12, 57, 73, 89, 92, 94, 98, 103, 104, 122, 146, 149, 163, 171, 175, 194, 196
Murphy, Daniel (Dan) 76
Murphy, Eddie 46
Murphy, Rod 12, 27
Murphy, William A. (Bill) 127
Myers, Elmer G. 62, 77

National Association of Baseball Leagues 43, 44, 66, 71, 81, 130, 132
National Board of Arbitration 67, 68, 71, 161
National Commission 21, 81
Navin, Frank 31
Nelson, Merton A. (Mert) 163, 172, 174
Nevers, Ernest A. (Ernie) 101, 163, 168, 169, 172
New Orleans (Southern Association franchise) 164
New York Giants 25, 39, 40, 43, 102, 120, 125, 165, 168, 184–186
New York Yankees 16, 17, 22, 32, 50, 82, 124, 125, 135–137, 163, 170, 182
Newark Bears 104
Niehoff, John A. (Bert) 5
Northwestern League 30, 31
Nutter, Frank 141

Oakland Oaks 14, 40, 44, 48, 53–55, 61, 75, 80, 85–86, 97, 112, 117–119, 123, 125, 129, 131–138, 155, 159, 160, 168, 181, 183, 184, 188
Oakland Tribune, covering the subject of: PCL as major league 46
Oaks *see* Oakland Oaks
Oaks Park: 1926 attendance at 119; Carlyle home run hit at 168; Dittmar on 181; history and description of 133–134; Jimmy Reese Day at 137; Lyn Lary Day at 137
O'Connell, James J. (Jimmy) 40, 43, 45, 48, 50, 57, 81
O'Doul, Francis J. (Lefty) 41, 42, 60, 77, 94, 95, 96, 104–105, 107, 114, 123–125, 139, 180, 191, 196
Oescheger, C. Joseph (Joe) 117

Ogden Gunners 138
Oldham, Red 12
O'Neil, Joseph Henry (Harry) 61, 77
Orr, Anson 183
Osborne, Frank R. 73, 86, 149, 150, 152, 155

Pacific Coast League: 1920 meeting for tougher gambling enforcement 13; 1921 roster expansion 34; 1922 bonus incentive plan 51–52; 1923 presidency battle and election of Harry Williams 65–71; 1928 first split season championship 154; 1928 playoff plan 141; all-stars of 1926 122; all-star team of 1928 158; attendance during 1920s 48; attendance for 1924 88; attendance for 1926 119; attendance woes of 1927 137; attendance for 1928 (by city) 155; dispute over Seattle ownership rights 67–71; draft status 138; early history 2–3, 132; final standings and leaders: (1920 season) 27–28, (1921 season) 42, (1922 season) 55–56, (1923 season) 71–72, (1924 season) 88–89, (1925 season) 107, (1926 season) 121–122, (1927 season) 139–140, (1928 season) 156–158, (1929 season) 176–177; first .400 batting average 106; first radio broadcasts 138; gambling charges against (1919) 5–14; gambling charges against (1924) 81; Ladies Day policy 159–161; Most Valuable Player Award for 1927 123; players, ethnic composition 3; population versus seating capacity in ballparks 47; President Harry Williams on his tenure 162; record for fielding chances set by Rhyne 101; record for worst record (season) set by Portland 36; record set for league batting average 168; records for hitting set by Bees 58; records held by Jigger Statz 115–116; records set by Ike Boone 166; roster sizes 138; salaries of players 48; season expanded to 28 weeks 16; spitball and "freak deliveries" policy 24–25; spring training

49; third major league, debate over 43–49; umpire support 79; Utah-Idaho League relations 138; war years 30; working relationship with major league teams 32
Pacific International League 60
Paten, Hazen 33
Patrick, Joseph (Joe) 78–79, 85, 111, 119, 130, 138
Payne, George W. 78, 111
Paynter, Norbert (Nobby) 95, 99, 183
Pearce, Walter 62
Pearl, Fred 149
Penner, W. Kenneth (Ken) 28, 76, 77, 89
Peoria (Indiana-Illinois-Iowa League franchise) 60
Peters, John W. (Shotgun) 62, 98
Pfeffer, Edward J. (Jeff) 91, 92, 93, 94, 95, 96, 103
Philadelphia Athletics 40, 61, 79, 82, 125
Philadelphia Phillies 92, 125, 133, 189
Phyle, Bill 99
Pick, Charles T. (Charlie) 41, 77
Piercy, William B. (Bill, Wild Bill) 27, 129, 139
Pillette, Herman P. (Old Folks) 26, 31, 33, 37–38, 42, 114, 139, 163, 171, 172, 173–174, 195
Pinelli, Ralph A. (Babe) 146, 148, 149, 152, 154, 155
Pipgras, Fred J. 58
Pittinger, Clark A. (Pinky) 61
Pittsburgh Pirates 32, 103, 104, 106, 145, 146
Plummer, William L. (Bill) 75
Pocatello Bannocks 138
Polo Grounds 191
Polson, Harry G. 31, 35
Ponder, Charles Elmer (Elmer) 52, 96
Poole, James R. (Jim, Easy) 32, 33, 35, 36, 77, 89, 196
Portland Beavers 13, 14, 29–40, 77, 79, 82–87, 94, 99, 112, 128, 143, 155, 167–168, 171, 178, 181
Portland Telegram 29
Powers, Johnny 11, 14, 15, 26, 41, 54
Prothro, James T. (Doc) 122, 128, 130
Prough, Herschel Clinton (Clint, Bill) 41, 58, 72

Pruett, Hubert S. (Hub) 117
Purdy, Everett V. (Pid) 127
Putnam, G.A. (Alfie) 43, 49, 50, 54, 92, 102, 146, 183, 190

Quincy (International League franchise) 183

Rachac, Max J. 128, 146, 152, 154
Rainier Valley Park: attendance improves at 23; Almada on 186; history and description of 83–84
Rath, Morris C. (Morrie) 35, 59
Ray, Robert (Bob) 86, 171
Raymond, Nate 12–13
Read, Addison J. 132
Recreation Park: 1924 final series at 87; 1925 Junior World Series attendance 102; 1928 playoff and championship series at 150–154; 1929 championship games attendance 173; action at (photos) 58, 91; Booze Cage 2, 90; Camilli on 191–192; continuous baseball at 159; description of 90; destruction of in 1906 131; Dittmar description of 180; expected receipts at 84; gambling locations at 6; Lefty O'Doul Day at 138; Missions play at 113; Missions rent to use 162; Oaks cost to use 54; Ping Bodie Day at 137; rightfield fence at 101, 163; semi-pro games at 54; Suhr on game at 183; Vernon Tigers possible move to 80; Waner secures .400 season at 106
Reese, James H. (Jimmy) 117, 132, 134, 135–137, 139, 168, 184, 195, 196
Rego, Antone (Tony) 151
Reichow, Oscar 69, 79, 81, 111, 119
Reinhart, Arthur C. 42
Rhyne, Harold J. (Hal) 50, 73, 92, 95, 99, 100, 101, 103, 104, 106, 114, 117, 147, 148, 149, 152, 155, 166, 193, 194, 195, 196
Richter, Francis 44
Rickey, Branch 110, 179
Ritchie, Peter (Pete) 92, 95, 99

Rohwer, Ray (Home Run Ray) 74–75, 86, 87, 129, 149, 151, 152, 155
Rollings, William Russell (Russ, Red) 173
Root, Charles H. (Charlie) 78, 87, 94–95, 111
Rose, Edward (Ed, Eddie) 139, 163
Rosebuds *see* Portland Beavers
Ross, Samuel I. (Sam) 31
Rourke, Bill 35
Rowland, Pants 189
Ruether, Walter H. (Dutch) 147, 150, 151, 153, 157, 158, 163, 172, 174
Rumler, William J. (Bill) 9–13, 22, 59, 170, 173, 174, 175
Runyon, Damon 120
Ruth, Babe (Bambino) 2, 43, 46, 50, 137
Ryan, John Bud (Buddy) 41, 77, 178

Sacramento (California League franchise) 132
Sacramento (California State League franchise) 126
Sacramento Bee, covering the subject of: 1928 championship series, game five 152–153; 1928 Senators loss of championship 155; attack on umpire Henry Fanning 151; Elmer Jacob attack on umpire Henry Fanning 151; Sacramento Chamber of Commerce supporting Senators 142
Sacramento Senators 21, 25, 26, 30, 37, 38, 41, 46, 49, 53, 57–58, 68–69, 76–77, 93, 94, 115, 128–129, 131, 138, 141–155, 167, 170, 178, 181, 184, 188, 189, 191, 192, 195
Sacramento Solons *see* Sacramento Senators
St. Louis Cardinals 32, 46, 110, 179
St. Paul (American Association franchise) 16, 88
Salt Lake Bees 5, 8, 10, 13, 14, 21, 22, 23, 25, 26, 30, 35, 40, 58–65, 77, 80, 93, 95–98, 99, 114, 125, 145, 159, 166, 170, 181
San Diego Padres 25, 38, 161, 175
San Francisco Chronicle, covering the subject of: 1924 Indians-Beavers game 86; 1924 Los Angeles Angels

81; 1925 Junior World Series 101; 1929 Missions 162; attendance at Bonneville Park 96; Bill Lane's reaction to winning 1929 pennant 175; Crosetti earning third base job 146; Oaks of 1927 137; Ping Bodie 125; San Francisco fans 91; Shellenback home run in championship series 174; umpiring 97
San Francisco Missions 38, 63, 80, 113–114, 117, 119, 126–127, 138, 155, 162–167, 170–175, 181, 188
San Francisco Seals 7, 11, 18, 19, 21, 23, 25, 26, 32, 35, 37, 40–41, 43, 48, 49–55, 57–58, 68–69, 73, 82–87, 90–106, 108, 110, 113, 114, 115, 117, 120, 123–125, 131–132, 137, 138, 141, 142, 146–155, 160, 162, 166, 180, 181, 183–184, 188, 190–192, 195
Sand, Heinie 81
Sawyer, Carl F. (Huck) 181
Saypo, Johnny 183
Schaller, Walter (Biff) 31
Schick, Maurice F. (Morrie) 27
Schmidt, Walter J. 113, 126
Schneider, Peter J. (Pete) 59, 181
Schroeder, Clyde M. 87
Schroth, Bob 46
Scott, Floyd J. (Pete) 163, 171, 173
Scott, James (Death Valley Jim) 28, 50
Seals *see* San Francisco Seals
Seaton, Tom 7–9, 21
Seattle Indians 5, 6, 13, 14, 18–19, 23–24, 25, 26, 30, 35, 38, 39, 53, 73–75, 82–87, 88, 93, 99, 112, 113, 127, 131, 141, 142, 146, 155, 167, 171, 181, 184, 186–188
See, Charles H. (Charlie, Chad) 50
Senators *see* Sacramento Senators
Severeid, Henry L. (Hank) 149, 152, 170, 173
Sexton, Mike 130
Shea, Elmer F. (Specs) 115, 132
Shea, Mervyn D.J. (Merv) 92
Shea, Patrick H. (Red) 50
Sheehan, Leslie (Les) 62, 72, 77, 95, 150, 153, 155
Sheely, Earl H. (Whitey) 22, 27, 59, 142, 145–146, 147, 149, 150, 152, 153, 155, 158

Sheiks *see* Hollywood Stars
Shellenback, Frank V. (Shelly) 24–25, 41, 75, 127, 140, 170, 173, 174–175, 177, 184, 188–189, 196
Sherlock, John C. (Jack, Monk) 171
Shibe, John 40, 77
Shinners, Ralph P. 119
Siebold, Harry (Socks) 23
Sigafoos, Francis L. (Frank) 128
Siglin, Wesley P. (Paddy) 12, 31, 42, 56, 195, 196
Singleton, John E. (Sheriff) 62, 96, 89, 129
Sittel, Al 109
Siwashes *see* Seattle Indians
Slade, Gordon L. (Oskie) 126, 171, 173, 195, 196
Smallwood, Walter C. (Walt) 20
Smith, Casey 7–9, 21, 22
Smith, Elmer J. 121, 128, 139
Smith, James Carlisle (Red) 17, 19
Solons *see* Sacramento Senators
Sommers, Charley 32
Southern Association 165
Southern League 8, 165, 181
Speaker, Tris 126
Spencer, Edward 12
Sporting News, covering the subject of: 1919 pennant 9; 1920 pennant race 18; 1920 Salt Lake Bees 22; 1921 incident at Portland 33–34; 1921 Portland Beavers 35; 1921 Salt Lake 31; 1923 "Civil War" 65; 1923 Salt Lake pitching 62; 1924 Seattle Indians 75; 1925 Seals infield 92; 1925 Seals on all-star team 104; Angel-Cub relations 111; Brazill's attack on umpire 129; Ellison addressing Seals 57; Ike Boone 165; Ladies Day policy costs and results 160; Missions' nickname 162; Moreing's ownership of Senators 144; Sacramento as the country's best baseball city 144; Salt Lake fans 96; Seattle fans 127–128; suspension of Seals players 7; West Coast baseball 44
Sprinz, Joseph C. (Joe, Mule) 146, 148, 152, 155, 166
Stafford, Harry 70–71
Staley, George Gaylord (Gale) 112

Stanford University 3, 101
Stanich, Vincent 49, 50
Stars *see* Hollywood Stars
Statz, Arnold J. (Jigger) 41, 52, 59, 94, 110, 111, 112, 114, 115–117, 119, 120, 129, 167, 180, 183, 184, 193, 195, 196
Stockton 47, 143, 144, 167
Strand, Paul E. 56, 58–61, 62, 72, 128, 166, 194, 196
Stroud, Ralph V. (Sailor) 9–10, 12, 22, 28
Strub, Dr. Charles 11, 14, 39, 43–44, 49–50, 54, 66, 67, 92, 102, 126, 146, 166, 183, 190
Stueland, George A. 73, 75, 84
Suds *see* Seattle Indians
Suhr, August R. (Gus) 50, 90, 123, 148, 149, 150, 152, 153, 154, 155, 166, 177, 182–184, 196
Sullivan, Prescott 174, 175
Sutherland, Harvey S. (Suds) 73, 74, 75, 84
Swanson, Ernest Evar (Evar, Swanny) 114, 121, 157, 184

Texas League 165, 181
Thomas, Charles G. (Babe) 86
Thomas, Claude A. (Lefty) 52, 76
Thompson, Harold (Harry) 58
Thorpe, James Frances (Jim) 102
Thurston, Hollis J. (Sloppy) 147, 148, 150, 152, 154, 155, 158, 166
Tigers *see* Vernon Tigers
Tincup, Ben 102
Tolson, Charles J. (Chick) 167
Tomlin, Edwin C. (Ed) 128
Toronto (International League franchise) 165
Turner, Tom 31, 40, 79, 128, 160–161, 167–168
Twin Falls Bruins 138
Twombley, Clarence E. (Babe) 52, 77, 127
Tyson, Ty 102

University of Alabama 164
University of California, Berkeley 3, 163

University of Southern California 3, 186
Utah-Idaho League 113, 138, 146, 190

Valla, Eugene (Gene) 50, 73, 92, 94, 99, 101, 104
Vaughn Street Park: history 30–31; 36 fans attending 1921 game at 36; proposed improvements to 39
Veeck, William (Bill), Jr. 31, 111
Veeck, William (Bill), Sr. 189
Vernon Tigers 5, 8, 10, 13, 15–28, 32, 38, 52–55, 59, 75–76, 85–86, 94, 99, 101, 108, 159, 161, 162, 163, 181, 195
Vinci, Lauri A. 115, 146, 149, 151, 152, 155, 184
Vitt, Oscar J. (Ossie, Ol' Os) 62, 77, 94, 98, 127, 170, 174

Wade, Charles W. 186
Waner, Lloyd J. (Little Poison) 1, 99, 103
Waner, Paul G. (Big Poison) 1, 50, 60, 73, 83, 92, 96, 99, 100, 102, 103, 104–106, 107, 110, 114, 149, 196
Warner, Pop 101
Washington Park: 1919 game at 5; 1920 Tigers-Seals series 21; 1924 gambling activity at 80–81; action at (photo) 22; Angels loss of territorial rights to 67; dilapidated state of 110; gamblers arrested at 8; Locker on 181; record 13-game series at 41; Salt Lake Bees using 80; Vernon's rights to 15
Washington Senators 83
Webb, William Earl (Earl) 167
Weis, Arthur J. (Butch) 111, 114, 116, 118, 127
Weiss, Bill 194–195
Weiss, George 80

Welsh, James C. (Jimmy) 75, 82
Western League 44, 61, 129, 146
Westerveldt, Fred 130
Wetzel, Charles E. (Buzz) 173, 174
Whitney, Rodney E. (Rod) 163
Wichita (Western League franchise) 61, 129
Wilhoit, Joseph W. (Joe) 61, 62
Wilie, Dennis E. (Denney) 27
Williams, Guy 92, 94, 97, 103
Williams, Harry 11, 69–71, 79–81, 85, 88, 97, 109, 129–131, 142, 151, 160–162
Williams, Nick 150–151, 152, 180, 190
Williams, Ted 25
Willis, Judge Frank 13–14
Wisterzil, George C. (Tex) 31, 35
Wolfer, Merle J. (Ike) 32, 33, 35, 37
Wright, Wayne B. (Rasty, Doc) 119, 122, 129
Wrigley, William 32, 41, 54, 65–68, 71, 80, 108–111, 112, 119, 120, 159, 170
Wrigley Field (Chicago) 109
Wrigley Field (Los Angeles): 1929 championship series at 174; dedication and description (photo) 108–110; Ernie Johnson Day at 138; Ladies Day policy at 159–161; Stars adjustment to 127; Stars play at 113; talk of building new stadium 80

Yakima (Pacific International League franchise) 60
Yarrison, Byron W. (Rube) 87, 111, 112, 118, 119
Yelle, Archie J. 50, 73, 92, 104
Yellowhorse, Moses J. (Chief) 58, 77
Young, Clyde 33

Zeider, Rollie H. (Bunions) 34–35
Zinn, James 149